*To the memory of Karl Brunner*

# Rational Expectations Macroeconomics

An Introductory Handbook

Patrick Minford

BLACKWELL
Oxford UK & Cambridge USA

First edition published in 1983 as Patrick Minford and David Peel, *Rational Expectations and the New Macroeconomics* by Martin Robertson & Company Ltd.

Second edition first published in 1992
Reprinted 1993

Blackwell Publishers
108 Cowley Road
Oxford OX4 1JF
UK

238 Main Street
Cambridge, Massachusetts 02142
USA

*British Library Cataloguing in Publication Data*

A CIP catalogue record for this book is available from the British Library.

*Library of Congress Cataloging-in-Publication Data*

Minford, Patrick.
    Rational Expectations Macroeconomics : An Introductory Handbook/
    Patrick Minford. – 2nd ed.
        p.    cm.
    Revision of: Rational Expectations and the New Macroeconomics, 1983.
    Includes bibliographical references and index.
    ISBN 0–631–17787–6 (acid-free)   ISBN 0–631–17788–4 (pbk. : acid-free)
    1. Rational expectations (Economic theory)   2. Macroeconomics.
    I. Minford, Patrick. Rational expectations and the new macroeconomics.   II. Title.
    HB172.5.M55   1992
    339–dc20   91–32311
    CIP

Typeset in 10½ on 12 pt Times
by Colset Private Limited, Singapore
Printed in Great Britain by T.J. Press Ltd, Padstow, Cornwall

This book is printed on acid-free paper.

# Contents

# Tables and Figures

# Preface to the Second Edition

The first edition of this book appeared in 1983 and of course was mainly written in 1980–2. In the best part of a decade since then the economics profession has fallen in love with the rational expectations hypothesis and the notion that it implies of the fully optimizing agent, optimizing intertemporally subject to his objective constraints (the 'model'), given his information at the time.

When a profession that can draw on such a mass of talent and sheer manpower moves into action, the results are awe-inspiring. There is now a mountainous literature exploring the hypothesis in most fields of macroeconomics. Most of it is of high quality and much of it also of considerable technical difficulty, whether it is ingenious theoretical extension or careful empirical testing. The sum total has been a dramatic change in the way we view the world. Faced with such a mountain, I have had to choose a path that would reveal its grandeur and challenges without totally exhausting both author and readers. The task is the harder since, to my great regret, David Peel was prevented by other commitments from joining me in preparing this second edition.

In our first edition we aimed to give the advanced undergraduate and the postgraduate a practical guide to the use of rational expectations models in macroeconomics. At the end of the book the student should be in a position to apply such a model to whatever economy he is involved with. He should also be aware of the policy and other issues frequently encountered in such applications. That remains my aim in this second edition. Practicality has remained my criterion for choice out of the voluminous material available.

That being so, I have not much disturbed the basic organization of the first edition. I have updated, extracted less interesting material and put in new topics. The main addition is two chapters on representative agent models, which are especially useful for analysing qualitative changes in economic behaviour as monetary and fiscal policy regimes change. Another addition is a chapter on modelling the open economy. Material on estimation and the empirical evidence bearing on the hypothesis is only sparingly included as before, sufficiently to convey the principles involved. I have tried to illustrate the argument better diagrammatically and cut down on the mass of algebra without too much handwaving.

In this second edition, I have accumulated further debts: to my research associates, especially Anupam Rastogi and Jon Riley; to students and colleagues who have discovered errors in the first edition; and to colleagues with whom I have worked on topics covered in this book, in particular to Martyn Andrews, Matt Canzoneri, Andrew Hughes Hallett and Kent Matthews. I am grateful to Jane Francis for putting the manuscript onto the wordprocessor and, last but not least, to my wife, Rosie, for putting up with the whole endeavour.

*Patrick Minford*

# Preface to the First Edition

This book is designed as an introduction to the use of rational expectations methods in macroeconomics. It will be suitable both for third-year undergraduate courses and for postgraduate teaching. It has arisen out of a course of lectures in macroeconomics we have been giving to third-year economics undergraduates at Liverpool for the last three years.

While this course covers some topics not dealt with in this book, its main emphasis is on rational expectations. It is taken by all economics students and optionally by some accounting and business studies students; our treatment has been conditioned by this. We have tended to use concrete examples of simple macroeconomic models to put across our points rather than to attempt generalization and abstraction. We also use discrete time throughout, since stochastic difference equations are now in the toolkit of economics students, while differential stochastic methods are not. We have found from experience that students are best able in this way both to follow the argument and then to use rational expectations methods themselves on simple models relevant to a variety of problems; while there are no class problems included as such, the chapters lend themselves easily to class discussion and problem-solving.

The level of difficulty is fairly consistent throughout, given the audience we have in mind. Our principal assumption is that the reader has mastered basic econometric concepts, as set out in a standard text such as Johnston (1972). We do not, however, assume that he has reached a high level of attainment in econometrics. Because of the organization by topics each chapter is fairly self-contained, though Chapter 2 on solution methods is required reading for all the rest. The book is a 'text', but, presumably like most texts, it contains some new and some controversial material; we think this adds to its interest and value, and have not tried to put a *cordon sanitaire* around these thoughts of ours.

We have aimed to cover the topics that an applied macroeconomist would need to understand, whether he is in teaching, business or government. Within the confines of space, this has led us to emphasize conceptual and policy issues and to give little space to the technical complexities either of estimation or of numerical solution. We justify this on the grounds that the applied macroeconomist who wants to carry out estimation and solution of a model on the computer should always seek expert advice on the details of his problem, and will in practice be guided to available software packages; and we do also include in Chapter 11, which describes our own work on a model of this sort, some preliminary hints that he may follow.

This book is not regrettably accessible to the layman, but it is accessible to economists in all walks of life, provided that they have a working knowledge of standard econometric techniques. We anticipate that it will therefore be useful to those economists whose training does not include the rational expectations methods so prevalent in macroeconomics today.

Our reason for writing this book is simple and compelling: the topic is of great importance to the applied macroeconomist of today and central in particular to forecasting and policy making, yet teachers and students of it have been handicapped by the difficulty of most of the material available and understanding of its appears to us to have been correspondingly held back, limited mainly to some rather simple propositions in the literature which have given a quite misleading impression of its implications. We hope they will find this book useful, and the true implications of rational expectations – at least as we see them – as exciting as we do.

We have incurred a number of debts in writing this book. We have had fruitful discussions over the years with Mike Beenstock, Matt Canzoneri, Ken Wallis and Mike Wickens on many of the issues we have covered: notably, solution, estimation, model building and stabilization policy. Ken Cleaver assisted in interpreting the work of George Shackle, Peter Pope commented helpfully on the draft of the chapter on market efficiency, and Martyn Hill did the same for the appendix to Chapter 9 on wealth effects, contributing the empirical section. The Liverpool work used in this book owes a great deal that is not explicitly cited to other members of the Liverpool Research Group in Macroeconomics, notably Chris Ioannidis, Satwant Marwaha, and Kent Matthews. They, and other members of the Liverpool department, have also contributed to an ongoing seminar on the topics of this book. Simon Blackman prepared the references and the index. The manuscript was typed often under considerable pressure by Jackie Fawcett and Maureen Kay. We thank – without implicating – these friends and colleagues for their help in this venture. We also gratefully acknowledge the continuing financial support – since 1977 – of the Social Science Research Council for the work on the Liverpool model described in Chapter 11 and other related work referred to elsewhere in this book. Our thanks, too, go to the fine team at Martin Robertson for their usual efficiency, speed and charm. Finally, we thank our students over the past six years for acting as (mostly) friendly critics of our efforts; ultimately, they provided the spur, even if we had the whip hand.

Patrick Minford and David Peel
Liverpool July 1983

# 1

# Introductory Ideas

Expectations are fundamental in economics. Every economic decision is about the *future*, given the existing situation. Even decisions apparently only involving the current situation such as choosing to buy apples rather than pears, implicitly involve a view of the future; in this case it is a view both about future income which underlies the budget one is prepared to allocate to apples and pears, and about future prices of apples and pears, which dictates whether it is worthwhile storing them in place of future purchases.

By definition the future is unknowable. Economics, the study of economic decision-making, therefore is concerned with how people deal with the unknowable.

The Liverpool University economist, George Shackle, made this a constant theme of his work. In his view (e.g. Shackle, 1958) each individual constructs in his imagination different scenarios or possible outcomes following on different actions he is contemplating. He knows *now* the pleasure given by the consequences he imagines for each course of action. The course which gives him the most pleasure when its consequences are imagined spurs him to action. So Shackle envisages a hedonistic calculus of the imagination as the basis for economic choice.

For Shackle the pleasure involved in a course of action will depend, not only on the 'expected pleasure' if the consequences anticipated were to occur, but also on the 'chances' of them occurring. A fine outcome will normally give less pleasure when imagined if it is fraught with uncertainty. But this will not always be true. For example, for some people the same outcome may seem the sweeter if it is accompanied by the challenge of possible failure. Too easy a victory may not inspire a sense of triumph at all and may not attract the decision-taker.

Shackle, therefore, regards economic decisions as entirely subjective, because they are the product of the individual's imagination interacting with the known facts of the past and present. Nor does he feel that we can predict how people will act except in matters where nature reproduces herself with regularity. For example, in inventory control where the product has a reliable distribution, the manager can and will stop production when a sample has a proportion of defective products higher than some percentage. In such cases Shackle says there is 'uncertainty': the rules of probability can be applied by people and we can infer what they will do from a knowledge of their objectives and of the probability distributions.

For many decisions the major elements in the future outcome are not subject to reliable distributions. For example, what the voters of Warrington would do in July 1981, faced for the first time in Britain with a Social Democratic candidate, could not be described by a probability distribution. It was not a regular event. No sense could be given to 'the' probability distribution. Such elements Shackle terms sources of 'potential surprise'. In evaluating future outcomes with such elements, each person will make his individual assessment and we cannot say what he will do without a complete knowledge of his psychology, even if we have access to exactly the same facts as he has.

Shackle's perceptions appear to be quite devastating to the use of statistical models in economics (i.e. econometrics). For these models assert that economic behaviour is predictable and regular. Their implication is that economic agents take decisions about future outcomes which are predictable and subject to well-defined probability distributions. The models are supposed to be derived from assumptions about agents' preferences, technology and the probability distributions they face.

The keystone of econometrics is the implicit assertion that, in the mass, individual decisions exhibit regularity, even though each individual decision will be quite unpredictable. Suppose we could define the probability distribution of future outcomes. Then econometrics asserts that there is a 'typical' individual who, faced with this distribution, will decide in a certain way; we might in particular say that he 'maximizes an expected utility function', where the utility function is a mathematical representation of his preferences. Individuals, when aggregated in a large sample, will behave like many typical individuals.

This assertion is supported up to a point by the central limit theorem, according to which the distribution of the mean of a sample of random variables will tend to normality as the sample gets larger, regardless of the distributions of each variable in the sample (see, for example, Hoel, 1962, p. 145). But although the assertion is supported in this way, it is still required that an individual decision can be regarded as a random variable with a defined mean, generated by a systematic decision process. Shackle denies this, while econometrics asserts it. Furthermore, it was supposed in the above argument that the future outcomes had a probability distribution. But for this to be the case it is necessary that individuals do behave in the aggregate in the regular manner just described. For the distribution of future outcomes is the product of the interaction of individuals' behaviour – e.g. the distribution of future prices and quantities for sugar results from the interaction of individuals' supplies and demands for sugar.

Thus the linchpin of the whole edifice of econometrics is the postulate of regularity in economic nature. That postulate in turn justifies the assumption that econometricians face regularities. Whether this postulate is 'true or false' can only be settled empirically, by evaluating the success and failure of econometrics in attempting to apply this basic assertion. But it is important to realize that the whole foundation of econometrics could be wrong. Indeed many economists regard it (as did Keynes – see, for example, Keynes, 1939) as an unfortunate development which has perverted policy on many important issues because of a false perception that numerical estimates of likely outcomes from different policies can be generated.

Some of the early hopes of econometricians were that econometrics would enable complex problems of decision-making by governments, firms and individuals to be reduced to the mere application of known techniques to models of the relevant economic environment. But these hopes have been cruelly dashed. Nowhere has this been more so than in macroeconomics. Macroeconomic models were built in great profusion in the 1960s for most major countries and used, especially in Britain and the United States, as the basis for forecasting and policy. Crude forms of 'optimal control' were used by governments: typically governments made forecasts, using their models, of inflation and unemployment over a horizon and modified policy to obtain better outcomes according to these models. By the mid-1970s disillusion with these methods was widespread, as the Western world grappled with a combination of high inflation and high unemployment which, in general, neither had been predicted by econometric models, nor had responded to policy in the manner predicted by these models.

The reaction to this disillusion has been varied, with the result that the consensus in macroeconomics that had appeared in the late 1960s had abruptly disappeared by the late 1970s. To some this was a vindication of their scepticism about econometrics. Others, however, have searched for reformulations of the models which failed in the 1970s.

**Rational Expectations**

In this book we are concerned with one particularly radical reformulation, rational expectations. Rational expectations takes one step further the basic assertion of econometrics that individuals in the aggregate act in a regular manner as if each was a typical individual following a systematic decision process. The step is to assert that in this decision process the individual utilizes efficiently the information available to him in forming expectations about future outcomes.

By 'efficient utilization' is meant that the typical individual's perception of the probability distribution of future outcomes (his 'subjective distribution'), conditional on the available information, coincides with the actual probability distribution conditional on that information.

It cannot be stressed too heavily – since this is a source of repeated misunderstanding – that this is an assertion about the 'typical' individual; in other words, it is to be used operationally with reference to the aggregate behaviour of individuals. It cannot be falsified by examples of behaviour by any actual individual. Clearly particular individuals may behave in ways that exhibit no systematic rational behaviour or expectations-formation according to normal criteria, and yet if the behaviour of other individuals, who contributed a dominant proportion of the variability in aggregate behaviour, were rational in this sense, this would be sufficient to generate aggregate behaviour that exhibited rationality.

A further point is that, like all assertions in econometrics, it is to be judged by statistical criteria which will be relative. Whether a relationship asserted to operate for the behaviour of a group 'exists' or not will depend upon how reliable it is statistically, relative to the uses to which it may be put. Such uses in turn may themselves evolve from the discovery of new relationships.

There is therefore no such thing as an objective criterion for judging whether an econometric assertion is valid. Rather there is a joint and interactive evolution of models and their uses. The 1970s crisis in macro-economic policy and modelling described earlier arose because the uses to which models were being put required properties that those models turned out not to have. Therefore, the question that the rational expectations research programme has to answer is: can models based on rational expectations be developed that are useful in application? If so, what are these uses, and how do they compare to the uses available for other modelling approaches?

The assertion (or 'hypothesis') of rational expectations in one sense vindicates Shackle's basic perception that expectations are at the centre of economic behaviour. For on this view behaviour reacts to expected future behaviour, which in turn depends on current behaviour; the capacity therefore exists for changes in the environment to affect current behaviour sharply, as individuals react to their perceptions of the changed environment and its implications for the future. Expectations are therefore completely integrated into behaviour.

In previous theories of expectations, this integration was incomplete. Econometric models used 'proxies' for expectations of particular types of outcomes. These proxies were based on what had been found in the past to correlate well with behaviour in a way that could reasonably be attributed to the operation of expectations rather than actual events. Hence for any particular problem in hand a proxy would be sought *ad hoc*. It is obvious enough that if changes in the environment disturbed the previous relationship between the proxy's behaviour and expectations, this would affect behaviour in a way that would be inaccurately captured by the effect of changes in the proxy. Hence only under the restricted set of circumstances where the previous relationship is unaffected will the proxies be useful. Unfortunately, the restricted set excludes most of the policy experiments that are of interest to governments.

In another sense the rational expectations hypothesis conflicts with Shackle's vision in that it is an attempt to use econometrics to capture the integration of expectations into behaviour. As such, it could be rated as even more foolhardy than basic econometrics. For whereas in well settled times patterns of behaviour might conceivably evolve which could give rise to some econometric relationships, in times of change when expectations are being disturbed in an unfamiliar way, then surely to model the effect of the changes on expectations and their interactions with behaviour must be a mad attempt. For there is the capacity for immense diversity of imagined outcomes from the changes taking place; the 'typically' imagined outcome will be a useless construct in this diversity, where different individuals will be behaving in unrelated and possibly conflicting ways.

This reaction correctly identifies the way in which rational expectations is a programme for pushing econometrics to the limits of its possibilities in the prediction of behaviour. At the same time the reaction correctly notes the ambition of this attempt. It is possible that the attempt is hopelessly over-ambitious. If it is proved to be so, then at least the limits of econometrics will have been clearly defined. For it will be the case that econometric relationships can at best only be useful in the restricted circumstances where the environment shows considerable stability. This would imply that they could be used to forecast existing trends in an unchanged environment, but not to predict the effects of changes in the environment, especially policy changes. If this were so, then it would equally invalidate attempts to use econometric models to design 'optimal' policy rules. Hence the implications flowing from a proper exploration of the potentialities of rational expectations are substantial and important.

We wrote in our first edition: 'While our own view is that these potentialities are considerable, it will only be a decade or so before we will know with reasonable clarity just what can be delivered from this approach.' The view of the economics profession today, judging from the widespread application of rational expectations, is that much has been delivered from it that is useful; the hypothesis has evolved its own set of uses as well as revealing the limits of some traditional ones. This book sets out to chart the high points of this evolution.

## Intellectual History of the Hypothesis – an Overview

As so often in economics, it turns out that early economists propounded ideas at different stages that bear a striking resemblance to the hypothesis. For example, Marshall (1887), in his evidence to a Royal Commission, argued that an increase in the supply of money would affect economic activity by lowering interest rates, increasing loans, expenditure and finally prices. However, he also added that if the increase in the supply of money was well known, then individuals would anticipate the consequent expansion in demand and the effect on prices would be much faster.[1]

Modigliani and Grunberg (1954) are credited by Robert Shiller (1978) with the earliest post-war promulgation of the ideas behind the hypothesis. However, it was one of Modigliani's collaborators, John Muth, who truly created the hypothesis (Muth, 1961), in the sense that he set it down in precise form and showed how it could be applied to specific problems.

Muth's article was written partly in order to defend the prevailing flagship of the 1960s in expectations modelling, adaptive expectations, according to which expectations of a variable are an exponentially weighted average of past values of this variable. It turns out that under certain circumstances this is the same as the rational expectation. These were the circumstances to which Muth seemed to draw attention. His other work published at the time was exclusively devoted to the use of exponentially weighted averages (Muth, 1960; Holt et al., 1960).

The use of a particular modelling technique depends as much on its perceived tractability by economists as on its inherent plausibility. It was in fact the best part of a decade before economists started to use Muth's concept in its own right in applied and theoretical work. Adaptive expectations seemed in the 1960s the best tool, partly perhaps because it was still new and relatively unexplored (it made its first journal appearance in Nerlove, 1958), partly because of its most convenient econometric transformation (due to Koyck, 1954) into a single lagged value of the dependent variable. By contrast, the techniques for using rational expectations (RE) were not widely available; the solution of models with RE presented difficulties, overcome by Muth in very simple models, but not readily dealt with in the larger models being developed in that decade. As we shall see, solution of larger models (and also estimation) required substantial computing power; and it may well be that the rapid quickening of interest in RE modelling from the mid-1970s has been due to the explosion in the capacity of the electronic computer.

The earliest published work in macroeconomics using Muth's concept seriously, if only to a limited extent, is that of Walters (1971) and Lucas (1972a). Walters showed that the effect of money on prices would be substantially quickened by RE. Lucas argued that under RE (unlike adaptive expectations) monetary expansion could not raise output above the natural rate on average (the 'natural rate hypothesis'), although the responses of money to lagged output and prices (feedback responses) could affect the time-path of output in response to shocks. Notice that neither author in these articles argued for the ineffectiveness of monetary policy feedback responses for influencing the time-path of output.

Another early paper was by Black (1973), who applied rational expectations to the foreign exchange market, an area which has seen many further and productive applications of the concept. Some of this subsequent work used Muth's original model in a partial equilibrium treatment of the market, treating macroeconomic variables exogenously (e.g. Minford, 1978; Bell and Beenstock, 1980). Other work (e.g. Frankel, 1979) has estimated reduced form models of the exchange rate derived from monetary models with rational expectations. Shiller (1973) applied it to the term structure of interest rates; here too a separate but closely related body of work has been extremely fruitful.

This has taken the form of tests of the 'efficient market hypothesis'. This is a combination of the rational expectations hypothesis (REH) and some hypothesis about market behaviour, which thus makes it possible to test rational expectations through the behaviour of market prices. Eugene Fama (e.g. 1970, 1976) and his collaborators at Chicago have been prolific in this area, and have covered not only financial markets but also a variety of commodity markets, with results which have at the least substantially revised the popular notions of the early post-war period that markets were irrational and highly inefficient.

Work on general macroeconomic applications (i.e. to inflation and output) in the early 1970s is substantially that of Lucas (1972a, b) and Sargent and Wallace (1975). Lucas's concern was to develop the rationale for fluctuations in money supply to affect output, his problem being that if information on money is available, then movements in money should immediately be discounted in prices, as everyone seeks to maintain relative prices unchanged. He developed a theme due to Milton Friedman (1968) that individuals perceive economy-wide data such as money and the general price level with an information lag, and are forced to estimate whether the price changes they currently perceive at the market level are relative price changes or merely reflect general price movements (inflation). A positive relationship between output and money or price movements (a 'Phillips curve') can occur because of mistakes made by individuals in estimating current inflation; they supply more output, mistakenly thinking that the relative price of their output has risen.

This 'surprise' supply function is an essential component of the small scale macro models used by Sargent and Wallace to illustrate the potential implications for policy-making of RE. They showed that in a 'Keynesian' model, if the Phillips curve (a standard Keynesian construct) is interpreted as a surprise supply function, then only monetary surprises can affect output; monetary plans, whatever they are, can only affect prices. Hence, in particular, sophisticated feedback rules (which, for example, raised money supply in response to a poor past output performance) would be ineffective in their output stabilization objective. However, Lucas and Sargent (1978) have pointed out that this work was not intended to imply that monetary policy was *in general* ineffective for output, merely that in a particular 'standard' model (which they did not in any case endorse) to which 'optimal' monetary control techniques were routinely applied, such techniques were in fact useless. The lesson they drew was cautionary: monetary policy rules should carefully allow for the reactions of private agents to the rules themselves.

Lucas (1975) and Sargent (1976a) proceeded in the later 1970s to develop an alternative to the standard model, the so-called 'equilibrium business cycle' model. In this model the information lag story is maintained, but all markets are treated as if they are auction markets in which all agents are atomistic competitive units. Households are consumers and suppliers of labour and, period by period, compute optimal intertemporal plans for consumption and work based on the price sequences they perceive themselves as facing. Firms, on the other side of the labour and goods markets from households, similarly compute (given their technology) optimal plans for hiring labour and producing goods based on the same price sequences. The price sequences that are perceived are the rational expectations equilibrium sequences that clear the markets today and are expected to clear them in the future. Because firms and households, once they have made a plan, incur 'sunk costs', there is an adjustment cost in changing plans as these past decisions are unwound. This imparts the correlation of prices and quantities over time that is a feature of business cycles. But the impulse to the cycle comes from shocks to the economy, whether from monetary policy, technological innovations or surprise shifts in household preferences. Models motivated in this way or parts of such models have been estimated by Sargent (1976a) and Barro (1977).

Such a model is by no means mandatory in the rational expectations research programme. The 'surprise' supply function is hard to sustain when information about prices is as up-to-date as it is in the modern economy. Also, while the 'as if' assumption of auction markets and automatic agents may work well for economies with highly competitive structures, monopoly power, in labour markets particularly, is widespread in Western economies, markedly so in Europe, and could require explicit modelling. Furthermore, the role of long-term contracts – in goods, labour and financial markets – may be inadequately captured by this 'as if' assumption; this assumption would imply that contracts were approximately 'fully contingent' (i.e. such that prices and quantities altered in response to shocks in just the manner that optimal plans would call for if there were no contracts), yet this apparently is not generally the case, for reasons that are still not well understood but may well be entirely consistent with rationality. Recently, 'menu costs' (the cost of changing prices, as on a printed menu) have been shown, in partial equilibrium models of one or more micro markets, to justify the setting of prices in nominal contracts (Parkin, 1986; Rotemberg, 1983); it has yet to be worked out whether this argument survives in general equilibrium when everyone allows for such costs.

Work by Phelps and Taylor (1977) and Fischer (1977a, b) has taken non-contingent contracts in goods and labour markets as *given* and set up simple models to explore the implications. The influential model of an 'overshooting' foreign exchange market in an open economy, by Dornbusch (1976), centres on the interaction of 'sticky' contracts in goods and labour markets with an auction foreign exchange market. The effect of changes in financial asset values due to the presence of financial contracts (such as long-term bonds) has similarly played an important role in the models of Blanchard (1981) and Minford (1980). Integration of labour monopoly power into these models has been carried out by Minford (1983). These developments imply a model different in many aspects from the narrowly defined equilibrium model of Lucas and Sargent, although it should be stressed that a model with contracts and monopolies where agents have rational expectations could perhaps most naturally be described as an equilibrium model, in that contracts have been voluntarily entered into and monopolies have agency rights on behalf of their members (and if the state legitimizes a closed shop, their non-members too). The policy properties differ substantially; there is in general more scope for stabilization, although whether it would be beneficial is another matter, requiring careful welfare analysis (see Chapter 5).

There are yet other strands in the ongoing RE research programme. B. Friedman (1979) and Brunner et al. (1980) have attempted to introduce the modelling of learning about the model, notably about the evolving 'permanent' elements in the model's structure. Research on learning and whether it converges to rational expectations equilibrium continues to be active (Frydman and Phelps, 1983), although as yet few tractable models have emerged.

Long and Plosser (1983) suggested that business cycles may be modelled without an appeal to information lags or the price supply function; they may stem from real shocks to consumer wealth which generate equilibrium cycles in consumption, production and relative prices. Correlations between money and output may be explainable by implication in terms of reverse causation (Long and Plosser, 1983).

This 'real business cycle' approach has the attraction that it relies on fewer *ad hoc* institutional restrictions than the new classical approach (where information on money and prices, though in principle available rapidly, is slow to arrive in practice) or the new Keynesian (where contracts have unexplained nominal rigidities). Recently, Kydland and Prescott (1982) have shown that a model of this type, calibrated to US data from cross-section studies, can replicate the time series properties of the US post-war economy; this does not yet amount to a statistical test of the model, but it is a start.

There is also an influential school led by Sims (1979) that despairs of modelling the economy's structure, but is interested in time series analysis for predictive purposes within stable structures using the vector autoregression, or VAR (the regression of a group of variables on the past of *all* members of the group). McNees (1986) and Litterman (1986) have found that such VAR models can predict as well as the main US commercial forecasters; however, in the UK during the 1980s VAR models have been out-performed by the main forecasters (Holden and Broomhead, 1990). Finally, there is a large and growing theoretical literature deriving from the work of Lucas (1978) and Wallace (1980) exploring the behaviour of artificial economies peopled by representative agents. These models give us insights into the role of money, taxes and government bonds in enabling exchanges between groups that may be separated by geography (as in Townsend's (1980) tribes travelling in opposite directions along a turnpike) or time (as in Samuelson's (1958) overlapping generations models, e.g. Wallace, 1980).

**The Plan of the Book**

The object of this book is to provide a basic working knowledge of the principles and application of the REH in macroeconomics. It omits an account of the many actual empirical applications and tests in the literature (referring to some of them in passing and indicating survey articles or books where such accounts can be found). It also stops short of many detailed complexities of technique, again referring to further more advanced books and articles where these are covered.

Hence chapters 2 and 3 explain the nature and solution of the most widely used RE models, those without partial information in chapter 2, those with it in chapter 3. Chapters 4 to 7 discuss the implications of the REH for monetary and fiscal policy. Chapters 4 and 5 deal with the central policy issue of stabilization: is it feasible (4) and is it desirable (5)? Chapter 6 considers the limits and desirable form of fiscal policy. Chapter 7 looks at how the political pressures of modern democracy shape policy. Chapter 8 extends these macro models to the open economy, a key component, of course, of the models in practical use.

In chapters 9 and 10 we introduce RE models which are not yet widely used in applied forecasting and policy analysis but which are likely to become increasingly so in the future. These are the representative-agent models, which predict macro behaviour from exact micro assumptions. Chapter 9 deals with models of non-monetary economies, chapter 10 with monetary versions.

Finally, we turn to methods of testing the REH. Chapter 11 treats the efficient market hypothesis, which combines the REH with a hypothesis about market equilibrium and tests the two together. Chapter 12 considers the attempts, initiated by Robert Barro, to test the REH via the reduced form equation relating output to the money supply and other exogenous variables. Chapter 13 briefly discusses direct tests of the REH through surveys of expectations before considering in some detail the estimation of RE models of the type covered in chapters 2 to 8; it concludes by arguing that full information maximum likelihood estimation permits powerful tests of the REH but noting the paucity up to now of such tests. Clearly the REH is still a vigorous field for research.

**Note**

1 This reference was pointed out to us by Richard Harrington.

# 2

# Solving Rational Expectations Models

In chapter 1 we defined the rational expectations hypothesis (REH) as the assumption that peoples' subjective probability distributions about future outcomes are the same as the actual probability distributions conditional on the information available to them. In practice we will be concerned with moments of these distributions, most frequently the mean, but also occasionally the variance, and very rarely the higher moments (the skewness, etc.). The mathematical term for the mean of a distribution is its 'expected value', and it is usual for applied work on the REH to identify the 'expectation of $x_{t+i}(x$ at time $t + i)$' with the mathematically expected value of $x_{t+i}$. In this book we will use the notation $E_{t+j} x_{t+i}$ for expectations framed for the period $t + i$, on the basis of information generally available at time $t + j$; $j, i$ can be positive or negative. E is the mathematical expectations operator, meaning 'mathematically expected value of'. Formally $E_{t+j} x_{t+i}$ is defined as $E(x_{t+i}|\Phi_{t+j})$ where $\Phi_{t+j}$ is the set of generally available information at time $t + j$. Of course, once $x_{t+i}$ is part of the information set $\Phi_{t+j}$, then $E_{t+j} x_{t+i} = x_{t+i}$ trivially.

If we wish to indicate that the information available to those framing expectations is restricted to a set $\theta_{t+j}$ at $t + j$, we will write $E_{t+j}(x_{t+i}|\theta_{t+j})$, i.e. the expectation of $x$ at $t + i$ framed on the basis of information set $\theta$ available at $t + j$. It is natural to think of $E_{t+j} x_{t+i}$ as 'expectations formed at $t + j$ of $x$ at $t + i$'; this will do for some purposes but it is not quite accurate. It is not in fact the date at which expectations are formed that matters but rather the date of the information set on the basis of which they are formed. Because of information lags, people may form expectations for this period on the basis of last period's information, and we would write this as $E_{t-1} x_t$.

Suppose for extreme simplicity that the model of $x_t$ is:

$$x_{t+1} = x_t + \varepsilon_{t+1} \tag{2.1}$$

where $\varepsilon_t$ is normally distributed with a mean of 0, a constant variance of $\sigma^2$, independence between successive values, and independence of all previous events; i.e. $\varepsilon_t : N(0, \sigma^2)$, $E(\varepsilon_{t+i} \ \varepsilon_{t+j}) = 0(i \neq j)$ and $E\varepsilon_{t+i}|\Phi_{t+j} = 0(i > j)$. Equation (2.1) states that $x_t$ follows a 'random walk' (the change in $x_t$ is random).

The expectation of $x_{t+1}$ at $t$ is $x_t$ if we assume that people know $x_t$ then. They cannot know $\varepsilon_{t+1}$ because it has not yet occurred and as a random variable its expected value is zero. If we write $\Phi_t$ as the total information set at $t$, then:

$$E_t x_{t+1} = E(x_{t+1}|\Phi_t) = E(x_t + \varepsilon_{t+1}|\Phi_t) = x_t + E(\varepsilon_{t+1}|\Phi_t) = x_t$$
(2.2)

$E_t x_{t+1}$ will be an unbiased predictor of $x_{t+1}$, i.e. the mean (or expected value) of the prediction error $x_{t+1} - E_t x_{t+1}$ is zero. Thus:

$$E(x_{t+1} - E_t x_{t+1}) = E(x_t + \varepsilon_{t+1} - x_t) = E\varepsilon_{t+1} = 0$$
(2.3)

$E_t x_{t+1}$ will also be the efficient predictor of $x_{t+1}$, i.e. the variance of the predictor error is smaller than that of any other predictor. Thus:

$$\text{Variance}(x_{t+1} - E_t x_{t+1}) = E(x_{t+1} - E_t x_{t+1})^2 = E(\varepsilon_{t+1})^2 = \sigma^2$$
(2.4)

This is the minimum variance possible in prediction of $x_{t+1}$ because $\varepsilon_{t+1}$ is distributed independently of previous events (the meaning of 'unpredictable'). Suppose we add any expression whatsoever, say $\beta z_t$, where $z_t$ is a variable taken from $\Phi_t$, to $E_t x_{t+1}$, making another predictor $\hat{x}_{t+1}$:

$$\hat{x}_{t+1} = x_t + \beta z_t$$
(2.5)

Then:

$$E(x_{t+1} - \hat{x}_{t+1}) = E(\varepsilon_{t+1} - \beta z_t)^2 = \sigma^2 + \beta^2 E z_t^2$$
(2.6)

The variance will be increased by the variance of the added expression, because this must be independent of $\varepsilon_{t+1}$.

The unbiasedness and efficiency of their forecasts are the two key properties of rational expectations forecasts that we will constantly return to in this book. However, for the time being, in this chapter, we will restrict ourselves to explaining how the rational expectation of variables determined in more complex models is to be found, and how those models are accordingly to be solved.

## The Basic Method

Now take a simple macro model (illustrated in figure 2.1):

$$m_t = p_t + y_t$$
(2.7)

$$p_t = E_{t-1} p_t + \delta(y_t - y^*)$$
(2.8)

$$m_t = \bar{m} + \varepsilon_t$$
(2.9)

where $m, p, y$ are the logarithms of money supply, the price level and output respectively; $y^*$ is normal output, $\bar{m}$ is the monetary target (both are assumed to be known constants). Equation (2.7) is a simple money demand function with a zero interest elasticity and a unit income elasticity: in figure 2.1 it is drawn as an aggregate demand curve with a slope of $-1$. Equation (2.9) is a money supply function in which the government aims for a monetary target with an error, $\varepsilon$, which has the properties of our previous $\varepsilon$ in (2.1). As the error shocks the economy, aggregate demand shifts up and down around $D^*D^*$, its steady state position set by $\bar{m}$. Equation (2.8) is a Phillips curve as can be seen by subtracting $p_{t-1}$ from both sides; in this case it states that the rate of inflation equals last period's expectation of the inflation rate plus a function of 'excess demand' We can think of the 'periods' as being 'quarters' and prices as being set, as quantities change, on the basis of last quarter's information about the general price level – hence we appeal to an information lag of one quarter and $E_{t-1}$ refers to this quarter's expectation formed (the operative element) on the basis of last quarter's information. In figure 2.1, equation (2.8) is drawn as the aggregate supply curve; rising output requires rising prices, given expected prices, because each producer wants his own relative price to be higher to compensate for the extra effort of higher supply. The vertical supply curve, $S^*S^*$, is the long-run Phillips curve, indicating that when producers know what the general price level is they will not

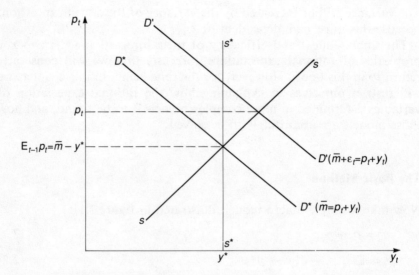

Figure 2.1 A simple macroeconomic model illustrated.

be 'fooled' into supplying more output as it rises because they realize their own relative price is unchanged.

This model is three linear equations with three endogenous variables, two exogenous variables, $\bar{m}$ and $\varepsilon$, and an expectation variable, $E_{t-1} p_t$. Given the expectation, we can solve it normally, e.g. by substitution. So substituting for $m_t$ and $p_t$ from (2.8) and (2.9) into (2.7) gives us:

$$\bar{m} + \varepsilon_t = E_{t-1} p_t + (1 + \delta)y_t - \delta y^* \tag{2.10}$$

This corresponds to the intersection of the $D'D'$ and $SS$ curves in figure 2.1. But we now need to find $E_{t-1} p_t$, to get the full solution.

To do this, we write the model in expected form (i.e. taking expectations at $t - 1$ thoughout) as:

$$E_{t-1} m_t = E_{t-1} p_t + E_{t-1} y_t \tag{2.7}^e$$

$$E_{t-1} p_t = E_{t-1} p_t + \delta(E_{t-1} y_t - y^*) \tag{2.8}^e$$

$$E_{t-1} m_t = \bar{m} \tag{2.9}^e$$

Substituting $(2.8)^e$ and $(2.9)^e$ into $(2.7)^e$ gives:

$$E_{t-1} p_t = \bar{m} - y^* \tag{2.11}$$

This is the intersection of the $D^*D^*$ and $S^*S^*$ curves in figure 2.1. $S^*S^*$ shows what producers will supply on the assumption that the prices they receive are those which they expect (this is an 'expected supply' surve); $D^*D^*$ shows what output will be demanded at different prices on the assumption that the money supply is $\bar{m}$, as expected (an 'expected demand' curve). Where these two curves intersect is accordingly expected output and prices. Equation (2.11) is substituted into (2.10) to give the full meaning of the $p_t$, $y_t$ intersection in figure 2.1:

$$y_t = y^* + (1/1 + \delta)\varepsilon_t \tag{2.12}$$

Consequently, from (2.8) and using (2.11):

$$p_t = \bar{m} - y^* + (\delta/1 + \delta)c_t \tag{2.13}$$

The solutions for $y_t$ and $p_t$ consist of an expected part ($y^*$ and $\bar{m} - y^*$ respectively) and an unexpected part (functions of $\varepsilon_t$). Rational expectations has incorporated anything known at $t - 1$ with implications for $p$ and $y$ at time $t$ into the expected part, so that the unexpected part is purely unpredictable.

This model, though simple, has an interesting implication, first pointed out by Sargent and Wallace (1975). The solution for $y_t$ is invariant to the parameters of the money supply rule. Output would in this model be at its normal level in the absence of surprises, which here are restricted to monetary surprises. If the government attempts to stabilize output by changing the money supply rule to, say,

$$m_t = \bar{m} - \beta(y_{t-1} - y^*) + \varepsilon_t \tag{2.14}$$

then still the solution for output is (2.12), because this money supply rule is incorporated into people's expectations at $t - 1$ and cannot cause any surprises. The only effect is on expected (and so also actual) prices:

$$E_{t-1}\, p_t = \bar{m} - \beta(y_{t-1} - y^*) - y^* = \bar{m} - y^* - (\beta/1 + \delta)\varepsilon_{t-1} \tag{2.15}$$

$$p_t = \bar{m} - y^* - (\beta/1 + \delta)\varepsilon_{t-1} + (\delta/1 + \delta)\varepsilon_t \tag{2.16}$$

Notice that this will raise the variance of prices around their long-run value $(\bar{m} - y^*)$ by $[\beta/(1 + \delta)]^2\sigma^2$. This is illustrated in figure 2.2, where we start this model out from steady state at period $t - 1$, letting $E_{t-1}\, p_0 = \bar{m} - y^*$, $E_{t-1}\, y_0 = y^*$; let there be a shock in period 0, $\varepsilon_0$.

The solution for $(p_0, y_0)$ is the same as before. But now the government responds in period 1 with a money supply contraction, reducing $m$ to $\bar{m} - \beta\varepsilon_0/(1 + \delta)$; this shifts the aggregate demand curve to $D''D''$. But because producers know in period 0 that this reaction will occur, they work out the intersection of their expected supply $S^*S^*$, and the expected demand, $D''D''$, correctly anticipating that $p_1 = \bar{m} - \beta\varepsilon_0/(1 + \delta) - y^*$. Where these curves intersect is accordingly expected output and prices.

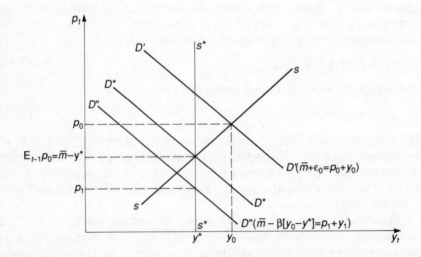

Figure 2.2   The simple model with an interventionist monetary rule.

This of course contradicts the well-known results for models with backward-looking expectations whereby stabilization policy by government can reduce fluctuations in output, provided the government chooses the appropriate monetary target. For example, suppose we had assumed in accordance with the popular practice of the 1960s that expectations of the price level were formed adaptively. The adaptive expectations hypothesis is that

$$x_t^e - x_{t-1}^e = \mu(x_{t-1} - x_{t-1}^e) \qquad 0 < \mu < 1 \tag{2.17}$$

or that expectations of $x_t$ change by some positive fraction, $\mu$, of last period's error. This can be written equivalently as:

$$x_t^e = \mu x_{t-1} + (1 - \mu)x_{t-1}^e = \mu x_{t-1} + (1 - \mu)[\mu x_{t-2} + (1 - \mu)x_{t-2}^e]$$

$$= \mu \sum_{i=0}^{\infty} (1 - \mu)^i x_{t-1-i} \tag{2.18}$$

by continuous substitution for $x_{t-2}^e, x_{t-3}^e, \dots$.

Substituting $p_t^e$ for $E_{t-1} p_t$ in our simple model of (2.7) to (2.9) turns it into an orthodox dynamic model to be solved by standard methods. Equation (2.8) becomes:

$$p_t = \mu \sum_{i=0}^{\infty} (1 - \mu)^i p_{t-1-i} + \delta(y_t - y^*) \tag{2.8}^a$$

We can see that expected prices depend not on planned money supply but on events known to the government last period. Consequently the government can plan a money supply for this period confident that it will not be 'frustrated' by a response from expectations. They can set a target $m^*$, such that $y_t = y^*$. This will be a target which accommodates prices at their expected level, delivering $p_t = p_t^e$; for $(2.8)^a$ assures us that when $p_t = p_t^e$, $y_t = y^*$. By (2.7), when $p_t = p_t^e$ and $y_t = y^*$, then:

$$m^* = p_t^e + y^* = \mu \sum_{i=0}^{\infty} (1 - \mu)^i p_{t-1-i} + y^* \tag{2.19}$$

We now find that the solution for output depends on the deviations of money supply from this optimal target:

$$y_t = y^* + 1/(1 + \delta)(m_t - m^*) \tag{2.20}$$

These deviations may be due either to unpredictable errors, $\varepsilon_t$, as in the RE case, or to a policy failure to plan $m_t$ at $m^*$; in other words:

$$m_t - m^* = \varepsilon_t + m^T - m^* \tag{2.21}$$

where $m^T$ is the actual policy target. But in this adaptive model both affect output, whereas in the RE version only $\varepsilon_t$, the error term, does. In other words, the monetary policy chosen affects output, not, as in RE, merely the monetary surprise.

We shall in subsequent chapters be examining this RE model and a number of considerably more complex RE models whose properties will differ from this one substantially. Nevertheless, it is a common feature of all these models that there is an important difference between the effects of an anticipated and of an unanticipated change in any exogenous variable; by contrast, in models where expectations are formed adaptively (or as any fixed function of past data) it makes no difference. This is probably the most fundamental result of rational expectations. It is the nature of the difference of these effects that forms the detailed study of RE models.

The method of solution set out above (the 'basic' method) will suffice for all RE models in which there are expectations (at any date in the past) of current events only. To repeat, this method involves three steps:

1  Solve the model, treating expectations as exogenous.
2  Take the expected value of this solution at the date of the expectations, and solve for the expectations.
3  Substitute the expectations solutions into the solution in 1, and obtain the complete solution.

**RE Models with Expectations of Future Variables (REFV Models)**

It will very often, in fact almost invariably, be the case – in the nature of economic decisions, which, as we have seen, involve a view of the future – that expectations of future events, whether formed currently or in the past, will enter the model. For these REFV models, our basic method must be supplemented and it can be replaced by more convenient alternatives.

For example, add to our previous simple model the assumption made by Cagan (1956), in his influential study of hyperinflation, that the demand for money responds negatively to expected inflation (we can think of this as approximating the effect of interest rates on money demand in less virulent inflations). Let the model now be:

$$m_t = p_t + y_t - \alpha[E_{t-1}\, p_{t+1} - E_{t-1}\, p_t] \qquad (\alpha > 0) \qquad (2.22)$$

$$p_t = E_{t-1}\, p_t + \delta(y_t - y^*) \qquad (2.8)$$

$$m_t = \bar{m} + \varepsilon_t \qquad (2.9)$$

We keep (2.8) and (2.9) as before. In (2.22) expectations of inflation in the current period are regarded as formed on the basis of last period's (quarter's) information; as in (2.8) we are appealing to an information lag.

Let us use our basic method and see how it has to be adapted for this model. Step 1 (solving given expectations as exogenous) gives us:

$$\bar{m} + \varepsilon_t = p_t + 1/\delta(p_t - E_{t-1}\, p_t) + y^* - \alpha(E_{t-1}\, p_{t+1} - E_{t-1}\, p_t)$$
(2.23)

This is the same intersection $(p_t, y_t)$ as in figure 2.1, except for the extra term $-\alpha(E_{t-1}\, p_{t+1} - E_{t-1}\, p_t)$, which shifts $D'D'$ relative to what is shown there. To find $E_{t-1}\, p_t$ and $E_{t-1}\, p_{t+1}$ we now take expectations of the model at $t - 1$ (step 2) to yield:

$$\bar{m} - y^* = (1 + \alpha)E_{t-1}\, p_t - \alpha\, E_{t-1}\, p_{t+1}$$
(2.24)

Equation (2.24) can solve for $E_{t-1}\, p_t$ in terms of $\bar{m}$, $y^*$, and $E_{t-1}\, p_{t+1}$. But this is not a solution because $E_{t-1}\, p_{t+1}$ is not solved out; we appear to have shifted the problem into the future.

To solve for $E_{t-1}\, p_{t+1}$ we may lead the model by one period (e.g. write (2.22) as $m_{t+1} = p_{t+1} + y_{t+1} - \alpha(E_t p_{t+2} - E_t p_{t+1}))$ and take expectations of it at $t - 1$ as before. This yields analogously:

$$\bar{m} - y^* = (1 + \alpha)E_{t-1}\, p_{t+1} - \alpha\, E_{t-1}\, p_{t+2}$$
(2.25)

We have now solved for $E_{t-1}\, p_{t+1}$ in terms of $\bar{m}$, $y^*$ and $E_{t-1}\, p_{t+2}$, again shifting the problem into the future.

In fact, we can carry on in this way indefinitely and it is easy to see that we obtain a series of equations which can be written as a sort of difference equation:

$$\bar{m} - y^* = (1 + \alpha)\, E_{t-1}\, p_{t+i} - \alpha\, E_{t-1}\, p_{t+i+1} \quad (i \geqslant 0)$$
(2.26)

This is actually a difference equation in a variable $p^e_{t+1}$, defined to be $p_{t+i}$ as expected from $t - 1$:

$$p^e_{t+i+1} - (1 + \alpha/\alpha)\, p^e_{t+i} = -(\bar{m} - y^*)/\alpha \quad (i \geqslant 0)$$
(2.27)

The solution of this first order non-homogenous difference equation is familiarly:

$$p^e_{t+i} = \bar{m} - y^* + [p^e_t - (\bar{m} - y^*)](1 + \alpha/\alpha)^i \quad (i \geqslant 0)$$
(2.28)

where $\bar{m} - y^*$ is the equilibrium of $p_t$ (the 'particular' solution), $(1 + \alpha)/\alpha$ is the root and $p^e_t - (\bar{m} - y^*)$ is the constant (determined by the initial value $p^e_t$) in the 'general' solution.

This can be understood from figure 2.3. Here we have drawn the long-run Phillips curve, $S^*S^*$, and the aggregate demand curve, $D^*D^*$, on the

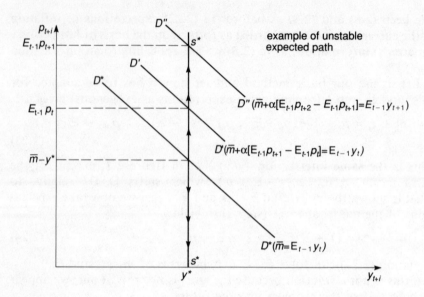

Figure 2.3   The solution expected at $t - 1$ of a simple REFV model, illustrated for an unstable path.

assumption that prices are not expected to change ($E_{t-1} \Delta p_{t+1} = 0$). On this assumption the expected price level is $\bar{m} - y^*$ as before (see figure 2.1). But we can rewrite the expected solution of equations (2.22) and (2.9) as $E_{t-1} \Delta p_{t+1} = (E_{t-1} p_t + y^* - \bar{m})/\alpha$, which shows that if expected aggregate demand ($E_{t-1} p_t + y^*$) exceeds the expected money supply, $\bar{m}$, then it must be because prices are expected to rise; and vice versa. So to the right of $D^* D^*$, prices are expected to rise, and to its left they are expected to fall, as shown by the arrows on figure 2.3. Since output is always expected to be $y^*$ on $S^* S^*$, the possible solution for $E_{t-1} p_t$ and subsequent $E_{t-1} p_{t+i}$ are shown by the arrows on $S^* S^*$. One such solution is shown by the intersection of the $D' D'$ dashed curve showing the expected aggregate demand curve, when prices are expected to rise.

## Choosing a Unique Expected Path

Equation (2.28) and figure 2.3 give an infinite number of solution paths for $p_{t+i}^e (i \geqslant 0)$. For we are free to choose any value of $p_t^e$ we like; the model does not restrict our choice. Another way of looking at (2.28) is to say that we can choose any future value for any $p_{t+i}^e$ we wish and work back from that to a solution for $p_t^e$. We could already have guessed that this would be so from (2.24) for, to obtain the expectation of a current value, we were compelled to take a view about $E_{t-1} p_{t+1}$. Any view of this future will then compel a present which is consistent with it; any set of expectations is therefore self-justifying.

REFV models (i.e. the vast majority) would be little better than *curiosa* if they did not carry with them additional restrictions sufficient to define a unique solution; for they would merely assert in effect that 'anything can happen provided it is expected, but what is expected is arbitrary'. Worse still, as (2.28) illustrates, these paths for events can be unstable; in fact, our model here implies that all paths for prices, except that for which $p_t^e = \bar{m} - y^*$, explode monotonically as shown in figure 2.4. Thus our particular REFV model would assert that only by accident would an equilibrium price level be established; otherwise prices would be propelled into either ever-deepening hyperdeflation or ever-accelerating hyperinflation, even though money supply is held rigid! (Output in this model is always expected to be equilibrium.) While such an assertion may appeal to some it has not impressed those who have espoused RE models; they have looked instead for additional restrictions.

We have already hinted at the source of an additional restriction in our model by noting the instability of all but one path. It is clear that the unstable paths are in some sense absurd. The question is: what would prevent them? It has to be the case that behaviour would alter in such a way as to prevent them.

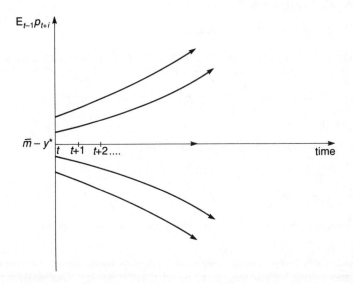

Figure 2.4  The solution paths for the price level expected at $t - 1$, as in equation (2.28).

Consider for example the path of ever-accelerating hyperinflation anticipated fully now (on the basis of last period's information). People deciding how much money to hold for transactions would expect now that in so many years they will need truckfuls of money to buy the daily groceries; they would therefore find an alternative means of carrying out transactions to avoid the investment in trucks they will otherwise anticipate. They would use beans or cows or sophisticated forms of barter to replace the old money. Ultimately the old money would not be used at all; prices would be defined in the new money, say beans.

But money has an issuer; it may be a bank or a government. The issuer derives profits from people's use of its money issue, and it will pay them to avoid its replacement. This it can only do by stopping any such hyperinflation 'bubbles' occurring. It turns out that a commitment on the issuer's part to put an end to any such inflation at some point, by decreasing the money supply at a sufficient rate to offset any decline in real money balances held, will do the trick. For if people expect that inflation will stop at some period $t + N$ (at which the bank will 'step in'), then this implies an arresting of the very on-going process that sustains the earlier path. Real money balances desired in $t + N$ will now be higher than anticipated in that path, so inflation must be lower in $t + N$. But if this is so, then real money balances in $t + N - 1$ will be similarly higher, so inflation will be lower then; and so on. The whole path will be invalidated.

In fact we can show this formally by imposing on the difference equation (2.27) the condition that:

$$p^e_{t+i+1} - p^e_{t+i} = 0 \quad (i \geqslant N) \tag{2.29}$$

and letting (2.27) run from $N \leqslant i \geqslant 0$, since $t + N$ is the period when the bank's new regime takes over. Using (2.27) for $i = N$, we have:

$$\bar{m} - y^* = p^e_{t+N} + \alpha(p^e_{t+N} - p^e_{t+N+1}) = \text{by (2.29)} \; p^e_{t+N} \tag{2.30}$$

By (2.28) this implies:

$$\bar{m} - y^* = \bar{m} - y^* + [p^e_t - (\bar{m} - y^*)](1 - \alpha/\alpha)^N \tag{2.31}$$

or

$$p^e_t = (\bar{m} - y^*) \tag{2.32}$$

It can be seen that (2.32) selects the unique stable path for $p^e_{t+i}$ so that

$$p^e_{t+i} = \bar{m} - y^* \quad (i \geqslant 0) \tag{2.33}$$

An analogous argument can be constructed for the path of ever-deepening hyperdeflation. In this case people will 'demand' infinite amounts of money because its return is infinite in the long term. The bank or government will have an incentive to issue money until the profit rate on the issue has returned to a normal level, i.e. the rate of deflation is zero. The knowledge that the issuer will go on issuing money until this occurs acts to impose the same condition (2.29) on the model.

We have constructed verbal arguments to justify the imposition of a 'terminal condition' such as (2.29) in our model. These arguments appeal to forces not explicitly in the model, but which would be brought into play by certain types of behaviour apparently allowed for by the model. These forces will differ from model to model; for example, we may appeal to legal controls or supervisory agencies to ensure 'orderly markets', or to competitive forces,[1] or to precepts upon government itself. But an RE model with expectations of the future (REFV model) is incomplete without some forces of this kind to supply an additional restriction, such as the terminal condition here.

Our terminal condition (2.29) has the effect in the model here of selecting the unique stable path. For REFV models with such a unique stable path (i.e. with the 'saddlepath' property, so called because any deviation from this path is unstable), the imposition of terminal stationarity on the expectations ensures the selection of this path. For such models, it is therefore only necessary to specify as a side-condition on the model that the solutions be stable or stationary; this condition is referred to variously in the literature as the 'stability' or 'stationarity' or 'convergence' condition, or 'ruling out speculative bubbles' or 'boundedness'. With other REFV models (i.e. without a unique stable path) this condition is either inadequate or over-strong and solution requires careful specification of the terminal conditions on the model. We revert to this issue, the 'uniqueness' problem, below.

Armed with our solution for $p^e_{t+i}$ in (2.33), we have now completed step 2 in our solution procedure, albeit in a more complex manner than before; call it step 2'. We proceed to step 3 and substitute for $E_{t-1} p_t$, $E_{t-1} p_{t+1}$ into (2.23). It turns out in this model that the solution is the same as for our earlier model, as the reader can easily verify.

We may now review our basic method for solving REFV models:

1   Solve the model, treating expectations as exogenous.
2'   Take the expected value of this solution at the date of the expectations. If the model generates a unique stable path for the expectational variables, impose the stability condition, and derive this solution for the expectations.
3   Substitute the expectations solutions into the solution in 1 and obtain the complete solution.

## Other Methods of Solution for REFV Models

Not surprisingly there are several other methods for finding the unique stable solution to an REFV model which has one. We shall explain three in detail because they have been widely used: the Sargent method of forward substitution, the Muth method of undetermined coefficients and the Lucas method of undermined coefficients.

### Sargent Method

The Sargent method, so called here because it has been used repeatedly by Thomas Sargent in his work on rational expectations, uses step 1 as above, obtaining (2.23). It continues as in step 2' to take expectations at $t - 1$, obtaining (2.24). Lead this one period to obtain (2.25) but write this as:

$$E_{t-1} p_{t+1} = (1/1 + \alpha)(\bar{m} - y^*) + (\alpha/1 + \alpha)E_{t-1} p_{t+2} \qquad (2.25)$$

Substitute successively (forwards) for $E_{t-1} p_{t+2}$, $E_{t-1} p_{t+3}$ and so on in (2.25) to obtain:

$$E_{t-1} p_{t+1} = (1/1 + \alpha) \sum_{i=0}^{N-1} (\alpha/1 + \alpha)^i (\bar{m} - y^*)$$

$$+ (\alpha/1 + \alpha)^N E_{t-1} p_{t+N+1} \qquad (2.34)$$

Let $N \to \infty$ and apply the stability condition to $E_{t-1} p_{t+i}$, so that $E_{t-1} p_{t+N+1} \to 0$ as $N \to \infty$. Since $[\alpha/(1 + \alpha)]^N \to 0$ also as $N \to \infty$ (2.34) becomes:

$$E_{t-1} p_{t+1} = 1/1 + \alpha \sum_{i=0}^{\infty} (\alpha/1 + \alpha)^i (\bar{m} - y^*) = \bar{m} - y^* \qquad (2.35)$$

By the same argument but starting from (2.24), $E_{t-1} p_t = \bar{m} - y^*$ also. We have therefore reached the same result as in step 2' and proceed to step 3 as in the basic method.

The Sargent method is more difficult to apply in models where the exogenous variables are not constant as here and where there are lagged endogenous variables. Sargent has evolved techniques using the lag operator to deal with these models; we will briefly explain these below.

### The Muth Method of Undetermined Coefficients

The Muth method starts from the proposition that the general solution of our model can be written

$$p_t = \bar{p} + \sum_{i=0}^{\infty} \pi_i \, \varepsilon_{t-i} \tag{2.36}$$

$$y_t = \bar{y} + \sum_{i=0}^{\infty} \phi_i \, \varepsilon_{t-i} \tag{2.37}$$

where $\bar{p}$, $\bar{y}$ are the equilibrium values of $p_t$, $y_t$.

Let us focus on the solution for $p_t$, since that for $y_t$ follows easily enough. $\bar{y} = y^*$ and $\bar{p} = \bar{m} - y^*$ by setting $\mathrm{E}_{t-1}\, p_t = \mathrm{E}_{t-1}\, p_{t+1} = p_t = \bar{p}$ and $y_t = \bar{y}$ in the model.

Having found the equilibrium in terms of the constants, we now drop these from the model and define $(p_t, y_t)$ in deviations from equilibrium. The model can now be written in terms of $p_t$ as:

$$\varepsilon_t = (1 + 1/\delta)\, p_t + (\alpha - 1/\delta)\, \mathrm{E}_{t-1}\, p_t - \alpha \, \mathrm{E}_{t-1}\, p_{t+1} \tag{2.38}$$

Using (2.36)

$$p_t = \sum_{i=0}^{\infty} \pi_i \, \varepsilon_{t-i} \tag{2.39}$$

$$\mathrm{E}_{t-1}\, p_t = \sum_{i=1}^{\infty} \pi_i \, \varepsilon_{t-i} \tag{2.40}$$

$$p_{t+1} = \sum_{i=0}^{\infty} \pi_i \, \varepsilon_{t-i+1} = \sum_{i=-1}^{\infty} \pi_{i+1} \, \varepsilon_{t-i} \tag{2.41}$$

$$\mathrm{E}_{t-1}\, p_{t+1} = \sum_{i=1}^{\infty} \pi_{i+1} \, \varepsilon_{t-i} \tag{2.42}$$

Equations (2.40) and (2.42) follow from (2.39) and (2.41) respectively because $\mathrm{E}_{t-1}\, \varepsilon_t = \mathrm{E}_{t-1}\, \varepsilon_{t+1} = 0$.

Substituting (2.39) to (2.42) into (2.38):

$$\varepsilon_t - (1 + 1/\delta) \sum_{i=0}^{\infty} \pi_i \, \varepsilon_{t-i} - (\alpha - 1/\delta) \sum_{i=1}^{\infty} \pi_i \, \varepsilon_{t-i} + \alpha \sum_{i=1}^{\infty} \pi_{i+1} \, \varepsilon_{t-i} = 0 \tag{2.43}$$

Each $\varepsilon_{t-i}$ can be any number so that (2.43) can hold if and only if the set of the coefficients on $\varepsilon_t$, on $\varepsilon_{t-1}$, on $\varepsilon_{t-2}$, ..., each individually sums to zero. These sets must satisfy:

$$(\text{on } \varepsilon_t) \quad 1 - (1 + 1/\delta)\, \pi_0 = 0 \tag{2.44}$$

$$(\text{on } \varepsilon_{t-i}, i \geqslant 1) \quad -(1 + \alpha)\, \pi_i + \alpha \pi_{i+1} = 0 \tag{2.45}$$

Equation (2.45) is a homogeneous, difference equation in $\pi_i$ with the same root as (2.27) above, and an analogous solution:

$$\pi_i = \pi_1 (1 + \alpha/\alpha)^{i-1} \quad (i \geqslant 1) \tag{2.46}$$

In (2.46) again we see that there are an infinity of solutions chosen here by selecting $\pi_1$ arbitrarily and that only one is stable, namely that where $\pi_1 = 0$. Invoking the stability condition we set $\pi_1 = 0$, so that $\pi_i = 0$ ($i \geqslant 1$). From (2.44) we obtain $\pi_0 = \delta/(1 + \delta)$. Our solution in $p_t$ is therefore:

$$p_t = \bar{m} - y^* + [\delta/(1 + \delta)]\, \varepsilon_t \tag{2.47}$$

as before.

The Muth method becomes unwieldy for larger models where there are several errors like $\varepsilon_t$ for each of which a sequence of coefficients must be determined, but it is often convenient for small illustrative models, and we will use it frequently for this purpose.

## Lucas Method of Undetermined Coefficients

A variant of the Muth method of undetermined coefficients has occasionally been used (e.g. Barro, 1976; Lucas, 1972a), whereby the solution for the endogenous variables, instead of being written in terms of the constants and the errors, is written in terms of the 'state' variables, i.e. current and past values of the exogenous variables (including the error terms of the model equations) and past values of the endogenous variables. The need to include all the state variables can make this method unnecessarily complicated, as the example of this model shows.

Write the solution for $p_t$ (on which we focus) as

$$p_t = \pi_1\, \varepsilon_t + \pi_2\, p_{t-1} + \pi_3\, y_{t-1} + \pi_4\, \varepsilon_{t-1} + \pi_5\, \bar{m} + \pi_6\, y^* \tag{2.37$^L$}$$

We have

$$\bar{m} + \varepsilon_t = p_t + 1/\delta(p_t - \mathrm{E}_{t-1}\, p_t) + y^* - \alpha(\mathrm{E}_{t-1}\, p_{t+1} - \mathrm{E}_{t-1}\, p_t) \tag{2.23}$$

Use (2.37)$^L$ to generate $\mathrm{E}_{t-1}\, p_t$, $\mathrm{E}_{t-1}\, p_{t+1}$ and substitute for these and $p_t$ in (2.23), obtaining

$$\bar{m} + \varepsilon_t = \pi_1\, \varepsilon_t + \pi_2\, p_{t-1} + \pi_3\, y_{t-1} + \pi_4\, \varepsilon_{t-1} + \pi_5\, \bar{m} + \pi_6\, y^*$$

$$+ 1/\delta(\pi_1\, \varepsilon_t) + y^* - \alpha[\,(\pi_2 - 1)(\pi_2\, p_{t-1} + \pi_3\, y_{t-1} + \pi_4\, \varepsilon_{t-1}$$

$$+ \pi_5\, \bar{m} + \pi_6\, y^*) + \pi_3\, y^* + \pi_5\, \bar{m} + \pi_6\, y^*\,] \tag{2.38$^L$}$$

We used $\mathrm{E}_{t-1}\, y_t = y^*$ in this, from the Phillips curve. Now by the same argument as with the Muth method, the terms in each of the state variables must equate. So we have

$$(\text{terms in } \varepsilon_t)\, 1 = \pi_1 + 1/\delta\, \pi_1$$

yielding

$$\pi_1 = 1/(1 + 1/\delta) = \delta/1 + \delta$$

(terms in $p_{t-1}$) $0 = \pi_2 - \alpha(\pi_2 - 1)\pi_2 = \pi_2(1 + \alpha) - \alpha\pi_2^2$

from which there are two solutions for $\pi_2 = 0$, $(1 + \alpha)/\alpha$. Of these, $(1 + \alpha)/\alpha$ violates the stability condition and is ruled out, leaving $\pi_2 = 0$.

(terms in $y_{t-1}$) $0 = \pi_3 - \alpha(\pi_2 - 1)\pi_3$, implying $\pi_3 = 0$

(terms in $\varepsilon_{t-1}$) $0 = \pi_4 - \alpha(\pi_2 - 1)\pi_4$, implying $\pi_4 = 0$

Given these solutions, the terms in $\bar{m}$ and $y^*$ yield $\pi_5 = 1$, $\pi_6 = -1$. Hence we have obtained, if by a somewhat roundabout route, the solution for $p_t$; that for $y_t$ follows simply using the Phillips curve.

Clearly the method of solution is a matter purely of convenience. We have discussed four, all of which have been extensively used according to the problem and tastes of the problem-solver. All have their advantages and disadvantages and are worth the reader's while to understand. We now turn to an important problem which may arise in the solution of REFV models.

## The Uniqueness Problem

We may illustrate this problem by supposing that for some reason $\alpha$ in our model is negative and $< -0.5$. Suppose, for example, that there is a rigid relationship of money to average transactions in a period; and that precautionary transactions demand is positively related to the rate of inflation, because of the irregularity of price changes and the correlation between the size of these changes when they occur and the inflation rate (e.g. I go to the doctor and find he had just put up his price by 30 per cent). This is implausible but not impossible.

Using our basic adjusted method we obtain the solution for $p_{t+i}^e$ in (2.28)

$$p_{t+i}^e = \bar{m} - y^* + [p_t^e - (\bar{m} - y^*)](1 + \alpha/\alpha)^i \quad (i \geqslant 0) \qquad (2.28)$$

Previously we used the stability condition to choose the unique stable path. However, now all the paths in (2.28) are stable, as shown in figures 2.5 and 2.6, because we have rigged it so that $|(1 + \alpha)/\alpha| < 1$. The stability condition is incapable of selecting a unique solution, therefore. This problem was first pointed out by Taylor (1977), and so far as we know there is nothing to rule out the possibility that REFV macroeconomic models will have an infinity of stable paths.

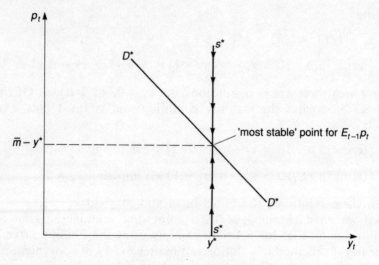

Figure 2.5   The uniqueness problem in ($p_t$, $y_t$) space.

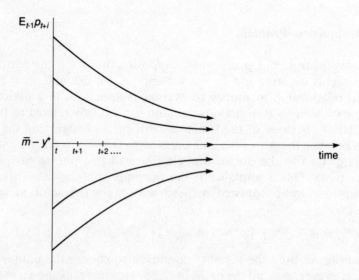

Figure 2.6   The uniqueness problem in ($p_t$, $t$) space.

There is no generally agreed procedure among those using REFV models for this problem, other than to avoid using the ones with this property. One solution has, however, been suggested by Minford et al. (1979). Suppose that, instead of the stability condition, the original terminal condition (2.29) is imposed.

$$p^e_{t+i+1} - p^e_{t+i} = 0 \quad (i \geqslant N) \tag{2.29}$$

This implies, as we saw earlier:

$$p^e_t = \bar{m} - y^* \tag{2.32}$$

This selects, out of the infinity of stable paths, the unique path closest to equilibrium (in this case this path is always in equilibrium) – a result much in the spirit of a suggestion by Taylor (1977) that the least variance path will be selected by 'collective rationality'.

We argued earlier that the stability condition was justified by the terminal conditions imposed by forces outside the model (whether social or governmental or competitive or whatever); these forces were argued to be unleashed if the model got off track in some way. If the model is unstable, then it is not hard to see why such forces would come into play. It may perhaps appear harder to justify that they would do so if the model is globally stable and merely has a non-unique solution.

Upon consideration it is equally justifiable. Non-uniqueness must cause quite as serious problems as instability. For the endogenous variables may in each period jump by unpredictably large (strictly unbounded) amounts; even though they will subsequently be expected to return to equilibrium, in all subsequent periods there will be shocks with infinite variance. Such uncertainty would be likely to provoke changes in behaviour sufficient to create an incentive for the money issuer to make a commitment such as is set out in the terminal condition. This commitment would then limit the uncertainty, as we have seen, to that associated with the 'most stable' path.[2]

## The Techniques in Application – a More Complicated Example

We now cease to develop the argument. Instead we use a slightly more elaborate REFV model (with a unique stable solution) to illustrate further the application of these solution methods. The model here is 'fully dynamic', that is to say it returns to its steady state gradually after a shock rather than immediately as our previous models did. As such it is a prototype for many macro models used in practical analysis.

We retain our Cagan-style money demand equation but date the expectations at $t$ for convenience in the money market.[3] We also retain our simple money supply equation (2.9); but we allow for adjustment costs in the response of output to unexpected price changes (our Phillips curve). So now we have a new model:

$$m_t = p_t + y_t - \alpha(E_t\, p_{t+1} - p_t) \qquad (\alpha > 0) \qquad (2.48)$$

$$y_t - y^* = 1/\delta(p_t - E_{t-1}\, p_t) + \mu(y_{t-1} - y^*)$$

$$= 1/\delta(p_t - E_{t-1}\, p_t)/(1 - \mu L) \qquad (2.49)$$

$$m_t = \bar{m} + \varepsilon_t \qquad (2.9)$$

where we have used the backward lag operator, $L$, in the second expression of (2.49) to facilitate our subsequent operations.

### Basic Method

Let us apply our adjusted method, focusing on the solution for $p_t$. Step 1 gives, substituting for (2.49) and (2.9) into (2.48):

$$\bar{m} + \varepsilon_t = (1 + \alpha)p_t + y^* + 1/\delta(p_t - E_{t-1}\, p_t)/(1 - \mu L) - \alpha E_t\, p_{t+1} \qquad (2.50)$$

Rearranging and multiplying through by $(1 - \mu L)$ yields:

$$(\bar{m} - y^*)(1 - \mu) + \varepsilon_t - \mu\, \varepsilon_{t-1} = -\alpha\, E_t\, p_{t+1} + (1 + \alpha + 1/\delta)p_t$$

$$+ (\alpha\mu - 1/\delta)E_{t-1}\, p_t - (\mu + \alpha\mu)p_{t-1} \qquad (2.51)$$

Notice that the lag of $E_t\, p_{t+1}$ is $E_{t-1}\, p_t$ and not, for example, $p_t$ or $E_{t-1}\, p_{t+1}$.

We now move to step 2′, where we must find $E_t\, p_{t+1}$ and $E_{t-1}\, p_{t+1}$. Accordingly, first we take expectations at $t - 1$ to obtain

$$(\bar{m} - y^*)(1 - \mu) - \mu\, \varepsilon_{t-1} = -\alpha\, E_{t-1}\, p_{t+1}$$

$$+ (1 + \alpha + \alpha\mu)E_{t-1}\, p_t - (\mu + \alpha\mu)p_{t-1} \qquad (2.52)$$

and

$$(\bar{m} - y^*)(1 - \mu) = -\alpha E_{t-1}\, p_{t+i+1} + (1 + \alpha + \alpha\mu)E_{t-1}\, p_{t+i}$$

$$- (\mu + \alpha\mu)E_{t-1}\, p_{t+i-1} \qquad (i \geqslant 1) \qquad (2.53)$$

The solution of (2.53) is:

$$E_{t-1}\, p_{t+i} = (\bar{m} - y^*) + A(1 + \alpha/\alpha)^i + B\mu^i \qquad (i \geqslant 0) \qquad (2.54)$$

where $A$ and $B$ are determined by the initial values $E_{t-1}\, p_{t+1}$, $E_{t-1}\, p_t$. However, we have only one equation (2.53) to determine both $E_{t-1}\, p_{t+1}$

and $E_{t-1}\, p_t$, so that there is an infinity of paths, all but one unstable. This model therefore has the saddlepath property. Impose the stability condition, then set $A = 0$, with the result that $B = E_{t-1}\, p_t - (\bar{m} - y^*)$, so defining

$$E_{t-1}\, p_{t+1} = \bar{m} - y^* + [E_{t-1}\, p_t - (\bar{m} - y^*)]\mu.$$

We can now use (2.52) to solve for $E_{t-1}\, p_t$ as

$$E_{t-1}\, p_t = (\bar{m} - y^*)(1 - \mu) - (\mu/1 + \alpha)\varepsilon_{t-1} + \mu\, p_{t-1} \qquad (2.55)$$

We can infer immediately from (2.55) that:

$$E_t\, p_{t+1} = (\bar{m} - y^*)(1 - \mu) - (\mu/1 + \alpha)\varepsilon_t + \mu\, p_t \qquad (2.56)$$

This can be verified by leading (2.51) one period, taking expectations at $t$, and repeating the operations in (2.52) to (2.55) but advanced one period.

We have now completed step $2'$ and proceed to step 3, substituting $E_{t-1}\, p_t$ and $E_t\, p_{t+1}$ from (2.55) and (2.56) into (2.51), to obtain after collecting terms:

$$p_t = (\bar{m} - y^*)(1 - \mu) - (\mu/1 + \alpha)\varepsilon_{t-1} + \mu\, p_{t-1}$$

$$+ (1 + \alpha - \alpha\mu)/\{(1 + \alpha)(1 + \alpha - \alpha\mu + 1/\delta)\}\, \varepsilon_t \qquad (2.57)$$

This model and its solution are illustrated in figure 2.7. The initial shock to demand, $\varepsilon_t$, shifts the aggregate demand curve out to $DD$ along the $SS$, short-run Phillips, curve. The position of $DD$ takes account of $E_t\, p_{t+1}$, the expected value of next period's price level. This expectation solution is found by locating the unique stable path (the analogue of the algebra in equations (2.54) to (2.56)). The $D^*D^*$ curve shows the combinations of $(p, y)$ for which prices are not expected to change: the equation of the $DD$ curve (2.48) is written as $E_t\, \Delta p_{t+i+1} = -1/\alpha\,(\bar{m} - E_t\, p_{t+i} - E_t\, y_{t+i}\ (i \geqslant 1)$. The $S^*S^*$ curve shows the combinations of $(p, y)$ for which output is not expected to change: the Phillips curve, equation (2.49), is written as $E_t\, \Delta y_{t+i+1} = (\mu - 1)(E_t\, y_{t+i} - y^*)$ $(i \geqslant 1)$.

The arrows show the implied motion of $(p, y)$ where they take values off these curves; the line with arrows pointing along it towards the steady state equilibrium at the intersection of $D^*D^*$ and $S^*S^*$ is the saddlepath, the unique stable solution. $E_t\, p_{t+1}$ 'jumps' from $p_t$ on to this line at the point where it intersects $S'S'$, the expected vertical Phillips curve given by the gradual adjustment of $y_t$ back to $y^*$. Going through this point accordingly is an aggregate demand curve whose equation is $\bar{m} - E_t\, y_{t+1} + \alpha\, E_t\, p_{t+2} = (1 + \alpha)E_t\, p_{t+1}$; it looks forward to $E_t\, p_{t+2}$, which can be found in a similar way as the point on the

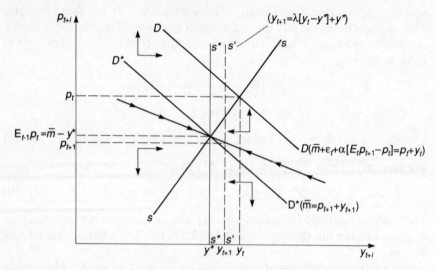

Figure 2.7   The solution of a fully dynamic model when a shock, $\varepsilon_t$, disturbs equilibrium.

saddlepath intersected by $E_t y_{t+2}$. Accordingly $(p, y)$ are expected to converge at the rate $\mu$ on $(\bar{m} - y^*, y^*)$ along this saddlepath, after their initial shock to $(p_t, y_t)$.

## Muth Method

The Muth method is probably the easiest to apply for this model. The general solution for $p$ will be as before

$$p_t = \bar{p} + \sum_{i=0}^{\infty} \pi_i \varepsilon_{t-i} \tag{2.58}$$

and it remains that:

$$\bar{p} = \bar{m} - y^*$$

We now substitute in (2.51), dropping constants to obtain the identities in the $\varepsilon_{t-i}$ from:

$$\varepsilon_t - \mu \, \varepsilon_{t-1} = -\alpha \sum_{i=0}^{\infty} \pi_{i+1} \, \varepsilon_{t-i} + (1 + \alpha + 1/\delta) \sum_{i=0}^{\infty} \pi_i \, \varepsilon_{t-i}$$

$$+ (\alpha\mu - 1/\delta) \sum_{i=1}^{\infty} \pi_i \, \varepsilon_{t-i} - (\mu + \alpha\mu) \sum_{i=1}^{\infty} \pi_{i-1} \, \varepsilon_{t-i} \tag{2.59}$$

The identities emerge as

$$(\varepsilon_t) \qquad 1 = -\alpha \pi_1 + (1 + \alpha + 1/\delta) \pi_0 \qquad (2.60)$$

$$(\varepsilon_{t-1}) \qquad -\mu = -\alpha \pi_2 + (1 + \alpha + \alpha\mu) \pi_1 - (\mu + \alpha\mu) \pi_0 \quad (2.61)$$

$$(\varepsilon_{t-i}, i \geqslant 2) \; 0 = -\alpha \pi_{i+1} + (1 + \alpha + \alpha\mu) \pi_i - (\mu + \alpha\mu) \pi_{i-1}$$
$$(2.62)$$

Applying the stability condition to the solution of (2.62):

$$\pi_i = A (1 + \alpha/\alpha)^{i-1} + B\mu^{i-1} \quad (i \geqslant 1) \qquad (2.63)$$

sets $A = 0$, so that:

$$\pi_i = \pi_1 \mu^{i-1} \quad (i \geqslant 1) \qquad (2.64)$$

Substituting this into (2.60) and (2.61) gives:

$$\pi_0 = (1 + \alpha - \alpha\mu)/\{(1 + \alpha)(1 + \alpha + 1/\delta - \alpha\mu)\} \qquad (2.65)$$

$$\pi_1 = -\mu/\{\delta(1 + \alpha)(1 + \alpha + 1/\delta - \alpha\mu)\} \qquad (2.66)$$

We can verify by expanding (2.57) that this is the solution arrived at previously.


*Sargent Method*

This parallels the basic method up to (2.53). Sargent now rewrites (2.53) as:

$$-1/\alpha(\bar{m} - y^*)(1 - \mu) = \{B^{-1} - ([1 + \alpha/\alpha] + \mu)$$
$$+ (1 + \alpha/\alpha)\mu B\} E_{t-1} \, p_{t+i} = \{1 - ([1 + \alpha/\alpha] + \mu)B$$
$$+ (1 + \alpha/\alpha)\mu B^2\} B^{-1} \, E_{t-1} \, p_{t+i} = (1 - [(1 + \alpha)/\alpha] B)$$
$$(1 - \mu B)B^{-1} \, E_{t-1} \, p_{t+i} \quad (i \geqslant 1) \qquad (2.67)$$

$B$ is the backward operator, instructing you to lag the expected variable but not the date of expectations (unlike with $L$ where both are to be lagged). Now note that there is an expansion of $(1/1 - \lambda B)$:

$$(1/1 - \lambda B) = [-(\lambda B)^{-1}/1 - (\lambda B)^{-1}] = -1/\lambda B[1 + 1/\lambda B^{-1}$$
$$+ (1/\lambda)^2 \, B^{-2} + \dots]$$

Equation (2.67) as it stands implies that $p^e_{t+i}$ will be unstable. However, we can conveniently use the alternative forward expansion of:

$$1/[1 - (1 + \alpha/\alpha) B] = -[(1 + \alpha/\alpha) B]^{-1} /1 - (1 + \alpha/\alpha B)^{-1}$$

and write (2.67) as:

$$(-1/\alpha)(\bar{m} - y^*)(1 - \mu)/\{1 - (1 + \alpha/\alpha \, B)^{-1}\}$$

$$= [(1 - \mu B) B^{-1} / -(1 + \alpha/\alpha B)^{-1}] E_{t-1} p_{t+i} \quad (i \geqslant 1) \quad (2.68)$$

On the right hand side the $B^{-1}$ cancel out; and if we impose stability, the left hand side generates an infinite forward expansion

$$-1/\alpha \ (\bar{m} - y^*)(1 - \mu)[1 + \alpha/1 + \alpha + (\alpha/1 + \alpha)^2 + \ldots]$$

$$= -1/\alpha \ (\bar{m} - y^*)(1 - \mu)/[1 - (1 + \alpha/\alpha)]$$

Cancelling and re-arranging terms and setting $i = 1$ yields:

$$E_{t-1} p_{t+1} = \mu E_{t-1} p_t + (\bar{m} - y^*)(1 - \mu) \quad (2.69)$$

which yields the rest of our solution as before. In this infinite forward expansion there was a remainder term $[\alpha/(1 + \alpha)]^N E_{t-1} p_{t+N+1} - \mu E_{t-1} p_{t+N}$ $(N \to \infty)$, which the stability condition forces to zero as $N \to \infty$.

The Sargent method thus represents a convenient extension of operator techniques to REFV models. Stable roots are projected backwards, i.e. kept in the form $1/(1 - \mu B)$; unstable roots are projected forwards, i.e. transformed to $[-(\mu B)^{-1}]/[1 - (\mu B)^{-1}]$; this procedure, under the stability condition, gives us the same result as before, but in a very compact manner.

Sargent's method is particularly useful for dealing with delayed shocks which are nevertheless anticipated from a date before they occur; so far we have considered only contemporaneous, unanticipated shocks. But, for example, it may become known now that the government plans to raise the money supply sharply in two years' time for some reason to do with anticipated public finance difficulties.

To allow for such a possibility let us in (2.9) allow $\varepsilon_t$ to be a shock which may be related to previous events, whereas before it was assumed to be unrelated. Now moving through the previous steps of our solution, we find that (2.51) is the same. Taking expectations at $t - 1$, however, yields

$$(\bar{m} - y^*)(1 - \mu) + E_{t-1} \varepsilon_t - \mu \varepsilon_{t-1} = -\alpha E_{t-1} p_{t+1}$$

$$+ (1 + \alpha + \alpha\mu) E_{t-1} p_t - (\mu + \alpha\mu) p_{t-1} \quad (2.52)'$$

and so

$$(\bar{m} - y^*)(1 - \mu) + E_{t-1} \varepsilon_{t+i} - \mu E_{t-1} \varepsilon_{t+i-1} = -\alpha E_{t-1} p_{t+i+1}$$

$$+ (1 + \alpha + \alpha\mu) E_{t-1} p_{t+i} - (\mu + \alpha\mu) E_{t-1} p_{t+i-1} \quad (i \geqslant 1)$$

$$(2.53)$$

Sargent's (2.67) now becomes

$$-1/\alpha(\bar{m} - y^*)(1 - \mu) - 1/\alpha(1 - \mu B) E_{t-1} \varepsilon_{t+i}$$

$$= (1 - [1 + \alpha/\alpha] \ B) \ (1 - \mu B) B^{-1} \ E_{t-1} \ p_{t+i} \quad (i \geqslant 1) \quad (2.67)'$$

And (2.68):

$$(\bar{m} - y^*)(1 - \mu) + 1/(1 + \alpha)(1 - \mu B)/\{1 - (1 + \alpha/\alpha \ B)^{-1}\}$$

$$E_{t-1} \ \varepsilon_{t+i} = (1 - \mu B) E_{t-1} \ p_{t+i} \quad (i \geqslant 1) \tag{2.68'}$$

The left hand side of this can be written:

$$(\bar{m} - y^*)(1 - \mu) + 1/(1 + \alpha) \sum_{j=0}^{\infty} (\alpha/1 + \alpha)^j$$

$$(E_{t-1} \ \varepsilon_{t+i+j} - \mu \ E_{t-1} \ \varepsilon_{t+i-1+j})$$

which implies for the case of $i = 1$ the solution for

$$E_{t-1} \ p_{t+1} = \mu \ E_{t-1} \ p_t + (\bar{m} - y^*)(1 - \mu)$$

$$+ \ 1/(1 + \alpha) \sum_{j=0}^{\infty} (\alpha/(1 + \alpha))^j (E_{t-1} \ \varepsilon_{t+j+1} - \mu \ E_{t-1} \ \varepsilon_{t+j})$$

$$\tag{2.69'}$$

We can also use (2.52)' to solve for $E_{t-1} \ p_t$ as:

$$E_{t-1} \ p_t = (\bar{m} - y^*)(1 - \mu) + 1/1 + \alpha \ E_{t-1} \ \varepsilon_t - \mu/1 + \alpha \ \varepsilon_{t-1} + \mu$$

$$p_{t-1} + 1/(1 + \alpha) \sum_{j=0}^{\infty} (\alpha/1 + \alpha)^{j+1} (E_{t-1} \ \varepsilon_{t+j+1} - \mu \ E_{t-1} \ \varepsilon_{t+j})$$

$$\tag{2.55'}$$

Now we see that the future shocks foreseen at $t - 1$ for $t + j$ enter the expected solution for $p_t$ with a coefficient of

$$[1/(1 + \alpha)] [ (\alpha/1 + \alpha)^j - \mu(\alpha/1 + \alpha)^{j+1}]$$

$$= (\alpha/1 + \alpha)^j (1 - \mu\alpha/1 + \alpha)(1/1 + \alpha).$$

Hence the inverse of the unstable root is 'thrown forwards', acting as a weight on the foreseen shock which diminishes the further ahead the shock occurs.

This is illustrated in figure 2.8 for a positive demand shock anticipated at time $t$ for three periods ahead. At $t(= 0$ on the figure) the expected future shock to demand raises prices unexpectedly, increases supply (a movement along $SS$) and stimulates demand (a shift in the aggregate demand curve) because the rise in future prices relative to present prices reduces the demand for money, so increasing money expenditure. Demand continues to rise in $t = 1$ and $t = 2$ because future prices exceed current prices by a greater amount in $t = 1$ than in $t = 0$ and in $t = 2$ than in $t = 1$; this is dictated by the dynamics (shown by the phase arrows) in that part of figure 2.8. At $t = 3$, the shock occurs and

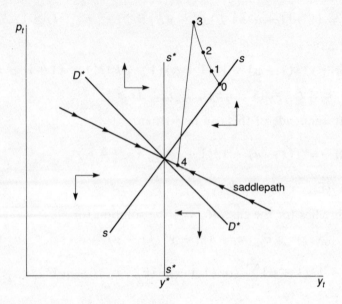

**Figure 2.8**   The effect of an anticipated shock.

Shock $\varepsilon_3$ occurs at $t = 3$, anticipated at $t = 0$. Numbers show the solution at each date, $t = 0, 1, \ldots$

increases demand further. Prices in $t = 4$ are expected to drop to exactly where they would have been (along the saddlepath) had the original shock to demand been an unanticipated one at $t = 0$ sufficient to stimulate output by the same amount as the anticipated shock did; so in $t = 3$ there are conflicting forces on demand, the positive effect of the $t = 3$ shock more than offsetting the effect from the expected future decline in prices.

The algebra for the illustration works out as follows if, for convenience, we set $E_{t-1}\, p_t = p_{t-1} = y_{t-1} = \varepsilon_{t-1} = \varepsilon_t = \bar{m} = y^* = 0$:

$$p_t = [\alpha/(1 + \alpha + 1/\delta)]\, E_t\, p_{t+1} \quad \text{from (2.51)}$$

$$E_t\, p_{t+1} = (1/1 + \alpha)(\alpha/1 + \alpha)^2 (1 - \mu\alpha/1 + \alpha)\, \varepsilon_{t+3} + \mu p_t$$

$$\text{from (2.55)}',$$

led by one period and taking expectations at time $t$ so that:

$$p_t = qx_t \quad \text{and} \quad E_t\, p_{t+1} = (1 + \mu q)\, x_t$$

where $x_t = (1/1 + \alpha)(\alpha/1 + \alpha)^2 (1 - \mu\alpha/1 + \alpha)\varepsilon_{t+3}$, $q = \alpha/(1 + \alpha - \alpha\mu + 1/\delta)$. Again from (2.55)'

$$E_t\, p_{t+2} = \mu\, E_t\, p_{t+1} + (1 + \alpha/\alpha)x_t = [\mu + \mu^2 q + (1 + \alpha/\alpha)]x_t$$

$$E_t\, p_{t+3} = \mu\, E_t\, p_{t+2} + (1 + \alpha/\alpha)x_t$$
$$= [\mu^2 + \mu^3 q + \mu(1 + \alpha/\alpha) + (1 + \alpha/\alpha)^2]\,x_t$$

$$E_t\, p_{t+4} = \mu\, E_t\, p_{t+3} - \mu(1/1 + \alpha)\varepsilon_{t+3}$$
$$= \mu\{\mu^2 + \mu^3 q + \mu(1 + \alpha)/\alpha + (1 + \alpha/\alpha)^2$$
$$- (1 + \alpha/\alpha)^2 (1 + \alpha/1 + \alpha - \alpha\mu)\}x_t$$

$$E_t\, p_{t+5} = \mu\, E_t\, p_{t+4}.$$ Both $E_t\, p_{t+4}$ and $E_t\, p_{t+5}$ are negative.

It is a useful exercise to assign numbers to the parameters and plot the resulting path as in figure 2.8.

In this model, non-uniqueness under the stability condition will occur if both $(1 + \alpha)/\alpha$ and $\mu$ are stable roots, i.e. if $\alpha < -0.5$. Here again, the terminal condition (2.29) will select the 'most stable' solution by, in effect, ruling out the root with the largest modulus.

If we insert (2.29) into (2.54), we obtain:

$$A/B = \alpha(1 - \mu)(\mu/(1 + \alpha)/\alpha)^N \tag{2.70}$$

For larger $N$, then if $\mu < |(1 + \alpha/\alpha|$, $A$ will be negligible and if $\mu > |(1 + \alpha)/\alpha|$, $B$ will be negligible. Hence powers of the root with the largest modulus will be multiplied by a negligible number.

In the case where the roots are stable and a complex pair, the terminal condition selects the phase of the oscillation in such a way that the cycle is at a stationary point at the terminal condition. It does not alter the damping factor or the amplitude of the oscillation. In this case the stable modulus is unique, and the non-uniqueness applies to the phase.

**Other Issues**

*The Case of Two Many Unstable Roots*

We have set up the REFV models so far so that they have had a stable solution, whether unique or not. However, it is possible for the REFV model to have no stable solution. For example, in our original model, instead of placing the adjustment parameter, $\mu$, in the Phillips curve, place it in the demand for money function so that our model is:

$$m_t - p_t = (1 - \mu)y_t - \alpha(E_{t-1} p_{t+1} - E_{t-1} p_t) + \mu(m - p)_{t-1}$$
$$(2.71)$$

$$y_t = y^* + 1/\delta(p_t - E_{t-1} p_t)$$
$$(2.72)$$

$$m_t = \bar{m} + \varepsilon_t$$
$$(2.73)$$

This gives an equation for $p$:

$$(\bar{m} - y^*)(1 - \mu) + \varepsilon_t - \mu\varepsilon_{t-1} = p_t + 1/\delta(p_t - E_{t-1} p_t)$$
$$- \alpha[(E_{t-1} p_{t+1} - E_{t-1} p_t)] - \mu p_{t-1}$$
$$(2.74)$$

Using the basic method, we take expectations at $t - 1$ to obtain

$$(\bar{m} - y^*)(1 - \mu) - \mu\varepsilon_{t-1} = -\alpha E_{t-1} p_{t+1}$$
$$+ (1 + \alpha)E_{t-1} p_t - \mu p_{t-1}$$
$$(2.75)$$

$$(\bar{m} - y^*)(1 - \mu) = -\alpha E_{t-1} p_{t+i+1} + (1 + \alpha)E_{t-1} p_{t+i}$$
$$- \mu E_{t-1} p_{t+i-1} \quad (1 \geqslant 1)$$
$$(2.76)$$

The roots of (2.76) are

$$(r_1, r_2) = \frac{1 + \alpha}{2\alpha} \pm \sqrt{\left[\left(\frac{1 + \alpha}{2\alpha}\right)^2 - \frac{\mu}{\alpha}\right]}$$

both of which may be unstable (e.g. $\alpha = -0.1$, $\mu = -0.9$) in the general solution:

$$E_{t-1} p_{t+i} = \bar{m} - y^* + Ar_1^i + Br_2^i \quad (i \geqslant 0)$$
$$(2.77)$$

Suppose they are both unstable. The initial values are $E_{t-1} p_t$, $E_{t-1} p_{t+1}$. If by the stability condition we set, say $B = 0$, we have $A = E_{t-1} p_t - (\bar{m} - y^*)$; but we must also set $A = 0$, hence $E_{t-1} p_t = \bar{m} - y^*$. It follows that:

$$E_{t-1} p_{t+i} = \bar{m} - y^* \quad (i \geqslant 0)$$
$$(2.78)$$

But this is impossible within this model. For substituting from (2.78) into (2.74) and into (2.75) yields respectively two incompatible solutions for $p_t$. Substituting into (2.74) we obtain:

$$p_t = \delta\mu/(1 + \delta)p_{t-1} + \delta/(1 + \delta)(\varepsilon_t - \mu\varepsilon_{t-1})$$
$$+ \delta(1 - \mu + 1/\delta)/(1 + \delta)(m - y^*)$$
$$(2.79)$$

Substituting into (2.75) gives:

$$p_{t-1} = \varepsilon_{t-1} + (\bar{m} - y^*)$$
$$(2.80)$$

and so (leading 2.80):

$$p_t = \varepsilon_t + (\bar{m} - y^*)$$
$$(2.81)$$

which contradicts (2.79). There is therefore no feasible stable solution for the model when $r_1$ and $r_2$ are both unstable. The stability condition over-determines the model, by placing two restrictions on it ($A = B = 0$) when only one is required.

Does this imply that REFV models cannot generate unstable behaviour? It might appear so. For, it seems, either we supply the stability condition, in which case only stable solutions are admitted, or we do not, in which case there will not be a unique solution.

This again, like the uniqueness issue, is a question on which there is no agreed answer within the profession (other than to avoid REFV models which pose it). However, as Minford et al. (1979) have pointed out, if the original terminal condition (2.29) is used in place of the stability condition, then for an REFV model without a stable condition, a unique solution will exist. It will of course be unstable, but this does give content to the idea of an unstable REFV model.

For example, in this model insert (2.29) into (2.77), to obtain

$$A/B = (r_2/r_1)^N (1 - r_2)/1 - r_1) \qquad (2.82)$$

For large $N$ this will set $A$ or $B$ to a negligible value according to which root has the largest modulus, in effect ruling out the one with the largest. Hence this condition selects the solution path which is the 'least unstable' in this sense. (If the unstable roots are complex the terminal condition selects the phase uniquely; the unique modulus of course remains unstable.)

One can visualize a world represented by this model and the terminal condition as one in which there is 'controlled instability'. The authorities (or other source of the terminal condition) intervene periodically to 'stop' the process; when it 'restarts', the instability resumes until the next stop. Whether such a world would continue for long without modifications that produced stability must be open to doubt. But it seems hard to assert its impossibility.

## 'Will o' the Wisp' Variables

It is possible to add arbitrary variables to the solution of REFV models provided they obey certain processes dictated by the coefficients in the model's future expectations (see e.g., Canzoneri, 1983; Gourieroux et al., 1982).

For example, take the model of (2.22), (2.8) and (2.9), our simplest Cagan model without lags. Suppose people believe at $t - 1$, for no good reason, that prices would be affected by $(1 + \alpha/\alpha)^i E_{t-1} z_{t+i}$ where:

$$E_{t-1} z_{t+i} = z_{t-1} \qquad (2.83)$$

(i.e. $z_t$ is a martingale). Their belief, though 'irrational', would formally be validated by the model, for

$$p_{t+i} = (\bar{m} - y^*) + \delta/(1 + \delta)\,\varepsilon_{t+i} + (1 + \alpha/\alpha)^i\,\mathsf{E}_{t-1}\,z_{t+i} \qquad (2.84)$$

is a solution to the model, as can be verified by substituting (2.84) and (2.83) into (2.23). Any 'will o' the wisp' variable, $z_{t-1}$, could therefore produce an irrational solution to an REFV model by this self-validating process.

This is simply an implication of the indeterminacy of $p_t^e$ we noted earlier in commenting on equation (2.28); so we can write $p_t^e - (m - y^*) = \mu_{t-1}$ where $\mu_{t-1}$ is *anything*. However, the solution to the 'will o' the wisp' problem is one and the same as that of the indeterminacy problem: we have to impose an additional restriction on the model to ensure determinacy.

Hence, in this model we notice that $[(1 + \alpha)/\alpha]^i\,\mathsf{E}_{t-1}\,z_{t+i}$ is an unstable process. So the stability condition rules it out. This objection does not rule it out in the generality of models. For example, suppose in the above that $\alpha < -0.5$. Then $[(1 + \alpha)/\alpha]^i\,\mathsf{E}_{t-1}\,z_{t+i}$ would be stable. However, the terminal condition in this non-uniqueness case does rule out $z_{t-1}$, although as we have seen this remains a controversial solution. Alternatively, some other restriction (such as that suggested by Peel, 1981; Taylor, 1977; or McCallum, 1983) would do the job.

## Conclusions

This has been a chapter designed to equip the reader with the techniques to solve rational expectations models in a manner useful to applied work.[4] We have shown how to use four main methods of solution: a basic method, the Sargent forward operator method, and the Muth and Lucas undetermined coefficients methods. We have also discussed the criterion for choosing a unique solution in these models, free of extraneous or 'will o' the wisp' variables. The criterion we propose, namely that terminal conditions are imposed on the model either by the authorities or by some other outside force, is not fully accepted by all practitioners. Nevertheless, all models in use for policy analysis and forecasting are solved by imposing terminal conditions (for UK practice, see Wallis et al., 1985), while in the USA the Fair and Taylor (1983) procedure of the 'extended path' (which pushes the terminal date as far ahead as necessary for the forecast to become insensitive to it) is generally used. Whatever criterion is used, the practical effect in the macroeconomic models likely to be encountered by applied macroeconomists will usually be the same as that of our criterion, namely to select the 'most stable' path (i.e. the roots with smallest modulus) and one free of extraneous variables. In many models to be encountered, there will be a unique stable path, which will in principle be the one selected on any of the criteria that have been proposed. The practitioner therefore will be almost invariably on safe ground if he uses the methodology described here.

## Notes

1 For example, in the competitive equilibrium model of the labour market of Lucas and Sargent, as set out in, for example, Sargent (1979, chapter 16), the transversality conditions of households and firms supply the necessary terminal conditions. These conditions are necessary for optimality; in other words, explosive paths for labour supply and demand are not followed by households or firms because they are sub-optimal.
2 There have been other suggestions, like Taylor's, as to how society would select such a path. Peel (1981) argues the monetary authorities will select a feedback rule generating uniqueness; however, it is not clear that they do select such rules in practice. McCallum (1983) argues that the solution chosen, when framed according to the Lucas undetermined coefficients method, will contain only the minimum set of state variables; this does, however, appear to be an arbitrary procedure.
3 This dating of expectations implies that agents in the money and bonds markets have access to all current information whereas those in the goods and labour markets only have access to last period's – not an assertion with much theoretical appeal. Exactly what information which agents have is discussed carefully below (especially in chapters 3 and 4). Here we make this assumption merely to illustrate our techniques with less complication.
4 There are a number of descriptions of solution methods available in the literature (see, e.g., Shiller, 1978; and the useful Aoki and Canzoneri, 1979). For more complex applications than those considered in this chapter, the reader will invariably use numerical methods on the computer.

# 3

# Partial Information and Signal Extraction

To this point, we have assumed that people had access to all relevant information on events up to a certain date in forming their expectations: for example, $E_t x_t$ or $E(x_t | \Phi_t)$ implied they know the whole contents of $\Phi_t$, the information set relating to period $t$ and before. If they did not have access to $\Phi_t$, then they might have access to $\Phi_{t-1}$, the previous period's information set. However, there is an intermediate possibility, which we have in this way ignored but which has important implications for the behaviour of people with rational expectations. This possibility is that they know a part of $\Phi_t$ only, as well as all of $\Phi_{t-1}$. For example, each individual might know the prices of certain goods which he or she trades (but not the general price level). This is 'micro' information. As for macro or aggregate information, in many economies capital market information, such as exchange rates or interest rates, is available essentially instantaneously.

When endowed with such partial knowledge, agents face a statistical inference problem. Observation of the current values of macroeconomic variables, given knowledge of the variance of disturbances in the economy, allows them to form an optimal expectation of the currently unobserved random variables using Kalman filter methods (Kalman, 1960). In particular, if a variable $z$ is observed which is the sum of two random variables $(u, e)$, i.e.

$$z_t = u_t + e_t \tag{3.1}$$

then the current expectations of $u$ and $e$ are respectively given by

$$E_t(u_t) = \{\sigma_u^2 / (\sigma_u^2 + \sigma_e^2)\} z_t \tag{3.2}$$

$$E_t(e_t) = \{\sigma_e^2 / (\sigma_u^2 + \sigma_e^2)\} z_t \tag{3.3}$$

where $\sigma_u^2, \sigma_e^2$ are the known variances of the disturbances (Graybill (1961) has a fuller discussion). The coefficient on $z_t$ in (3.2) or (3.3) can be thought of as that of a simple ordinary least squares regression of $u_t$ on $z_t$ (carried out over an infinite sample).

The purpose of this chapter is to consider two examples of how partial information alters the solution of rational expectations models; these will both illustrate the method of solution and explain the workings of two models important in their own right. The first example is the Phillips curve in Lucas's (1972b) 'islands story', where people know individual prices but not the general price level – a case of partial micro information. The second example is a general macro model where people have some capital market information – a case of partial macro information.

## The New Classical Phillips Curve

In the original formulation of the Phillips curve (Phillips, 1958; Lipsey, 1960), some rigidity of money wages was assumed. The curve related the change in wages to a measure of excess demand at wages that were not clearing the market. This relationship was later 'augmented' by Phelps (1970) and Friedman (1968) with the addition of expected inflation: the idea was that people were bidding up wages at a rate expected to reduce excess demand but since excess demand would only fall if wages rose in real terms, nominal wages must be bid up by an amount equal to the expected necessary rise in real wages plus the expected rise in general prices. To the resulting wage equation was usually added a price equation relating prices to costs, from which a Phillips curve in price inflation could be obtained.

The New Classical reinterpretation consists of five elements:

1   The labour market is assumed to clear: there is no wage rigidity.
2   People and firms observe prices in their own markets continuously but observe prices in other markets after a time lag. This implies that firms continuously observe the prices of their inputs and outputs, workers only their wages and some local prices (e.g. of groceries for which they continuously shop). Workers must form an expectation of the general price level.
3   Workers' expectations are rational and in particular use signal extraction to infer the current general price level from the local prices they observe.
4   Workers' supply of labour has a substantial elasticity to current real wages; this is usually supported by the idea of intertemporal substitution of labour supply (although it could also occur when labour has a reservation wage for other reasons, such as unemployment benefits or 'shadow economy' earnings).
5   Firms continuously maximize profits; they relate prices to (marginal) cost, capital usually being taken as fixed, and they hire labour to the point at which its marginal value product equals its wage.

These ideas were developed by Lucas in a series of papers (Lucas and Rapping, 1969; Lucas, 1972a, b, 1973). They can be seen as a response to the difficulties of integrating rational expectations into the original Phillips curve formulation: it is hard to see why rational workers and firms should permit rigidity of wages. Later, as we shall see in chapter 4, Keynesian theorists attempted to overcome this difficulty by the assumption of nominal contracts of long maturity; however, that assumption is not easy to reconcile with the idea of voluntary contracting by agents free to exploit all opportunities for trade, and Lucas's theory has the advantage of full consistency with that paradigm. These remarks do not prejudge the empirical performance of either approach: we return to empirical issues much later in the book.

Let us begin with workers' intertemporal substitution. If one writes down a worker-consumer's general utility function, including terms in both consumption and leisure now and in all future periods, the first order conditions for a maximum will among other things set the marginal rate of transformation between present and future labour supply equal to the gross real rate of interest – for the formal maximization procedure, see chapter 9, and for its application in a model of labour supply see Sargent (1979, chapter 16).

This is illustrated in figure 3.1, where for simplicity the worker is assumed to have a fixed present value of consumption, $\bar{c}$, which can be achieved in a two period life by working either this period or next: his

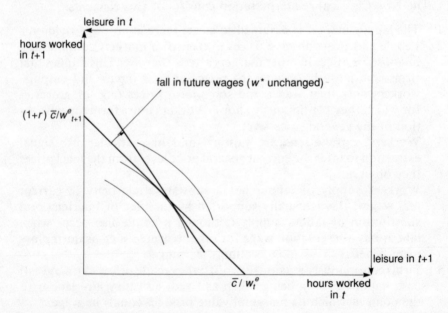

Figure 3.1   Intertemporal substitution by workers.

indifference curves between leisure (work) are tangent to the trade-off between minimum current and future hours required to achieve $\bar{c}$. $\bar{c}$ divided by next period's expected real wages, $w^e_{t+1}$ and multiplied by $1 + r$ (the gross real interest rate), gives the number of hours needed to provide $\bar{c}$ by working entirely in $t + 1$ and borrowing against that income to consume in $t$. The tangency condition is:

$$(U'_{t+1} \cdot w^e_t)/(U'_t \cdot w^e_{t+1}) = 1/(1 + r)$$

where $U'$ is the marginal utility of leisure.

Hence for a normally behaved utility function, higher current or $(U'_{t+1}/U'_t)$ real wages will have an income effect if 'permanent' real wages rise as a result, diminishing work effort, and a substitution effect (relative to future real wages), raising it. Lucas's argument is that these movements in current real wages generally leave permanent real wages unchanged and so the substitution effect is dominant, and large enough to account for the empirically observed Phillips curve correlation between prices and output.

Firms' profit maximization leads to a downward sloping demand for labour from the first order condition that the marginal product of labour, $f'$, equals the real wage, or $f' = W/P$, which in the simplest case where labour is the only variable factor also expresses the price = marginal cost condition, $P = W/f'$; if $f$ is a normally behaved production function, $f'$ will fall as labour input increases.

The complete Phillips curve derivation is illustrated in figure 3.2, a four quadrant diagram due to Parkin and Bade (1988). Quadrant (a) shows the labour $(L)$ market: the supply by workers is conditional on expected prices, $p^e$ (as well as permanent real wages, $w^*$, and $r$, both of which we hold constant here), the demand by firms depends on their own actual prices, which they continuously observe. Quadrant (b) shows the short run production function relating output $(y)$ to labour, capital being fixed. Quadrant (c) transfers the implied output to quadrant (d), which summarizes the resulting PP relationship between prices, $p$, and output. This is illustrated for an increase of $p$ from $p_0 = p^e$ to $p_1$, with workers continuing to expect prices of $p^e = p_0$. This raises labour demand to $D'D'$ but leaves the supply curve where it is. Employment expands and more output is produced: the rise in prices has raised wages and so 'fooled' workers into thinking they are being paid higher real wages, so supplying more labour to firms who are actually enjoying lower real wage costs.

Suppose $p_1$ is maintained in the next period and $p^e$ rises to this new level, then $SS$ too shifts upwards. It will do so by exactly the same (vertical) distance as $DD$, namely a rise in $W$ that is of the same proportion as the rise in $p$; this leaves both actual and expected real wages the same as at our starting point ($p = p_0 = w^e$, $W = W_0$), and

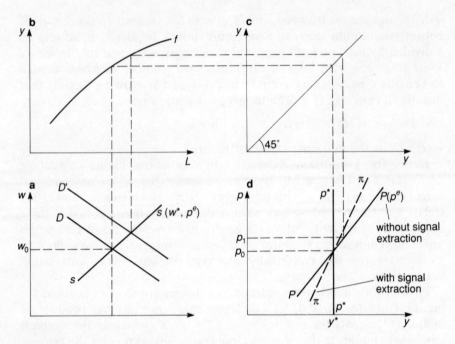

Figure 3.2   The New Classical Phillips curve.

hence of course labour supply and demand will be the same as then. The resulting relationship between $p$ and $y$, the 'long-run' Phillips curve obtained when $p = p^e$, is shown as $P^*P^*$ and is vertical: consistently with neo-classical theory in which people and prices care about real quantities and relative prices, having no 'money illusion', rises in prices when fully anticipated or perceived have no real impact. In this simple model with no lags or adjustment in production or labour supply the economy is at its natural rate when $p = p^e$.

Let us write the resulting Phillips curve relationship between $y$ and $p$ as:

$$y_t - y^* = 1/\delta(p_t - p_t^e) \tag{3.4}$$

This immediately brings out the formal equivalence between the traditional Phillips curve we used in chapter 2, in which prices are the dependent variable, and the New Classical formulation here in which output is. Although the derivations are clearly different, the result is formally the same.

Now let us graft on to this process the one assumption we have so far left out, signal extraction. Workers can use their current information on local prices they observe in their regular shopping to improve their expectation of the general price level. Denote the $i$th (of $N$) group of workers' local price as $p_{it}$ and assume that it is governed by

$$p_{it} = v_{it} + p_t \tag{3.5}$$

where $v_{it}$ is a random error with variance of $\sigma_v^2$.[1]

The problem faced by the $i$th group of workers is to forecast $p_t - E(p_t|\Phi_{t-1})$ from $p_{it} - E(p_{it}|\Phi_{t-1})$ where $\Phi_{t-1}$ is all last period's data assumed available to all $i$ groups by the current period. To do this, they compute the least squares regression of $p_t - E_t(p_t|\Phi_{t-1})$ on $p_{it} - E(p_{it}|\Phi_{t-1})$ and predict from it.

We know that

$$p_t = \sum_{i=0}^{\infty} \pi_i \varepsilon_{t-i} + p^* \tag{3.6}$$

$$E(p_t|\Phi_{t-1}) = \sum_{i=1}^{\infty} \pi_i \varepsilon_{t-i} + p^* \tag{3.7}$$

and

$$E(p_{it}|\Phi_{t-1}) = E[(p_t + v_{it})|\Phi_{t-1}] = E(p_t|\Phi_{t-1}) \tag{3.8}$$

since all $i$ groups have the same $t - 1$ information and cannot predict $v_{it}$ from it. So our regression will be:

$$\pi_0 \varepsilon_t = \phi_0 + \phi(\pi_0 \varepsilon_t + v_{it}) \tag{3.9}$$

Assuming our workers had a large sample, so that we can ignore sampling error for simplicity, they will obtain (all $i$ groups since $\sigma_v^2$ is the same for all $v_{it}$) $\phi_0 = 0$ because $\varepsilon_t$ and $v_{it}$ have zero means, and

$$\phi = \frac{E(\pi_0 \varepsilon_t, \pi_0 \varepsilon_t + v_{it})}{E(\pi_0 \varepsilon_t + v_{it})^2} = \frac{\pi_0^2 \sigma_\varepsilon^2}{\pi_0^2 \sigma_\varepsilon^2 + \sigma_v^2}$$

Armed with this regression, the $i$th group's *current* expectation of $p_t$, $p_{t,i}^e = E(p_t|\theta_{it}, \Phi_{t-1})$ where $\theta_{it}$ is this period's data available in the current period to the $i$th group, now can be written as:

$$p_{t,i}^e = E(p_t|\Phi_{t-1}) + \phi(p_{it} - E[p_t|\Phi_{t-1}]) \tag{3.10}$$

Averaging expectations over all i groups gives us:

$$p_t^e = \sum_i p_{t,i}^e/N = (1 - \phi)E(p_t|\Phi_{t-1}) + \phi p_t \tag{3.11}$$

In passing, notice that $p_t^e$ implies an average expectation of $\varepsilon_t$. Since all i groups know that $p_t = \pi_0 \varepsilon_t + E(p_t | \Phi_{t-1})$, their expectation of $\varepsilon_t$ will be given by:

$$E(\varepsilon_t | \theta_{it}, \Phi_{t-1}) = [E(p_t | \theta_{it}, \Phi_{t-1}) - E(p_t | \Phi_{t-1})]/\pi_0$$

$$= [p_{t,i}^e - E(p_t | \Phi_{t-1})]/\pi_0$$

$$= \phi(p_{it} - E(p_t | \Phi_{t-1}))/\pi_0 \qquad (3.12)$$

Averaging (3.12) over all $i$ gives:

$$\varepsilon_t^e = \phi \pi_0 \varepsilon_t / \pi_0 = \phi \varepsilon_t \qquad (3.13)$$

We may now integrate $p_t^e$ into our New Classical Phillips curve:

$$y_t - y^* = 1/\delta(p_t - p_t^e) = \left(\frac{1-\phi}{\delta}\right)(p_t - E[p_t | \Phi_{t-1}]) \qquad (3.14)$$

The dashed $\pi\pi$ curve in figure 3.2 shows the resulting full New Classical Phillips curve: signal extraction steepens its slope, since now as actual prices rise workers react by altering $p_t^e$.

Let us work out the values of $\phi$ and $\pi_0$ for a simple model:

$$\bar{m} + \varepsilon_t = p_t + y_t \qquad (3.15)$$

$$y_t - y^* = \left(\frac{1-\phi}{\delta}\right)(p_t - Ep_t | \Phi_{t-1}) \qquad (3.16)$$

Using the Muth solution we obtain: $\pi_i = 0 (i \geqslant 1)$ and $\pi_0 = \delta/(\delta + 1 - \phi)$. The slope of the Phillips curve is $(1 - \phi)/\delta$ and must lie between 0 and $1/\delta$, since $0 < \phi < 1$. With $\phi$ given above, we can see that the solution for $\pi_0$ and $\phi$ is in general a cubic, with the extreme values of $\pi_0 = 1, \phi = 1$ (vertical Phillips curve) and $\pi_0 = \delta/1 + \delta, \phi = 0$ (the $PP$ curve in figure 3.2).

The main implication of signal extraction is therefore that the Phillips curve's slope depends on the behaviour of monetary policy. This determines $\varepsilon_t$ in our simple models to this point; but even in more complex models where many influences impact on the 'surprise' term ($p_t - E(p_t | \Phi_{t-1})$), including all demand and supply shocks, money supply shocks will play a major role (a more complex model of this sort in which the problem is to disentangle permanent from temporary money supply shocks is set out by Brunner et al., 1980). If the money supply is volatile, then workers will assume that the current movements in prices they observe are largely monetary in origin: $\phi$ will be close to 1 as $\pi_0^2 \sigma_\varepsilon^2$ is large relative to $\sigma_v^2$. The Phillips curve will be close to vertical. By contrast, countries with monetary stability will have flatter Phillips curves, with workers interpreting local price movements as predominantly relative price movements. Lucas (1973) turned up convincing evidence of this in a large cross-country sample of Phillips curves, and much subsequent evidence has confirmed it. One particularly obvious way in which the Phillips curve steepens is through the spread of indexation in countries with poor monetary control: indexation for a group of workers typically replaces $p_t^e$ by a weighted average of $p_t^e$ and $p_t$ (or $p_{t-k}$ where $k$ is made as small as possible given information-gathering costs). Ironically, though, in countries with extreme monetary volatility indexation is handicapped both by the necessary lag in information and by poor or even fraudulent government information about the general price level.

## The Supply Side: Integrating Macro with Micro

Most of this book is concerned with the behaviour of the economy in response to monetary shocks, in the sense of shocks which disturb the absolute price level. These set up reactions through the Phillips or supply curve on output and so on other variables, for example in the way we have just examined. Yet there is a wide variety and scale of real shocks, which regardless of their effects on the price level, cause important effects on the economy. One of the key changes in our thinking produced by the rational expectations hypothesis has been a renewed emphasis on the 'supply side'; that is, the mechanisms through which the economy responds to real shocks.

One branch of rational expectations research, real business cycle theory, dismisses monetary shocks altogether as a source of variation in output, explaining it entirely in terms of real shocks (e.g. Kydland and Prescott, 1982; Long and Plosser, 1983); these economists argue that people have sufficiently up-to-date information on the price level to avoid being fooled as in the New Classical supply curve, and that any contracts they sign are fully indexed to the price level, again avoiding any real effects of unexpected price changes as in the New Keynesian supply curve. The price level on this view will vary if the money supply increases (e.g. through expansion in bank credit and deposits) but this will have no real effects. Only if there is some shock to payments technology which disturbs real plans (for example, by credit controls creating a 'credit crunch') will monetary shocks have a real effect: but this is not a normal money supply shock in our terms.

The real business cycle school may or may not be going too far in denying any effect of monetary shocks: testing its assertions is difficult because it can in principle account for the same correlations we observe, such as that between prices and output in the Phillips curve, by appealing to reverse causation – real shocks move output, which induces monetary expansion, which raises prices. Nevertheless, what is undoubtedly important is the focus on real shocks and the supply side as of primary interest to macroeconomists. We have just set out a basic model of the supply side, to explain the full New Classical model. This model can be developed to explain unemployment in terms of people's voluntary choices confronted with the opportunities they face (not necessarily attractive ones of course); a further factor which may frustrate their choices, however, is the power of unions. Analysis of unemployment along these lines for the UK is to be found in Minford (1983), Minford et al. (1985) and Layard and Nickell (1985), for Germany in Davis and Minford (1986) and for a variety of other countries in Bean et al. (1989). In chapter 8 we will extend the supply side to the open economy, to explain the real exchange rate and the current account of the balance of payments.

Rational expectations has re-united macro and micro economics into a single subject. Keynes (1936) divided off, indeed created, the subject of macroeconomics with its own aggregate laws, not derivable from micro behaviour and subject to regular aggregate 'market failure'. Since his intervention we have learned much about aggregate behaviour, which had never previously been much studied by the classical economists. Essentially, rational expectations has enabled us to account for macro behaviour in terms of micro laws.

## Capital Markets and Partial Macro Information

We now consider our second example of signal extraction. Here we assume that there is no useful local information ($\sigma_v^2$ is large relative to $\sigma_\varepsilon^2$) but that there is current macro information from capital markets. Clearly a relevant model of most economies will contain both sorts of information but it helps our exposition to focus on each separately.

Our illustrative example supposes that people know the interest rate currently. They wish to derive from this estimates of other current macroeconomic variables – the price level and output, and so on. They do this just as in the local information case by predicting from a regression of these variables on the interest rate, any variable $x_t$ being expressed as $x_t - E(x_t | \Phi_{t-1})$. Again, as in the local case, the regression parameters enter the model through their effect on the expected variables: there is an additional feedback in the model from current events to expectations, altering the impact effect of shocks to the economy.

We saw in the local case that the true regression parameter (i.e. in a large sample), $\phi$, was determined by the other ('primitive') parameters of the model and the variances of the errors $\varepsilon_t$ and $v_{it}$. So it is here. Let us now work out here too the signal extraction parameters and how the model will behave in their presence.

To give our example enough complexity to be of interest we move to a fairly general macro model. We express all variables in deviations from equilibrium, so all constants such as $\bar{m}$ and $y^*$ are dropped. For short $E_t x_t$ is used to note the current expectation conditional on last period's full data and this period's partial data (consisting of $R_t$, the interest rate). The model (from Minford and Peel, 1983) is:

$$y_t = a(p_t - E_t\, p_t) + u_t \qquad (3.17)$$

$$m_t = p_t + y_t - c\, R_t \qquad (3.18)$$

$$m_t = \mu\, m_{t-1} + e_t \qquad (3.19)$$

$$y_t = -\alpha\, R_t + \alpha\, E_t\, p_{t+1} - \alpha\, E_t\, p_t + v_t \qquad (3.20)$$

$c, \alpha, a, \mu$ are constants; $u_t, v_t$ and $e_t$ are independent random shocks with known variances $\sigma_u^2, \sigma_v^2$ and $\sigma_e^2$; (3.17) is aggregate output supply; (3.18) is money demand; (3.19) is money supply; (3.20) is demand for aggregate output.

To solve this model, we first obtain a basic equation in the errors as deviations from their expected values. Taking expectations of (3.17) and subtracting from (3.17) yields:

$$y_t - E_t\, y_t = a(p_t - E_t\, p_t) + u_t - E_t\, u_t \qquad (3.21)$$

Equating (3.18) with (3.19) and following the same procedure as with (3.17) yields:

$$e_t - E_t\, e_t = p_t - E_t\, p_t + y_t - E_t\, y_t - c(R_t - E_t\, R_t) \qquad (3.22)$$

(3.20) analogously gives:

$$y_t - E_t\, y_t = -\alpha(R_t - E_t\, R_t) + v_t - E_t\, v_t = v_t - E_t\, v_t \qquad (3.23)$$

since $R_t = E_t\, R_t$, $R_t$ being known. Simple manipulation then yields our basic equation in the errors:

$$(1 + a)(v_t - E_t\, v_t) = a(e_t - E_t\, e_t) + u_t - E_t\, u_t \qquad (3.24)$$

This formal restriction across the expected and actual values of the errors results from the fact that people know $R_t$. Therefore the actual solution of $R_t$ (based on the actual and expected errors) must coincide with the expected solution (based only on the expected errors). The parameters $\alpha$ and $c$ drop out because when deviations from expectations are taken these multiply variables that must be zero (since $R_t = E_t\, R_t$, $E_t(E_t\, p_t) = E_t\, p_t$, $E_t(E_t\, p_{t+1}) = E_t\, p_{t+1}$).

This linear model has a general linear solution for $R_t$ in terms of the current shocks and lagged information:

$$R_t = Au_t + Bv_t + De_t + Zm_{t-1} \tag{3.25}$$

$A, B, D$ and $Z$ are the coefficients to be solved for. Consequently, using the Graybill formula, the best estimates of $u_t, v_t, e_t$, given $R_t - Zm_{t-1}$, are:

$$E_t\, u_t = \frac{1}{A}\, \phi_u\,(Au_t + Bv_t + De_t) \tag{3.26}$$

$$E_t\, v_t = \frac{1}{B}\, \phi_v\,(Au_t + Bv_t + De_t) \tag{3.27}$$

$$E_t\, e_t = \frac{1}{D}\, \phi_e\,(Au_t + Bv_t + De_t) \tag{3.28}$$

where

$$\phi_u = A^2\sigma_u^2/X;\; \phi_v = B^2\sigma_v^2/X;\; \phi_e = D^2\sigma_e^2/X$$

and

$$X = A^2\sigma_u^2 + B^2\sigma_v^2 + D^2\sigma_e^2$$

Substituting (3.26), (3.27) and (3.28) into (3.24) we obtain:

$$(1 + a)v_t - ae_t - u_t = \left\{(1 + a)\frac{\phi_v}{B} - \frac{a\phi_e}{D} - \frac{\phi_u}{A}\right\}(Au_t + Bv_t + De_t) \tag{3.29}$$

Since $v_t$, $e_t$ and $u_t$ may each be any real number, (3.29) is only satisfied if the coefficients on each alone equate, that is if, for example,

$$1 = \phi_v - a/(1 + a)\frac{B}{D}\phi_e - 1/(1 + a)\frac{B}{A}\phi_u \quad \text{(on } v_t) \tag{3.30}$$

Further, since we know that $\phi_v + \phi_e + \phi_u = 1$ it follows at once that

$$\frac{D}{A} = a;\; \frac{D}{B} = -a/(1 + a);\; \frac{A}{B} = -1/(1 + a) \tag{3.31}$$

Consequently

$$\phi_u = \sigma_u^2/X';\; \phi_v = \sigma_v^2(1 + a)^2/X';\; \phi_e = a^2\sigma_e^2/X' \tag{3.32}$$

where

$$X' = \sigma_u^2 + (1 + a)^2\, \sigma_v^2 + a^2\sigma_e^2$$

The full solution of this model can now be found. From (3.17), (3.18) and (3.19) we have:

$$p_t + a(p_t - E_t\, p_t) + u_t - cR_t = e_t + \mu\, m_{t-1} \tag{3.33}$$

from which we obtain, taking expectations and using $R_t = E_t R_t$:

$$R_t = \frac{1}{c}(E_t \, p_t + E_t \, u_t - E_t \, e_t - \mu \, m_{t-1}) \tag{3.34}$$

Equating (3.17) and (3.18), taking expectations and substituting for $R_t$ from (3.34) we get:

$$E_t \, u_t - E_t \, v_t = -\alpha/c(E_t \, p_t + E_t \, u_t - E_t \, e_t - \mu \, m_{t-1})$$
$$- \alpha E_t \, p_t + \alpha E_t \, p_{t+1}$$

or rearranging:

$$E_t \, p_{t+1} - (1 + c/c) E_t \, p_t = (\alpha + c)/\alpha c \, E_t \, u_t$$
$$+ 1/\alpha \, E_t \, v_t + 1/c \, E_t \, e_t - \mu/c \, m_{t-1} \tag{3.35}$$

Following Sargent's procedure (see chapter 2), we write the left hand side of (3.35) as:

$$B^{-1} \frac{1 - [(1 + c)/c]^{-1} B^{-1}}{-[(1 + c)/c]^{-1} B^{-1}} E_t \, p_t =$$
$$-(1 + c/c) \, [1 - c/(1 + c) \, B^{-1}] E_t \, p_t \tag{3.36}$$

where $B$ is the backward operator instructing one to lag variables but not the expectations date (e.g. $BE_t P_t = E_t P_{t-1}$). Equation (3.36) can now be written as:

$$E_t \, p_t = -c/(1 + c) \, . \, 1/[1 - c/(1 + c) \, B^{-1}] \, .$$
$$(\alpha + c/\alpha c \, E_t \, u_t - 1/\alpha \, E_t \, v_t - 1/c \, E_t \, e_t - \mu/c \, m_{t-1})$$
$$= -(\alpha + c)/\alpha(1 + c) \, E_t \, u_t + c/\alpha(1 + c) \, E_t \, v_t$$
$$+ 1/(1 + c) \, E_t \, e_t + \mu/(1 + c) \sum_{i=0}^{\infty} \{c/(1 + c)\}^i \, E_t \, m_{t-1+i} \tag{3.37}$$

Since $E_t \, m_{t-1+i} = m_{t-1}, \mu \, m_{t-1} + E_t \, e_t, \mu^2 \, m_{t-1} + \mu \, E_t \, e_t, \ldots$, for $i = 0, 1, 2,\ldots$, (3.37) becomes:

$$E_t \, p_t = \frac{-(\alpha + c)}{\alpha(1 + c)} E_t \, u_t + \frac{c}{\alpha(1 + c)} E_t \, v_t$$
$$+ \frac{1}{1 + c(1 - \mu)} E_t \, e_t + \frac{\mu}{1 + c(1 - \mu)} m_{t-1} \tag{3.38}$$

whence:

$$E_t \, p_{t+1} = \frac{\mu^2 \, m_{t-1} + \mu \, E_t \, e_t}{1 + c(1 - \mu)} \tag{3.39}$$

To find $R_t$ substitute from (3.38) into (3.34) to obtain

$$R_t = \frac{-(1 - \alpha)}{\alpha(1 + c)} \, E_t \, u_t + \frac{1}{\alpha(1 + c)} \, E_t \, v_t$$

$$- \frac{1 - \mu}{1 + c(1 - \mu)} \, E_t \, e_t - \frac{\mu(1 - \mu)}{1 + c(1 - \mu)} \, m_{t-1} \qquad (3.40)$$

We can write

$$E_t \, u_t = \phi_u \, Q_t; \ E_t \, v_t = -\phi_v/(1 + a) Q_t; \ E_t \, e_t = \phi_e/a \, Q_t \qquad (3.41)$$

where

$$Q_t = u_t - (1 + a) v_t + a \, e_t$$

Hence

$$A = -[\alpha(1 + c)]^{-1}[(1 - \alpha)\phi_u + (1 + a)^{-1} \, \phi_v]$$

$$- \{a[1 + c(1 - \mu)]\}^{-1}[1 - \mu] \, \phi_e$$

$$B = -(1 + a) A; \ D = aA \qquad (3.42)$$

**Paradoxical Responses to Shocks**

It is of some interest to compare the reaction of this 'economy' when $R_t$ is known with that when $R_t$ is not known. Table 3.1 shows the reactions of output to the three shocks. When $R_t$ is not known, all shocks have 'normal' positive effects on output. Clearly the sizes of the coefficients are quite different when $R_t$ is known. This is hardly surprising since now output only responds – see equation (3.25) – to expected supply shocks ($E_t \, u_t$) and the *difference* of demand shocks, $v_t$, from their expected level. However, now even the sign of effect can be different for the various shocks. We can understand this as follows.

Suppose the noise in $e_t$ dominates; then $\phi_e \to 1$, $(\phi_u, \phi_v) \to 0$ and $u_t$ has no effect because $E_t \, u_t \to 0$, $E_t \, v_t \to 0$. Suppose noise in $v_t$ dominates; then $(\phi_e, \phi_u) \to 0$ and $v_t$ has no effect. But suppose noise in $u_t$ dominates; then $E_t \, v_t \to 0$, $\phi_u \to 1$, so that $\delta(v_t + E_t \, u_t)/\delta v_t = -a$.

Table 3.1  Output reactions to shocks

|  | $u_t$ | $v_t$ | $e_t$ |
|---|---|---|---|
| $y_t(R_t$ not known) | $W$ | $a(c/\alpha)W$ | $aW$ |
| $y_t(R_t$ known) | $\phi_u + (1 + a)^{-1}\phi_v$ | $\phi_e - a\phi_u$ | $a\phi_u + a(1 + a)^{-1}\phi_v$ |
| where $W = [1 + a\{1 + (c/\alpha)\}]^{-1}$ | | | |

Table 3.2  Price and interest rate reaction to shocks

|  | $u_t$ | $v_t$ | $e_t$ |
|---|---|---|---|
| $p_t(R_t$ not known) | $-(1 + c/\alpha)W$ | $c/\alpha W$ | $W$ |
| $p_t(R_t$ known) | $-S$ | $(1 + a)S - 1$ | $1 - aS$ |
| $R_t(R_t$ not known) | $(-a/\alpha)W$ | $\{1 + (ac/\alpha)\}W/\alpha$ | $(-a/\alpha)W$ |
| $R_t(R_t$ known) | $A$ | $B$ | $D$ |

where

$$S = \frac{\alpha + c}{\alpha(1 + c)}\phi_u + \frac{[c + \alpha(1 + c)]}{\alpha(1 + c)(1 + a)}\phi_v + \frac{c(1 - \mu)}{a(1 + c(1 - \mu))}\phi_e$$

Hence a demand shock has a negative effect on output if supply shocks predominate, because agents misinterpret the effect of the positive demand shock on interest rates as that of a negative supply shock; expected prices consequently rise more than actual prices and supply of output is reduced.

Similar peculiarities can occur in the reactions of $p_t$ and $R_t$; table 3.2 documents them. It is worth stressing therefore that the economy's

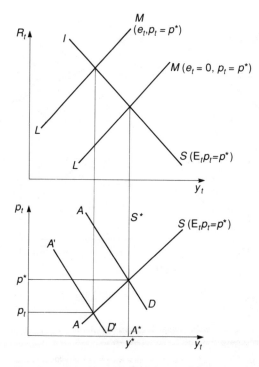

Figure 3.3  The case where $R_t$ is not currently observed and a negative $e_t$ shock occurs.

behaviour in response to shocks can be paradoxical if the shocks are misinterpreted. Such effects are well known at the level of everyday comment (cf. the behaviour of the UK economy in 1980, when the interest rates were interpreted as responding to 'overshooting' of its target by the money supply; subsequently it turned out that the money supply, truly measured, had contracted substantially). It is of interest that they can be rationalized within a stylized framework.

One such case is illustrated in figures 3.3 and 3.4. In figure 3.3, it is assumed that a negative monetary shock, $e_t$, occurs but that $R_t$ is not currently known; so normal results are obtained. The *LM* curve shifts leftwards in the upper $(R_t, y_t)$ half, shifting left the aggregate demand curve in the lower $(p_t, y_t)$ half. Prices and output fall and the interest rate rises; expectations of course are undisturbed.

In figure 3.4 the same shock occurs when $R_t$ is currently observed (so that $E_t\,p_t$ now reacts); we illustrate the paradoxical case just discussed where people expect only variations in the supply shock, $u_t$, of any significance, so they misinterpret the shock as a negative supply shock. The left side of figure 3.4 shows actual outcomes, the right side shows expected ones: across the two, expected outcomes are of course the same. The expected outcome is a rise in the interest rate and in prices,

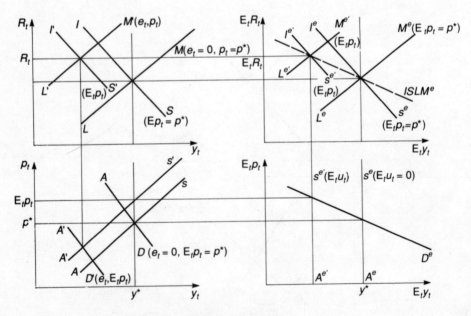

Figure 3.4  The case where $R_t$ is currently observed.

A negative $e_t$ shock occurs but $\sigma_v^2$, $\sigma_e^2$ are small so that a $u_t$ shock is expected ($\phi_u \to 1$). The $e_t$ shock is interpreted as a $u_t$ shock ($E_t\,p_{t+1} = p^*$; i.e. $\mu = 0$).

together with a fall in output because of a negative $u_t$. The rise in $E_t p_t$ shifts both the expected $IS$ and $LM$ curves, $IS^e$ and $LM^e$, along the $ISLM^e$ curve which plots their intersection as $E_t p_t$ changes. In $(E_t p_t, E_t y_t)$ space, the $AS$ curve shifts leftwards from the fall in $E_t u_t$, along $A^e D^e$, the expected aggregate demand curve.

The actual outcome can be broken down into two parts: the shifts in the curves because $E_t p_t$ rises, and the shifts because $e_t$ falls. The rise in $E_t p_t$ shifts the $AS$ curve up and the $AD$ curve leftwards in $(p, y)$ space, the latter being produced by the IS curve shifting leftwards in $(R, y)$ space. The fall in $e_t$ shifts the $LM$ leftwards in $(R, y)$ space and so the $AD$ leftwards in $(p, y)$ space. These various shifts are shown on the graphs by labelling each curve according to the value of $e_t$, $p_t$ and $E_t p_t$.

In effect, the expected supply shock drives expected prices up (because of fears of shortage) so that even though prices may fall by much the same as in the normal case, the contraction in output is much greater. In this example, the misinterpretation of the monetary shock has seriously worsened recession (somewhat reminiscent of the 1980 British recession).

## Conclusions

We have seen that signal extraction has potentially important effects on economic behaviour. How people interpret shocks conditions their behaviour, whether in the slope of the Phillips curve or more generally. In this chapter we have illustrated these effects and shown how models can be solved allowing for the signal extraction feedback. In subsequent chapters we shall be applying the techniques of chapters 2 and 3 to the analysis of a variety of policy issues.

## Note

1   $\sum_i v_{it} = 0$ by definition since $\sum_i p_{it}/N = p_t$ by definition;

hence $v_{it}$ is a relative price shock in the $i$th market and there are $N - 1$ independent $v_{it}$, the $N$th being given as

$$-\sum_{i=1}^{N-1} v_{it} = v_{Nt}.$$

We have 'fixed' the covariances between $v_{it}$, however, so that they all have the same variance, $\sigma_v^2$.

# 4

# Stabilization Policy

In this chapter we will outline the implications for stabilization policy if agents in an economy form their expectations rationally. Stabilization policies are typically defined as policies aimed at reducing deviations (the variance usually) of output and employment from their full-employment ('natural' or 'equilibrium') levels. We will initially use this definition.

Stabilization policies are usefully classified into two groups, namely fixed and flexible rules. Fixed rules are rules setting policy instruments on a trajectory that will not be altered whatever happens. Perhaps the best known example is Milton Friedman's proposal that the authorities should adopt a policy of a fixed rate of growth of the nominal money stock (Friedman, 1968). Flexible rules, by contrast, are rules with 'feedback': that is, they are contingent on certain outcomes in the economy. One simple example of a flexible rule would be one in which the money stock deviates around some target level as the rate of unemployment $U$, deviates from the equilibrium or natural rate, $U^n$:

$$m_t = \bar{m} + \mu(U_{t-1} - U^N) \tag{4.1}$$

There has been a long-running academic debate as to the relative merits of fixed versus flexible rules, or 'rules versus discretion'. We will return to this normative issue in chapter 5. However, this chapter discusses the positive issue of how stabilization policies affect the behaviour of economies with rational expectations. We assume that the government's stabilizing behaviour can be summarized by linear functions relating (or not, as the case may be) the money supply and the budget deficit to past economic outcomes – the rules in question, fixed or flexible.

There are conditions under which this is not the case: for example, a government maximizing some general welfare function each period subject to a non-linear economic model will decide a new set of policies (i.e. settings for the money supply and the deficit) for the future each period and that new set will be affected by the whole path of the model's exogenous and endogenous variables. However, these conditions are not particularly relevant, as no government is likely to have the information or resources to carry out such an exercise. Where the model is linear and the welfare function is quadratic, it is possible to compute the rule an optimizing government will follow; even in this case, the full optimal rule may be a function of many variables and it is usual to find a simple version that captures the main benefits in stabilization. The discussion in this chapter uses some such illustrative simple rules.

In rational expectations models we will find – and will discuss fully in chapter 5 – that the optimal rules a government will follow depend on what binding advance commitments it is prepared to make. These advance commitments influence expectations and behaviour, often in a beneficial way, but they also limit the room for flexible reaction to new events. The optimal extent of this discretionary freedom is an important issue for chapter 5. But whatever choice a government makes, it is still possible to compute, in the linear quadratic case we assume, the rule it will follow; and it will in general be a flexible rule, because in general it will be optimal to react to new events in some way or other. A fixed rule is a special case of an advance commitment, where any sort of reaction to new events is ruled out. It is this special case of the fixed rule that in this chapter we are contrasting with flexible rules of all types.

## Models with the Sargent–Wallace Supply Curve

An early result, due to Sargent and Wallace (1975), is that stabilization policy has no impact on either real output or unemployment in classical equilibrium models if they embody a supply function relating deviations of output to surprise movements in the price level, and further that (a) both private and public agents have identical information sets and (b) are able to act on these information sets. We discussed this result briefly in chapter 2 in the context of a simple monetary model, which we now extend somewhat.

Consider the following simple model:

$$y_t = -\alpha(R_t - E_{t-1}\, p_{t+1} + E_{t-1}\, p_t) + \mu_f\, (y_{t-1} - y^*) \qquad (4.2)$$

$$y_t = y^* + \beta(p_t - E_{t-1}\, p_t) \qquad (4.3)$$

$$m_t = p_t + y_t - cR_t + v_t \qquad (4.4)$$

$$m_t = \bar{m} + \mu_m(y_{t-1} - y^*) + u_t \qquad (4.5)$$

$\alpha, \beta, \mu_f, \mu_m$ and $c$ are constants ($\mu_f, \mu_m$ would typically be negative in Keynesian policy rules), $u_t$ and $v_t$ are random errors, $R_t$ is the nominal interest rate.

Equation (4.2) is the aggregate demand schedule. It includes a fiscal feedback response $\mu_f(y_{t-1} - y^*)$ representing government counter-cyclical variations in spending or tax rates.

Equation (4.3) is the Sargent and Wallace Phillips (or supply) curve. This is derived as in chapter 3. The only difference is that it assumes that people can obtain no useful information about the general price level from their current local prices; so there is no signal extraction in this case – hence the dating of expectations at $t - 1$. The same assumption is used throughout the model. It turns out, as we shall see later, to be an important restriction.

Another way of looking at (4.3) is as an 'old', Keynesian, augmented Phillips curve in which inflation equals expected inflation plus an effect of excess demand proxied by $y - y^*$. Sargent and Wallace stressed that their result could be viewed as an implication of orthodox Keynesian models, if rational expectations were substituted for adaptive expectations.

Equation (4.5) is a money supply rule with a feedback response $\mu_m (y_{t-1} - y^*)$. On substituting (4.2) for $R_t$ into (4.4) and equating (4.5) to the result, we obtain:

$$\bar{m} + \mu(y_{t-1} - y^*) + w_t = p_t + (1 + c/\alpha)y_t$$
$$- c(E_{t-1} \, p_{t+1} - E_{t-1} \, p_t) \qquad (4.6)$$

where $w_t = u_t - v_t$ and $\mu = [\mu_f(c/\alpha) + \mu_m]$. Substitution of (4.3) into (4.6) for $y_t$ and $y_{t-1}$ yields:

$$\bar{m} + \beta\mu(p_{t-1} - E_{t-1} \, p_{t-1}) + w_t = p_t + (1 + c/\alpha)\beta \, (p_t - E_{t-1} \, p_t)$$
$$- c(E_{t-1} \, p_{t+1} - E_{t-1} \, p_t) + (1 + c/\alpha)y^* \qquad (4.7)$$

To solve (4.7) for prices, we use the Muth solution method discussed in chapter 2, writing:

$$p_t = \bar{p} + \sum_{i=0}^{\infty} \pi_i \, w_{t-i} \qquad (4.8)$$

We find that the identities yield:

$$\bar{p} = \bar{m} - (1 + c/\alpha)y^* \qquad (4.9)$$

(terms in $w_t$)

$$1 = (\pi_0[1 + \beta(1 + c/\alpha)] \qquad (4.10)$$

The identities in the other errors are irrelevant for our purposes here. Since

$$p_t - E_{t-1} \, p_t = \pi_0 \, w_t \qquad (4.11)$$

substitution in (4.3) yields

$$y_t = y^* + \beta\pi_0 \, w_t \qquad (4.12)$$

From (4.10) we see that $\pi_0$ does not depend on either $\mu_m$ or $\mu_f$ and consequently we see from (4.12) that systematic monetary policy does not influence the variance of output in this model. Unanticipated monetary change is of course equal to $m_t - E_{t-1} m_t$.

Since $E_{t-1} m_t = \bar{m} + \mu_m (y_{t-1} - y^*)$,

$$m_t - E_{t-1} m_t = u_t \tag{4.13}$$

which is a component of $w_t$. Consequently, *unanticipated* monetary policy does influence output in the Sargent–Wallace model, but not anticipated monetary policy.

This result stems from the nature of the supply curve. Output is set by supply considerations (relative prices, technology, producers' preferences, etc.) and is only influenced by macroeconomic events if these cause surprise movements in absolute prices which in turn are partially (mis)interpreted as relative price movements. Government by definition cannot plan surprises (if it tried to, the 'surprise' would be – under our assumptions here – part of available information at $t - 1$ and so would be fully anticipated, and no surprise at all); its feedback responses are *planned* variations in net spending or money supply.

A basic extension of the result occurs if there are adjustment costs in supply; allowance for these in a standard way (e.g. a quadratic cost function) adds a term $+ \mu(y_{t-1} - y^*)$ to (4.3) $(0 < \mu < 1)$. A shock to output now persists, and in principle the business cycle in output can be accounted for by the interaction of a variety of shocks with such a 'persistence mechanism' (various forms of it have been suggested by Lucas, 1975; Sargent, 1976a; Barro, 1980).

Even though a macroeconomic shock now affects output for the indefinite future, it is still impossible for fiscal or monetary feedback rules to affect its variance because they can neither affect the impact of the shock itself, being a surprise, nor alter the adjustment parameter(s) which determine the lagged effects, these parameters being fixed by technology, etc. We leave the demonstration of this – by substituting for $y_t$ and $y_{t-1}$ in (4.6) from the new supply curve in (4.3) – as an exercise for the reader.

## Different Information Sets

It is crucial for this neutrality proposition that, even in a model embodying a Sargent–Wallace supply curve, both private and public agents have the same information set.

If, for example, the government has an information superiority, then it can use this to modify the 'surprise' faced by the private sector. For suppose private agents have access only to last period's data in the current period, but the government knows the true price level (assume it collects price statistics over the period and waits before releasing them).

Then it may in principle let its net spending or the money supply react to this information; its reactions will modify the price surprises to suppliers. Formally, add $-a_f(p_t - E_{t-1}\, p_t)$ into (4.2) and $-a_m(p_t - E_{t-1}\, p_t)$ into (4.5) where $a_f, a_m$ (both positive) are fiscal and monetary responses respectively. To simplify matters set $\mu_f = \mu_m = 0$. Equation (4.7) now becomes

$$\bar{m} - (a_m + ca_f/\alpha)(p_t - E_{t-1}\, p_t) + w_t = p_t$$
$$+ (1 + c/\alpha)\beta(p_t - E_{t-1}\, p_t) - c(E_{t-1}\, p_{t+1} - E_{t-1}\, p_t)$$
$$+ (1 + c/\alpha)y^* \tag{4.14}$$

so that from the terms in $w_t$ we have:

$$\pi_0 = [1 + (1 + c/\alpha)\beta + a_m + ca_f/\alpha]^{-1} \tag{4.15}$$

from which it is apparent that the higher $a_m, a_f$ the smaller the price surprise and hence the output variance.

One may ask, however, why a government in possession of macro information should not release it rapidly as an alternative to implementing such (presumably costly) rules. If it did so, private agents would be able to make better informed judgements about current macroeconomic events, increasing the economy's stability. In the example here, if price data are released rapidly, then $p_t$ will be effectively known in period $t$ and the economy will be in continuous equilibrium – perfect stability!

A further information asymmetry, which may violate neutrality and has had some attention (Turnovsky, 1980; Weiss, 1980), is that where one group of private agents has superior information to that possessed by suppliers and by the government. The simplest method of illustrating this possibility is to modify the aggregate demand schedule (4.2) in the above model to

$$y_t = -\alpha(R_t - E_t\, p_{t+1} + p_t) + \mu_f(y_{t-1} - y^*) \tag{4.16}$$

The interpretation of this aggregate demand schedule (4.16) is that investors have instantaneous access to current information on all relevant macro data while other agents, such as the government or suppliers of goods, receive this information with a one-period lag.

While this particular example, used by Turnovsky (1980), is perhaps somewhat strained, the salient point he makes regarding the efficacy of stabilization policy is applicable in any macro model embodying a Sargent–Wallace supply curve in which the expectation of any future variable, such as the exchange rate or interest rate, is conditioned by an information set dated at time $t$. In defence of this, it is argued that agents in regular contact with asset markets receive global information (such as interest rates and asset prices) almost instantaneously, by contrast with those in the labour market.

Substitution of (4.16) into our model in place of (4.2) yields the following reduced form:

$$\bar{m} + \mu\beta(p_{t-1} - E_{t-2}\, p_{t-1}) + w_t = (1 + c)p_t$$

$$+ (1 + c/\alpha)\beta(p_t - E_{t-1}\, p_t) - c\, E_t\, p_{t+1} + (1 + c/\alpha)y^* \qquad (4.17)$$

where $\mu = (\mu_m + \mu_f\, c/\alpha)$ as before. Using the Muth solution the identities are given by:

$$\bar{p} = \bar{m} - (1 + c/\alpha)y^* \qquad (4.18)$$

(terms in $w_t$)

$$1 = \pi_0(1 + c + \beta(1 + c/\alpha)) - c\pi_1 \qquad (4.19)$$

(terms in $w_{t-1}$)

$$\mu\beta\pi_0 = \pi_1(1 + c) - c\pi_2 \qquad (4.20)$$

(terms in $w_{t-i}, i \geqslant 2$)

$$0 = \pi_i(1 + c) - c\pi_{i+1} \qquad (4.21)$$

Equation (4.21) defines an unstable process. Consequently applying the stability condition, we set $\pi_i = 0\,(i \geqslant 2)$. Therefore we can simultaneously solve (4.19) and (4.20) to obtain $\pi_0$ and $\pi_1$. The important point is that $\pi_0$, the coefficient on the current innovation, will depend on $\mu$. Consequently the variance of output depends on the feedback rules.

The basis of this result is that the agents in the goods market with superior information demand goods this period in reaction to expected future prices because these affect the real interest rate they expect to pay. Even though expected future *output* is invariant to the feedback rule, expected future prices are not in these models – clearly not, since the *demand* for output is affected by feedback and this in turn has to be equated with given output supply by prices and interest rates. So current demand for goods is affected by the feedback parameters via their effect on expected future prices, and the response of goods demand, and so of prices and so of output, to shocks is correspondingly modified. The government can thus exploit these agents' information without itself having to access it. This second asymmetry result is, however, subject to questioning of a similar type to the first: namely, the basis for the restriction of such macroeconomic information to one set of agents. The case for macroeconomic information on individual markets being so restricted seems more secure, although this is communicable through asset prices. But macroeconomic information, once available, is a public good which, first, it is usual for the government to insist be made available at low cost; second, even if it is not so provided, it would pay the possessors to divulge it for a fee to other agents, since this maximizes the overall possibilities for its exploitation; third, asset prices themselves will communicate this information indirectly to other agents. The model just used furthermore makes the strong assumption that people operating in asset goods markets know all current macro data (this is implicit in taking expectations based on current period data), which is clearly implausible.

In short, the overall set-up here is generally implausible in both the asymmetry and the comprehensiveness of the group's information set.

## Partial Information

The result above can be refined to deal with the two objections under certain conditions. Suppose we let everyone in the economy have access to some partial current information, as discussed in chapter 3. When that information is micro, it turns out that flexible rules will affect the variance of output. The reason is the same as in the Turnovsky–Weiss case: people react to current shocks because they have incomplete information but the flexible policy rule affects expected future prices, which in turn condition those reactions. Of course, if people could disentangle from their current information exactly what the current money supply shock was, then they could protect their real wages, relative prices and real supplies and demands against mere monetary noise and a flexible money supply rule would be ineffective; but they cannot, and so it is effective. As for a flexible fiscal rule, that too is effective provided people cannot disentangle the shocks well enough to predict the current price level exactly: in other words, they have less than full current information, which is guaranteed by assumption.

To illustrate policy effectiveness in the presence of micro partial information, take the model of chapter 3 (p. 48), in which people know their local prices only (models of this sort with policy effectiveness were first set out in Marini (1985, 1986) and Minford (1986)). Let us modify the model, equations (3.15) and (3.16), by the addition in (3.15) of a flexible money supply response to output, $-\mu(y_{t-1} - y^*)$ and a Cagan-style demand response to expected inflation. The model now becomes:

$$\bar{m} + \varepsilon_t - \mu(y_{t-1} - y^*) = p_t + y_t - \alpha(\mathsf{E}_t\, p_{t+1} - \mathsf{E}_t\, p_t) \qquad (4.22)$$

$$y_t - y^* = \frac{1 - \phi}{\delta}\,(p_t - \mathsf{E}\, p_t\,|\,\Phi_{t-1}) \qquad (4.23)$$

where as before $\phi = 1/(1 + \sigma_v^2/\pi_0^2\sigma_\varepsilon^2)$. Using the Muth solution method and our previous results that $E_t \varepsilon_t = \phi \varepsilon_t$, we can substitute for $y_t$ from (4.23) into (4.22) to obtain:

$$\bar{m} + \varepsilon_t - [\mu(1 - \phi)/\delta] \, \pi_0 \varepsilon_{t-1} = \sum_{t=0}^{\infty} \pi_i \varepsilon_{t-i} + y^*$$

$$+ [(1 - \phi)/\delta] \, \pi_0 \varepsilon_t - \alpha(\pi_1 \phi \varepsilon_t - \pi_0 \phi \varepsilon_t) + \alpha \sum_{i=1}^{\infty} (\pi_{i+1} - \pi_i) \varepsilon_{t-i}$$

$$(4.24)$$

The identities yield:

$$1 = \pi_0 + \frac{1}{\delta}(1 - \phi)\pi_0 - \alpha(\pi_1 \phi - \pi_0 \phi) \qquad (\varepsilon_t) \qquad (4.25)$$

$$\frac{-\mu}{\delta}(1 - \phi)\pi_0 = \pi_1 - \alpha(\pi_2 - \pi_1) \qquad (\varepsilon_{t-1}) \qquad (4.26)$$

$$0 = (1 + \alpha)\pi_i - \alpha\pi_{i+1} \qquad (\varepsilon_{t-i}, i \geqslant 2) \qquad (4.27)$$

Imposing the terminal condition $\pi_N = 0$ ($N > 2$) yields $\pi_i = 0$ ($i \geqslant 2$); $\pi_1 = -\mu(1 - \phi)\pi_0/[\delta(1 + \alpha)]$; and

$$\pi_0 = [1 + (1 - \phi)/\delta + \alpha\phi + \alpha\mu\phi(1 - \phi)/\delta(1 + \alpha)]^{-1} \qquad (4.28)$$

It is clear from (4.28) that the parameter $\mu$ of the flexible rule affects $\pi_0$ and so output's response to the monetary shock, which is $(1 - \phi)$ $\pi_0/\delta$. It turns out, when $\phi$ is substituted out in terms of $\pi_0$, that (4.28) is a quintic in $\pi_0$. Computer solutions for a wide variety of possible parameter values indicate that $\pi_0$ has only one real root, which is reduced as $\mu$ rises: this yields the commonsense result that the more policy 'leans against' the recent business cycle, the more it stabilizes output. Suppose a monetary expansion, $\varepsilon_t$, raises output through a surprise rise in prices; this causes an expected money supply contraction through the flexible rule, implying expected future deflation, which in turn raises the current demand for money, lowers that for goods and so partially counteracts the upward pressure on current prices exerted by the current monetary expansion.

The process is illustrated in figure 4.1. $A'D'$ shows the aggregate demand curve shift from $\varepsilon_t$ alone. But next period's $AD$ curve, $A_1D_1$, shifts leftwards generating an expected price fall to $E_t P_{t+1}$. This also shifts current aggregate demand to $A_0D_0$. The expected path of prices and output is marked by the arrows. The point of the illustration is to show that $y_t$ rises by less than it would reach without the rule.

When people have only partial macro information as in our second model in chapter 3 (p. 51), this same effect does not in fact occur. Consider the effect of $\mu$, the flexible response of money to past events, in that model. While the solution for prices and interest rates reflects the

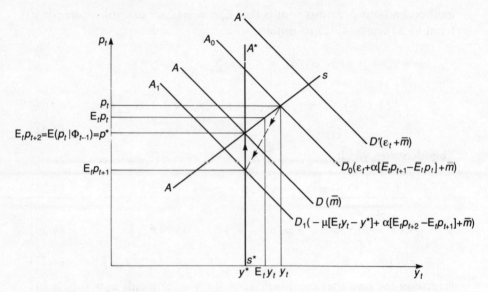

Figure 4.1   A monetary shock, $\varepsilon_t$, with a monetary feedback rule and local price information.

response parameter, $\mu$, that for output does not. The reason is that the current information on interest rates allows people to work out exactly what the effect of the feedback response is on expected future prices; since it can be worked out exactly, it is impounded into $E_t p_t$ and cannot affect output, which depends on producers being surprised by prices.

However, when people have *both* micro information on local prices *and* macro information on interest rates, effectiveness is restored (see, for example, Barro, 1980; King, 1982). Let us take as a representative model the one above and add local price information, so that $p_{it} = p_t + v_{it}$: this is essentially the model of Barro (1980). There are now two pieces of information, $p_{it}$ and $R_t$. For simplicity, let $v_t = 0$ so that there are only two macro errors $e_t$ and $u_t$.

One might think that both $p_{it}$ and $R_t$ would be used to estimate $e_t$ and $u_t$. In this case we would have

$$E\, u_t = \alpha_u p_{it} + \beta_u R_t \tag{4.29}$$

$$E\, e_t = \alpha_e p_{it} + \beta_e R_t \tag{4.30}$$

where the $\alpha$s and $\beta$s would be derived from the regressions of $u_t$ and $e_t$ on $p_{it}$ and $R_t$; $R_t = Au_t + De_t + Zm_{t-1}$ and $p_{it} = q_0 u_t + \pi_0 e_t + v_{it} + \pi_m m_{t-1}$. It turns out from the regression formulae that:

$$\alpha_u = DK/\Delta \tag{4.31}$$

$$\alpha_e = -AK/\Delta \tag{4.32}$$

$$\beta_e = (q_0 K + D\sigma_v^2 \sigma_e^2)/\Delta \tag{4.33}$$

$$\beta_u = (-\pi_0 K + A\sigma_v^2 \sigma_u^2)/\Delta \tag{4.34}$$

where $\Delta = (q_0 D - A\pi_0)^2 \sigma_u^2 \sigma_e^2 + \sigma_v^2 (A^2 \sigma_u^2 + D^2 \sigma_e^2)$
and $K = (q_0 D - A\pi_0)\sigma_u^2 \sigma_e^2$.
It follows that

$$A\alpha_u + D\alpha_e = 0 \tag{4.35}$$

and

$$D\beta_e + A\beta_u = 1 \tag{4.36}$$

Equation (3.24) holds as before so that here

$$ae_t + u_t = a\, E_t\, e_t + E_t\, u_t \tag{4.37}$$

Substituting from $E_t\, e_t$ and $E_t\, u_t$ gives:

$$ae_t + u_t = [(a\alpha_e + a_u)q_0 + (q\beta_e + \beta_u)A]u_t$$
$$+ [(a\alpha_e + \alpha_u)\pi_0 + (\alpha\beta_e + \beta_u)D]e_t \tag{4.38}$$

yielding two identities in $u_t, e_t$ as

$$1 = q_0 a\alpha_e + \alpha_u q_0 + a\beta_e + A\beta_u \tag{4.39}$$

$$1 = \alpha_e \pi_0 + (a_u \pi_0)/a + D\beta_e + \beta_u D/a \tag{4.40}$$

Letting, from (4.35), $\alpha_u = -D/A\, \alpha_e$ and, from (4.36), $\beta_u = 1/A - D\beta_e/A$, and substituting these into (4.39) and (4.40), implies that $D/A = a$.

Consequently the regression coefficients simplify to

$$\alpha_u = aK/\Delta; \quad \alpha_e = -K/\Delta; \quad \beta_e = [q_0 K + a\sigma_v^2 \sigma_e^2]/A\Delta;$$

$$\beta_u = [-\pi_0 K + \sigma_v^2 \sigma_u^2]/A\Delta$$

where $K = (aq_0 - \pi_0)\sigma_u^2 \sigma_e^2$ and $\Delta = (aq_0 - \pi_0)^2 \sigma_u^2 \sigma_e^2 + \sigma_v^2 (\sigma_u^2 + a^2 \sigma_e^2)$.
The solution is then worked out for $R_t$ as before in chapter 3, yielding:

$$A = -\{(1 - \alpha)(1 - aW)(1 + c[1 - \mu])$$
$$+ \alpha(1 + c)(1 - \mu)W\}/X;$$

$$D = \{-[(1 - \alpha)a(1 + c[1 - \mu])V + \alpha(1 + c)(1 - \mu)(1 - V)\}/X$$

where $W = a\sigma_v^2 \sigma_e^2/\Delta$; $V = \sigma_v^2 \sigma_u^2/\Delta$; and $X = \alpha(1 + c)(1 + c[1 - \mu])$.

Finally, using the expression for $p_t = \pi_0 e_t + q_0 u_t + \pi_m m_{t-1}, \pi_0, q_0$

and $\pi_m$ are found by the undetermined coefficients method (the solution is non-linear, as above for $\pi_0$ in (4.28)). We then find that

$$y_t = (1 - aW)u_t + aVe_t \tag{4.41}$$

It turns out therefore that $\mu$ indeed enters the determination of $y_t = E_t u_t$ because it affects the weight of $R_t$ and $p_{it}$ in forming expectations of $u_t$ and so also $\pi_0, q_0, A$ and $D$.

## Automatic Stabilizers – an Aside

Before going on to consider alternative assumptions about the supply curve we digress briefly to discuss the potential goal of 'automatic' stabilizers. By an automatic stabilizer we mean a mechanism in which a variable (for instance, tax liabilities) responds to current income levels, and therefore provides an automatic and immediate adjustment to current disturbances.

This is to be distinguished from policy actions in response to global information, such as we have been considering hitherto; 'automatic' implies that the response is effected at the microeconomic level, without recourse to macroeconomic information or to higher political authority. Tax liabilities, when tax rates are set, are of this sort: only the taxpayer, his income and the tax man are involved. In the monetary area, certain open market procedures – such as pegging Central Bank liabilities by Treasury bill sales – also fall into this category. The work of Poole (1970) on monetary policy in a closed economy and of Parkin (1978) on monetary and exchange rate intervention in an open economy can be regarded as dealing with these types of stabilizer.

McCallum and Whittaker (1979) considered the properties of automatic tax stabilizers and showed that they do influence the variance of output. Their point can most easily be demonstrated by writing the aggregate demand schedule as:

$$y_t = \alpha' (R_t - E_{t-1} p_{t+1} + p_t) - \sigma t y_t \tag{4.42}$$

where $t$ is the direct tax elasticity and $\sigma$ is the elasticity of spending to temporary variations in tax liabilities. The tax elasticity, $\delta$ log tax receipts/$\delta$ log output $= (\delta$ tax/$\delta$ output) (tax/output), is the marginal tax rate divided by the average tax rate.

If we define

$$\alpha = \alpha'/(1 + \sigma t) \tag{4.43}$$

then the solution of the model (4.2), (4.3), (4.4) and (4.5) is the same as (4.9) and (4.10), but where $\alpha$ is defined as here in (4.43). Consequently the solution for output is not independent of the automatic stabilizer, given this orthodox aggregate demand function;[1] a higher tax elasticity reduces the variance of output. However, although a high tax elasticity contributes to a reduction in output fluctuations, it does so at the cost of distortions to the operations of markets at the micro level: the highest tax elasticity of all is obtained when the marginal rate is 100 per cent!

The role of automatic stabilizers of this sort is quite distinct from that of feedback policy, although sometimes they are confused in popular discussion. It is, as we have seen, preserved within the Sargent and Wallace model considered above. However, there is one interesting set of conditions under which a particular monetary stabilizer is ineffective. This is where people have access to the same partial macro (or micro) information responded to by the monetary authorities.

Consider an 'automatic response' to the current interest rate, as discussed by Poole (1970), in the context of the macro model with partial macro information in chapter 3: equations (3.17) to (3.20). Suppose we rewrite the money supply function (3.19) as

$$m_t = \mu m_{t-1} + \eta R_t + e_t \qquad (3.19)'$$

Assume first that the monetary authorities can respond at a micro level (e.g. in the treasury bill market) to a market interest rate, with the effect aggregated over the whole security market of $\eta R_t$; assume also that no one observes the aggregate interest rate, $R_t$. Then the effect is to augment $c$, whenever it occurs in the solution, to $c' = c + \eta$. This will, as Poole suggested, dampen the effect on output of monetary shocks (and increase that of demand shocks) — see table 3.1, line 1.

Now suppose $R_t$ to be known to all as partial macro information; then the same policy (now no longer a response to micro data, but one to macroeconomic information) has no effect on output at all, as can be seen from the second line of table 3.1 where $c$ does not enter. We therefore have the result that interest rate stabilization is rendered ineffective (on output) in a Sargent–Wallace framework when the interest rate is universally observed. The reason is that any such response is impounded into $E_t\, p_t$ (because people can work out the money change due to $\eta R_t$) and cannot affect the surprise element $p_t - E_t\, p_t$.

This would not be true of any variable to which the monetary authorities could respond at a micro level and which was not universally observed, as in the case above with $R_t$ when unobserved. In this case people could not work out the money change to this response, and it could affect the surprise element, $p_t - E_t\, p_t$. However, plausible candidates for such a variable are hard to think of.

Nevertheless, the interesting possibility is introduced by macro information that the authorities can reduce the variance of output by raising the variance of the money supply shock, $e_t$, i.e. by deliberately making large rather than smaller mistakes. Previously this was impossible; higher var $e$ necessarily implied higher var $y$ since $e_t$ entered $y_t$ additively. But now var $e$ affects the coefficients of the $y$ expression via $\phi_u, \phi_v, \phi_e$.

Consider the asymptotic variance of $y$, $\sigma_y^2$. Substituting for $\phi_u, \phi_v, \phi_c$ from (3.23) in the $y$ expression (table 3.1, line 2) we obtain:

$$\sigma_y^2 = \sigma_v^2 + [(a^2\sigma_e^2 - a\sigma_u^2)/X']^2$$
$$+ [(\sigma_u^2 + (1+a)\sigma_v^2)/X']^2[\sigma_u^2 + a^2\sigma_e^2] \tag{4.44}$$

Now we find that as $\sigma_e^2 \to \infty$, $\phi_e \to 1$ and $\sigma_y^2 \to \sigma_v^2$, the variance of the demand shock: since $E_t y_t = E_t u_t = 0$, the $IS$ and $LM$ curves must be expected to intersect at $(E_t R_t, E_t y_t = 0)$. The actual $IS$ curve shifts by $v_t$ more than the expected one, hence the actual intersection is at $(R_t = E_t R_t, y_t = E_t y_t + v_t = v_t)$. It is clear that this may reduce the variance of output compared to the no monetary noise model; thus as $\sigma_e^2 \to 0$,

$$\sigma_y^2 \to \{a^2\sigma_v^2(\sigma_u^2)^2 + [\sigma_u^2 + (1+a)\sigma_v^2]^2\sigma_u^2\}/[\sigma_u^2 + (1+a)^2\sigma_v^2]^2 \tag{4.45}$$

which, depending on $\sigma_u^2$ and $a$, can exceed $\sigma_v^2$. Yet it can be shown that $\sigma_y^2$ is an inappropriate indicator of welfare and that the optimal policy is, commonsensically, to minimize $\sigma_e^2$ (i.e. for the Central Bank cashiers to make as few and as small mistakes as possible).

Abstracting from the usual problems (public goods, externalities, incomplete markets, etc.) the Pareto-optimal situation under uncertainty is one of Walrasian equilibrium when all the shocks are known to all agents (this is discussed at greater length in chapter 5). In the context of our model output would in this situation be simply $y_t = u_t$, because $E_t p_t = p_t$ and $u_t$, the supply shock, would shift our vertical supply curve fully along the quantity axis.

The optimal outcome under uncertainty, under normal assumptions for social welfare, is one which minimizes the variance of output from this outcome, as well as ensuring that this is the expected outcome: i.e. such that $E_t y_t = E_t u_t$ and $\sigma_{yu}^2 = E(y - u)^2$ is a minimum. All rational expectations outcomes, whatever the information set, guarantee that $E_t y_t = E_t u_t$. The problem therefore reduces to choosing $\sigma_e^2$ to minimize $\sigma_{yu}^2$. However $\sigma_{yu}^2 = a^2 E(p_t - E_t p_t)^2$, so that the optimal policy is equivalently to minimize the variance of unanticipated price changes $\sigma_{pe}^2$.

Using our earlier expression for $y_t$ (table 3.1, line 2), we find that

$$(p_t - E_t p_t) = (y_t - u_t)/a = [a(1+a)]^{-1}\{-[\phi_e + a(1 - \phi_u)]u_t$$
$$+ ((1+a)\phi_u + \phi_v)ae_t + [(1+a)\phi_e - a(1+a)\phi_v]v_t\} \tag{4.46}$$

Hence

$$\sigma_{pe}^2 = [a(1 + a)]^{-2}\{[\phi_e^2 + a^2(1 - \phi_u)^2 + 2a\phi_e(1 - \phi_u)]\sigma_u^2$$
$$+ [(1 + a)^2\phi_u^2 + \phi_v^2 + 2(1 + a)\phi_u\phi_v]a^2\sigma_e^2 + [(1 + a)^2\phi_e^2$$
$$+ a^2(1 + a)^2\phi_u^2 - 2a(1 + a)^2\phi_e\phi_u]\sigma_v^2\} \tag{4.47}$$

As $\sigma_e^2 \to 0$, we find that

$$\sigma_{pe}^2 \to \sigma_v^2\sigma_u^2/\{\sigma_u^2 + (1 + a)^2\sigma_v^2\} \tag{4.48}$$

and that as $\sigma_e^2 \to \infty$

$$\sigma_{pe}^2 \to (\sigma_v^2 + \sigma_u^2)/a^2 \tag{4.49}$$

The ratio of (4.49) to (4.48), $K$, is given by

$$K = (\sigma_v^2 + \sigma_u^2)[\sigma_u^2 + (1 + a)^2\sigma_v^2]/(a^2\sigma_v^2\sigma_u^2) > 1 \tag{4.50}$$

so that the low extreme dominates the high extreme. We can also show that minimizing $\sigma_e^2$ minimizes $\sigma_{pe}^2$; for $\delta\sigma_{pe}^2/\delta\sigma_e^2 > 0$ throughout the range of $\sigma_e^2$. Differentiating (4.47) yields:

$$\delta\sigma_{pe}^2/\delta\sigma_e^2 = (1 + a)^{-2}\{\phi_u^2\phi_e[1 + a^2 + 2a(\phi_e + \phi_v)] + 4a^2\phi_u^2\phi_v$$
$$+ \phi_v^2\phi_e + 4a\phi_e\phi_u\phi_v + (\phi_u + \phi_v)[(1 + a)\phi_u + \phi_v]^2\} > 0$$
$$\tag{4.51}$$

Hence welfare is unambiguously maximized by minimizing the variance of the money supply, as we would instinctively expect to be the case.

## Models with Long-term Non-contingent Contracts – the New Keynesian Phillips Curve

One of the assumptions required for anticipated monetary policy to have no effect on output in the Sargent–Wallace model is that agents are able to act on their information sets. If we have a situation where, for instance, private agents cannot respond to new information by changing their consumption, wage-price decisions, etc., as quickly as the public sector can change any (at least one) of its controls, then scope once again emerges for systematic stabilization policy to have real effects. This insight was developed principally by Fischer (1977a, b) and Phelps and Taylor (1977) in the context of multi-period non-contingent wage or price contracts.

Suppose we have a situation where all wage contracts run for two periods and the contract drawn in period $t$ specifies nominal wages for periods $t + 1$ and $t + 2$. At each period of time, half the labour force is covered by a pre-existing contract. As long as the contracts are not contingent on new information that accrues during the contract period, this raises the possibility of stabilization policy. Firms respond to changes in their environment (say, unpredictable changes in demand which were unanticipated at the time of the pre-existing contract) by altering output and employment at the pre-contracted wage; only contracts which are up for renewal can reflect prevailing information. If the monetary authorities can respond to new information that has accrued between the time the two-period contract is drawn up and the last period of the operation of the contract, then systematic stabilization policy is possible. In other words, while there are no information differences between public and private agents, the speed of response to the new information is different.

The essentials of this argument involve replacing the Sargent–Wallace supply equation (4.3) with one based on overlapping contracts. Suppose, following Fischer (1977a, b), that wages are set for two periods so as to maintain expected real wages constant at a 'normal' level. Denote (the log of nominal) wages set in period $t - i$ for period $t$ as $_{t-i}W_t$. Then

$$_{t-i}W_t = \mathrm{E}_{t-i}\, p_t \tag{4.52}$$

(where the log of normal wages is set to zero) and current nominal wages are

$$W_t = 0.5(_{t-2}W_t + {}_{t-1}W_t) = 0.5(\mathrm{E}_{t-2}\, p_t + \mathrm{E}_{t-1}\, p_t) \tag{4.53}$$

Now let output supply be a declining function of the real wage (from firms maximizing profits subject to a production function with labour input and some fixed overheads):

$$y_t = -q(W_t - p_t) + y^* \tag{4.54}$$

We derive from these the new supply equation:

$$y_t = 0.5q((p_t - \mathrm{E}_{t-2}\, p_t) + (p_t - \mathrm{E}_{t-1}\, p_t)) + y^* \tag{4.55}$$

This equation, the New Keynesian (NK) Phillips curve, and its derivation are illustrated in figure 4.2, which also contrasts it with the New Classical (NC) Phillips curve, in a diagram again taken from Parkin and Bade (1988). In figure 4.2, as $p$ rises from its expected level $p_0$ to $p_1$, $MPL + p$ (the wage offer for labour, where $MPL$ is the log of labour's marginal product) shifts: under NC, nominal wages are bid up along $SS$; under NK, wages are fixed at the contract level $W_0$. Hence the NK Phillips curve, $S_{NK}$, is flatter than the NC Phillips curve, $S_{NC}$.

Let us use (4.55) in place of (4.3), together with the rest of the model (4.1), (4.2) and (4.5); then it can conveniently be written in terms of the Muth solution as:

$$y_t = q(\pi_0 w_t + 0.5\pi_1 w_{t-1}) + y^* \tag{4.56}$$

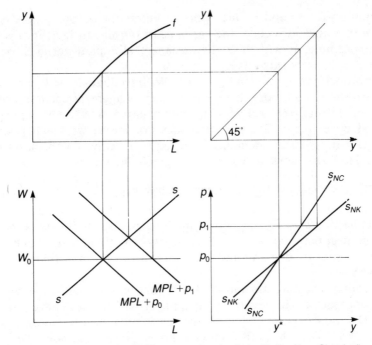

Figure 4.2   The New Keynesian Phillips curve (contrasted with the New Classical).

The model solution equation can now be written:

$$\bar{m} + q\mu(\pi_0 w_{t-1} + 0.5\pi_1 w_{t-2}) + w_t = p_t + q(1 + c/\alpha)(\pi_0 w_t$$
$$+ 0.5\pi_1 w_{t-1}) - c(E_{t-1} p_{t+1} - E_{t-1} p_t) + (1 + c/\alpha)y^* \quad (4.57)$$

The identities in the $w_{t-i}$ are now:

(terms in $w_t$)

$$1 = \pi_0[1 + q(1 + c/\alpha)] \quad (4.58)$$

(terms in $w_{t-1}$)

$$\mu q \pi_0 = \pi_1 + 0.5q(1 + c/\alpha)\pi_1 - c(\pi_2 - \pi_1) \quad (4.59)$$

(terms in $w_{t-2}$)

$$0.5q\mu\pi_1 = \pi_2 - c(\pi_3 - \pi_2) \quad (4.60)$$

(terms in $w_{t-i}$, $i \geqslant 3$)

$$0 = (1 + c)\pi_i - c\pi_{i+1} \quad (4.61)$$

Equation (4.61) gives $\pi_i = 0$ ($i \geqslant 3$) applying the stability condition, whence we can solve the other three equations for $\pi_2, \pi_1, \pi_0$. $\mu$ enters the solution for $\pi_1$ and $\pi_2$ and, since $\pi_1$ enters the output supply equation, $\mu$ therefore influences the variance of output. In fact, in this particular example, it will raise the variance; minimum variance occurs where $\mu = 0$, since this sets $\pi_1 = \pi_2 = 0$.

The model is illustrated in figure 4.3. With feedback, $\mu \neq 0$, we obtain the path shown. Suppose there is a temporary aggregate demand shock in $t = 0$, shifting $AD$ to $A_0D_0$. The supply curve, $S^*S^*$, whose position is fixed by $E_{t-2} p_t = E_{t-1} p_t = p^*$, does not move; we reach point 0. Next period, aggregate demand is shifted by negative feedback on $y_0$ to $A_1D_1$. Half the workers have now renegotiated wages in $t = 0$ with $E_0 p_1 = p_1$ (their expectations of $p_1$ in period 0), so the supply curve shifts to $S_1S_1$. Next period aggregate demand shifts to $A_2D_2$ as feedback now raises it in response to $y_1$. All workers have renegotiated wages, fully expecting $p_2 = E_0 p_2$ (there is no further surprise in prices relative to wage negotiations); so $y_2 = y^*$. In period 3, finally, feedback stops so both aggregate demand and supply return to normal, that is $A^*D^*$ and $S^*S^*$.

Of course, the diagram shows clearly that had the aggregate demand curve not reacted with feedback, then in period 1 it would have returned to $A^*D^*$ and workers would not have needed to renegotiate wages, staying on $S^*S^*$. Thus the path would have been direct from point 0 to point 3, clearly more stable than the path with feedback.

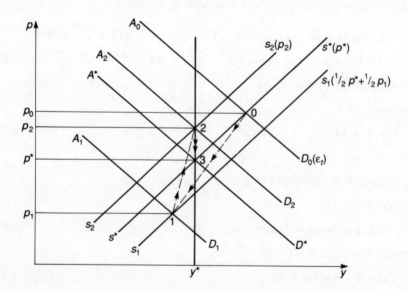

Figure 4.3  The effectiveness of feedback response in the New Keynesian model.

The path with feedback is shown by numbers; the path without feedback is 0, 3, 3. . . .

This example illustrates the obvious point that the case for stabilization policy does not rest with showing effectiveness; it is also necessary to show optimality. Nevertheless, it is easy to construct examples where $\mu \neq 0$ minimizes output variance; the reader should investigate one such as an exercise, namely when an adjustment term $+j(y_{t-1} - y^*)$ is added to (4.55). The reader should find that, while $\pi_0$ is unaltered, the expression for $\pi_1$ becomes:

$$\pi_1 = [q\mu\pi_0 + j(\pi_0 - 1)]/[1 + c(1 - j)$$
$$+ 0.5q(1 + c/\alpha - c\mu/(1 + c))] \tag{4.62}$$

The optimal value of $\mu$ found by minimizing the variance of $y - y^*$ sets $(y_{t+1} - y^*) = 0$ after a shock in $t = 0$, implying that $\pi_0 j + 0.5\pi_1 = 0$. It turns out that the optimal value of $\mu = -j(1 + c)/(0.5q)$ is negative, representing the normal 'leaning into the wind' response.

Models with overlapping contracting have been developed by Taylor (1979a, b, 1980) in a series of papers in order to show that important features of the business cycle can be captured by integrating this type of supply curve into standard macroeconomic analysis, and to exhibit examples of optimal policy design in such an economy.

Three points of weakness remain in this approach. First, the theoretical basis of non-contingent contracts, in which the nominal wage or price is fixed and quantity is set by demand, has not been established to universal satisfaction. One promising approach is to assume 'menu costs', that is transactions costs in fixing, negotiating and changing prices which are reduced by periodic contracts: this approach (assumed by earlier authors such as Barro (1972), Mussa (1981) and Canzoneri (1980)) has been explored theoretically by, for example, Rotemberg (1983) and Parkin (1986). What is harder to establish is how large these menu costs are and why, given that non-contingent contracts risk losses in the face of shocks, the contracts do not build in contingency clauses (which may be less expensive to write in than the potential losses they avoid). The humdrum answer may be that people are approximately risk-neutral for small risks and so reduce menu costs by writing non-contingent contracts that expose them totally to these risks: they only bother with contingency clauses (or other insurance) for the large risks. This tallies with other insurance practices, such as excess clauses and no-claims bonuses, which effectively exclude the small risks.

If this is so, then the appearance of non-contingent contracts may be deceptive, the second weakness in this approach. They may be truly non-contingent for only rather trivial shocks. Indeed, closer inspection reveals that actual contracts are exceedingly complex once implicit elements are taken into account. For example, they will typically include bonus, discount and lay-off elements for quantity variation, and index-ation (whether formal or informal via shop-floor renegotiation) is fre-quently found.

The third and related weakness is that, if the authorities were system-atically to exploit these contracts in a way not envisaged at the time the contracts were set, then this would presumably lead to differences in the way contracts were written (contract length and indexation clauses are clearly endogenous). In the limit, if the government systematically exploited them in a way that altered agents' outcomes excessively from what they wished, then long-run contracts would be written in such a way that they were equivalent to a succession of single-period contracts so that the scope for stabilization policy would disappear.

For all these reasons there remains considerable doubt as to whether non-contingent contracts can be regarded as a firm basis for modelling and policy formulation. Nevertheless, in practice they are widely used in macroeconomic modelling, since they both appear to be widely used and do pick up usefully the short-term nominal rigidity observed in wages: clearly this implies that we must treat analysis based on such models with caution – but then what is new about that?

One final point: the 'New Keynesian' and 'New Classical' supply curves are often presented as a contrast between 'disequilibrium' and 'market clearing' approaches. This can be misleading. The fact that people may sign non-contingent contracts does not imply either that they are in dis-equilibrium or that markets do not clear when shocks occur later on during the contract period. Obviously they were aware this could happen (hence no 'disequilibrium') and planned not to vary their price in res-ponse to changed demand (hence their supply is elastic, 'clearing' the market). We are dealing with a different (non-auction) market structure entered into voluntarily by rational agents: this implies different proper-ties in response to shocks, that is all. It is quite different from the Keynesian or old Phillips curve assumptions that we briefly described at the start of chapter 3.

## New Classical Models with Intertemporal Substitution

The last group of models we wish to examine for feedback effectiveness is New Classical models with intertemporal substitution fully operative. The earlier New Classical models of this chapter suppressed one mechan-ism, the role of real interest rates in varying labour supply; empirically, this mechanism itself is of doubtful significance but in the open economy movements in real interest rates are associated with movements in the real exchange rate, and these are found to have powerful effects on labour supply, as is discussed in chapter 8. We can think of this closed economy mechanism as a proxy for that powerful open economy mechanism. It has some interesting theoretical implications for policy effectiveness.

As explained in chapter 3, the New Classical supply function is derived from workers or consumers maximizing expected utility subject to a lifetime budget constraint (a nicely tractable set-up, which has been explored by Sargent (e.g. 1979a, chapter 16), is the quadratic utility function with quadratic adjustment costs). From such a framework one can obtain a formal supply of labour equation of the form:

$$n_t = f(w_t^e, w_{t+1}^e - w_t - r_t, n_{t-1}) \qquad (4.63)$$

where $w$ is the real wage, $n$ is labour supply (both in logarithms) and $r$ is the real interest rate, which we now treat as a variable. The $e$ superscript denotes expected at time $t$. The information set assumed in this is last period's macroeconomic information and each worker also observes at the micro level his or her current nominal wages; but we assume that no micro information is usable for signal extraction about macro data. So

$$w_t^e = W_t - E_{t-1} p_t = w_t + p_t - E_{t-1} p_t$$

where $W_t$ is nominal wages (in logs). The first term represents the long-term effect of rising wages on supply, while the second represents inter-temporal substitution with a single-period 'future' for simplicity; the third represents costs of adjustment. $w_{t+1}^e$ is standing in for the whole future path of real wages and it will be helpful for our purpose here to treat it as a constant, 'the future normal real wage'.

Let us write the equation in (log) linear form as:

$$n_t = \sigma_0 + \sigma_1 (w_t + p_t - E_{t-1} p_t) + \sigma_2 r_t + jn_{t-1} \quad (0 < j < 1) \quad (4.64)$$

Now juxtapose this with a demand for labour function (4.65) derived from a simple Cobb–Douglas production function (4.66) with a fixed overhead element $k_t$

$$n_t = y_t - w_t \qquad (4.65)$$

$$y_t = \delta k_t + (1 - \delta)n_t \qquad (4.66)$$

From these last two we have

$$n_t = k_t - \delta^{-1} w_t$$

or

$$w_t = -\delta n_t + \delta k_t \qquad (4.67)$$

Substituting for $w_t$ from this into (4.64) gives

$$n_t = (1 + a)^{-1} [ak_t + \sigma_0 + \sigma_2 r_t + \sigma_1 (p_t - E_{t-1} p_t)]/(1 - qL)$$

$$(4.68)$$

where $q = j/(1 + a)$, $a = \delta \sigma_1$. Using (4.66) gives us:

$$y_t = (1 - qL)\delta k_t + (1 - \delta)(1 + a)^{-1} [ak_t + \sigma_0 + \sigma_2 r_t$$

$$+ \sigma_1 (p_t - E_{t-1} p_t)] + qy_{t-1} \qquad (4.69)$$

The equilibrium values of $r_t$ and $y_t$ will depend on the whole model; for simplicity we will normalize them at zero in what follows, since we do not focus on them.

Now write the full model as:

$$y_t = -\alpha r_t + \mu_f (y_{t-1}) \qquad (4.70)$$

$$y_t = dr_t + \beta (p_t - E_{t-1} p_t) + qy_{t-1} \qquad (4.71)$$

$$m_t = p_t + y_t - cR_t + v_t \qquad (4.72)$$

$$m_t = \bar{m} + \mu_m y_{t-1} + u_t \qquad (4.73)$$

$$R_t = r_t + E_{t-1} p_{t+1} - E_{t-1} p_t \qquad (4.74)$$

Equation (4.70) is the IS curve with the fiscal feedback parameter $\mu_f$; (4.71) is the supply curve with $d, \beta, q$ taken from (4.69) (e.g. $d = (1 - \delta)$ $(1 + a)^{-1}\sigma_2$); (4.72) is money demand; (4.73) is money supply with feedback parameter $\mu_m$; (4.74) is the Fisher identity.

We can immediately establish by (4.70) and (4.71) that fiscal feedback is effective, but monetary feedback is not. We obtain

$$r_t = -\beta (1 - \mu_f L)(p_t - E_{t-1} p_t)/$$

$$(\alpha + d)\{1 - [(q\alpha + \mu_f d)/(\alpha + d)]L\} \qquad (4.75)$$

This expression for $r_t$ than can be substituted into (4.70) to obtain $y_t$: clearly the reaction of $y_t$ to unanticipated prices depends importantly on $\mu_f$ but not on $\mu_m$. As for $p_t - E_{t-1} p_t$, this is quickly found as:

$$p_t - E_{t-1} p_t = [1 + \{\beta(\alpha + c)/(\alpha + d)\}]^{-1}(u_t - v_t) \qquad (4.76)$$

The intuition behind this result is that fiscal policy is causing *intertemporal substitution* of supply, in order to offset the 'cyclical' effects of shocks. Incidentally, this effect of fiscal feedback is quite independent of whether government bonds are net wealth (discussed in chapter 6). For example, even if private consumption depends only on permanent income and not on transitory income, the government expenditure pattern over time could be altered without affecting the present value of the tax stream, so altering the pattern of total demand over time. Of course, if private consumption depends also on transitory income, then alteration of the temporal pattern of taxes, holding the present value of the tax stream constant, would also have this effect. Such alteration of the patterns of aggregate demand over time then sets off the movement in real interest rates which creates intertemporal substitution in supply.

These points are illustrated in figure 4.4, where it is assumed that $q \approx 0.5$ and $\mu_f \approx -1$; the diagram is in $(r, y)$ space instead of more usual $(p, y)$ space, to focus on real interest rate movements. Initially, we assume some money supply shock drives prices up, unexpectedly shifting the SS New Classical supply curve rightwards; real interest rates drop to point 0 along the original IS curve. Now, if there were no fiscal feedback, $\mu_f = 0$, the SS curve would shift back to $S^*S^*$ at the rate of 50 per cent of $(y_{t-1} - y^*)$ per period. The path would be traced by the arrows along the $I^*S^*$ curve. With fiscal feedback, the IS shifts leftwards to $I_1S_1$, reaching point 1, where output is at $y^*$; hence in period 2 we return to $I^*S^*$ and $S^*S^*$, with full equilibrium restored (plainly faster in this example than with no feedback). The path of output is seen to be fully determined by this diagram; monetary feedback policy enters neither curve, so is ineffective. Only the shock to the money supply enters through $p_t - E_{t-1} p_t$.

The ineffectiveness of monetary feedback policy is negated by the introduction of wealth effects into the IS curve (or the supply curve). Assume that consumers hold long maturity bonds with fixed coupons

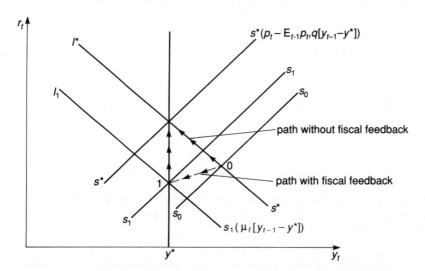

Figure 4.4 The effectiveness of fiscal policy with intertemporal substitution in supply.

(Monetary feedback is ineffective because only inflation surprise enters the SS curve.)

denominated in money terms: these must be government bonds in this closed economy, since any private sector bonds would net out in a consolidated private sector balance sheet; hence this commits us to the view that government bonds are net wealth (chapter 6). Variations in the price level brought about by monetary policy, future government expenditure constant, will alter the real value of these and so net wealth and spending.

The point can be seen by adding the term $f(b - p_t)$ into (4.70).[2] We set $\mu_f = 0$ since fiscal policy will remain effective as before; and to simplify the algebra here we set $q = 0 = b$. Using (4.70) and (4.71) we now obtain:

$$r_t = -f'p_t - \beta'(p_t - E_{t-1} p_t) \tag{4.77}$$

where $f' = f/(\alpha + d)$, $\beta' = \beta/(\alpha + d)$. Equating (4.72) and (4.73) and substituting into the result (4.77) for $r_t$ and (4.71) for $y_t$ we obtain the following equation in $p_t$.

$$(1 - f'd + f'c)p_t + f'\mu_m dp_{t-1} - c \, E_{t-1} \, p_{t+1} + c \, E_{t-1} \, p_t$$
$$+ (\beta - \beta'd + \beta'c)(p_t - E_{t-1} \, p_t)$$
$$- \mu_m(\beta - \beta'd)(p_{t-1} - E_{t-1} \, p_{t-1}) = \bar{m} + u_t - v_t \tag{4.78}$$

If $p_t = \sum_{i=0}^{\infty} \pi_i w_{t-i} + \bar{p}$

where $w_t = u_t - v_t$, then the identities in the $w_{t-i}$ are:

$(w_t)$

$$[(1 - f'd + f'c) + (\beta - \beta'd + \beta'c)]\pi_0 = 1 \tag{4.79}$$

$(w_{t-1})$

$$(1 - f'd + f'c)\pi_1 + f'\mu_m \, d\pi_0 - c\pi_2 + c\pi_1 - \mu_m(\beta - \beta'd)\pi_0 = 0 \tag{4.80}$$

$(w_{t-i}, i \geq 2)$

$$\pi_{i+1} - ([1 - f'd]/c + 1 + f')\pi_i - (f'\mu_m \, d/c)\pi_{i-1} = 0 \tag{4.81}$$

Suppose (4.81) has a unique stable root $\delta$: then $\pi_2 = \delta\pi_1$, where $\delta$ depends on $\mu_m$. $\pi_1$ also depends on $\mu_m$ from (4.80). Now output is given by (4.71) using (4.77), as:

$$y_t = -df'p_t + \alpha\beta'(p_t - E_{t-1} p_t) \tag{4.82}$$

from which it is apparent that $\mu_m$ enters the solution for output too. Wealth effects make monetary feedback policy effective.

The full classical model of labour supply therefore yields two interesting propositions. First, without wealth effects fiscal feedback is effective but monetary feedback is not (this is noted by Sargent, 1979, chapter 16). Secondly, with wealth effects both are effective. Again, this by no means establishes that feedback rules are beneficial. Sargent (1979), for example, shows that if welfare is measured by the sum of identical consumers' expected utility, then with no wealth effects zero fiscal feedback is optimal in the case of quadratic utility and production functions. That issue we defer. As for the existence of wealth effects, on which the effectiveness of monetary policy turns, that too is an issue requiring separate discussion; theoretically and empirically it is at this point an open question (chapter 6). Nevertheless, as a minimum it is of some interest that, even without signal extraction from local prices, new classical models in general give scope for fiscal feedback and across a potentially broad class also give scope for monetary feedback. This is contrary to the impression given (no doubt unintentionally) by much of the early literature, although subsequently corrected by Lucas and Sargent (1978).

## Conclusions

We have shown in the context of equilibrium linear models that there is one main set of assumptions under which neither monetary nor fiscal feedback policies have an impact on the variance of output: these are a New Classical (or old Keynesian with rational expectations) Phillips curve of the sort assumed by Sargent and Wallace, without signal extraction from local prices, without intertemporal substitution in supply induced by real interest rates, and without information asymmetries. It would be turgid and counter-productive to list here again all the conditions under which effectiveness of either fiscal or monetary feedback policy is or is not preserved.

The general proposition in this chapter is that rational expectations as such do not rule out counter-cyclical policy, but rather they alter its impact,[3] leaving it as an empirical matter whether they do or do not reduce the variance of relevant macroeconomic variables, and as a further issue whether they do or do not improve welfare. We also considered automatic stabilizers briefly and showed that their distinct role was not nullified by rational expectations, except in the specific New Classical case where people have current access to the same information that triggers the stabilizing mechanism; in this case output will be invariant because people will incorporate the response into their price expectations. Once it is appreciated that stabilization policy is in general not ruled out by rational expectations models, whether New Classical or not, the issue of whether the economy is subject to 'disequilibrium' (a

misnomer for non-contingent contracts) ceases to be of special significance: it is just one of a number of questions that have to be confronted
in the detailed specification of a rational expectations model. It is the
rationality of expectations itself that carries the really powerful implications for the nature of the impact of stabilization policy.

## Notes

1 In fact to obtain such a function we require a situation of incomplete debt
  neutrality – see the appendix to chapter 6. In brief, if taxpayers completely
  capitalize future tax liability, and consumption depends on permanent
  income, then these tax changes will exert no influence on total spending.
2 This could be, for example, a bond issue at £100 face value which promises
  to pay £100 × $R_i$ each $i$th period, $i = 1, 2, \ldots, \infty$; its present value will
  always be £100 (approximately). The point made here goes through for all
  types of *nominal* bonds; only if bonds are indexed will it not do so, for the
  obvious reason that the path of prices becomes irrelevant to the value of net
  wealth.
3 This viewpoint is in principle reinforced by work (e.g. Dickinson et al., 1982)
  which has taken up a suggestion of Shiller (1978) and shown that if a non-
  linear version of the Sargent–Wallace supply function replaced their original
  linear version then, even retaining all other assumptions, stabilization policy
  is feasible. Clearly non-linearity will be a typical feature of models of national
  economies; nevertheless, it seems doubtful that this source of stabilization
  leverage is of much practical importance.

# 5

# Problems in Choosing Optimal Policies

In chapters 3 and 4 we discussed the potential *effectiveness* (for output) of stabilization policy. We have shown that in general such policy can be effective. The question then arises of whether any such policy is optimal and, if so, how it should be designed. We will discuss three issues that bear on this: the welfare *criterion*, the *evaluation* of policy effects and, finally, how optimal policies might be *designed* (given a welfare criterion and a model appropriate for evaluation). We will find that this discussion will carry us far away from the conventional post-war ideas of 'optimal control' in economic policy; indeed, we will have few conclusions other than that 'optimal' policies are hard to identify except as a broad class and that changeable policies which undermine government credibility should be ruled out. In our present state of knowledge, a modest aim would be to choose simple rules of government behaviour that minimize private sector uncertainty about the things that government controls: tax rates, money supply, government spending and deficits. No doubt better (and optimal) ones exist; but we cannot pin them down and the attempt to do so with wrong parameter estimates[1] could be very costly.

## The Welfare Criterion

The yardstick of welfare that is most widely used by economists is the Pareto criterion. Pareto-optimality is the condition in which no one can be made better off without someone else being made worse off; it can be illustrated for a two-person world by an Edgeworth box diagram (figure 5.1), in which the 'contract curve' joins the points of tangency of the two sets of indifference curves, these points being all Pareto-optimal. If it is then assumed that distributional considerations are absent, either because they do not matter or because the government achieves the socially desired distribution at all times, there can be a unique Pareto-optimum for the specified distribution, illustrated by the circled dot in figure 5.1.

The proof that, for a given distribution function, there exists a unique Pareto-optimum has been established for an economy with well-behaved

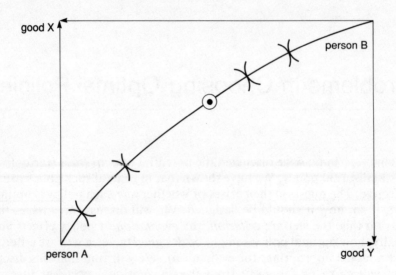

Figure 5.1   Edgeworth box.

preferences and technology in a Walrasian equilibrium when markets are competitive and complete, and there are no distortions (discrepancies between private social costs due, for example, to externalities); the proof is due to Arrow, Debreu and Hahn (see Arrow and Hahn, 1971). In an economy of this type, the steady state level of output at the Pareto-optimum would be the $y^*$ in our models.

Of course, in actual economies, with incomplete and some mono-polistic markets and with distortions, $y^*$, the equilibrium level of output, will not be at a Pareto-optimum. However, it is usual in macroeconomics to assume that these problems are the province of 'micro' policies, and that there should be no attempt by macroeconomic policy to push $y$ systematically away from $y^*$; indeed, we have already seen that any such attempt in an adaptive expectations model would cause ever-accelerating or ever-decelerating prices and in a rational expectations model would be completely frustrated. Instead $y^*$ is taken, from the viewpoint of macroeconomic policy, to be the optimum output level in a steady state.

Supposing this to be so, the question arises of what is the optimum short-run output level. In Keynesian disequilibrium models with adap-tive (or other backward-looking) expectations, if output is less (or more) than $y^*$, this is involuntary and suboptimal, the result of 'market failure'; hence the variation of output around $y^*$ is a natural criterion for minimization.[2] Since output tends to $y^*$ in the long run, but $y^*$ will typically be growing over time, we can measure this as the variance of output around its moving trend, var $(y - y^*)$. This is the one on which we focused in the discussion of effectiveness in chapter 4.

Sometimes, in these models, other measures have also been included in the minimand to represent the costs due to loss of consumer surplus not included in GDP – for example, the variance of inflation or interest rates as proxies for consumer and financial uncertainty. However, it is usually assumed in the context of stabilization policy that the variations in these costs across alternative policies are relatively small; this would also be our assumption.

In equilibrium models with adaptive expectations (such as that implicit in Milton Friedman's AEA address; Friedman, 1968), output deviations from $y^*$ arise because of expectations errors which could have been avoided by efficient use of available information. Again var $(y - y^*)$ is a natural minimand because agents would wish they had made output decisions on the basis of good forecasts.

In equilibrium models with rational expectations, however, $y$ only departs from $y^*$ because of unavoidable expectations errors. Such models include the New Keynesian ones of chapter 4, because the nominal wage contracts in these models are voluntarily negotiated, in the full knowledge that when shocks occur the response to them will be constrained by the contract.

Output is always at its 'desired' level in these models in the sense that, given available information, agents are maximizing their welfare subject to their private constraints, including the effects of shocks and associated expectations errors. Then, provided the level of distortion in the economy does not increase with $(y - y^*)^2$, government cannot improve and may reduce welfare by reducing var $(y - y^*)$ for the simple reason that it was already being maximized; an example of this is given by Sargent (1979, chapter 16) in a classical labour supply model where fiscal policy is effective because of intertemporal substitution, as discussed in chapter 4, and the same point has been stressed by Beenstock (1980).[3]

The proviso that the level of distortion does not increase with $(y - y^*)^2$ will be violated in practice when unemployment benefits do not vary with wages; for when depressive shocks reduce output and employment, the integral of the gap between the private and social cost of unemployment will increase. This is illustrated in figure 5.2, where $b$ is the fixed real benefit level, $SS$ is the 'undistorted' supply curve of labour, $S_b S_b$ is the supply curve in the presence of the fixed benefit level, $DD$ the demand curve in normal conditions, so that $L^*$ is the normal level of employment corresponding to $y^*$; $D'D'$ is the curve after the shock. The shaded areas, $a$ and $a'$, are respectively the distortion from benefits before and after the shock; $a'$ is clearly greater than $a$. It

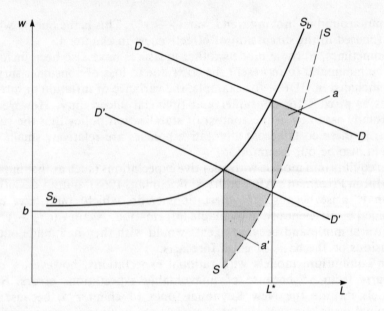

Figure 5.2   Benefit distortions and stabilization.

follows that var $(y - y^*)$ should be a minimand even in equilibrium RE models, if distortions behave in this way.[4]

In fact, strictly the minimand is var $(y - \bar{y})$ where $\bar{y}$ is the undistorted level of output, typically *above* $y^*$, as in figure 5.2 (where the distortion diminishes as $L$ increases). However, stabilization policies which attempt to boost $y$ above $y^*$ systematically will be frustrated in the attempt and will create other problems for the economy (inflation in the case of monetary policy and high taxation in the case of fiscal policy). Hence var $(y - y^*)^2$ is the minimand subject to the constraint that stabilization policies are not on average biased away from $y^*$.

To sum up, in rational expectations models, there are prima facie reasons to believe that in general stabilization policy, even if effective, will not improve welfare, the main exception being where distortions are positively correlated with the cycle; the importance of this exception will vary with the nature of the benefit system.

This fundamental argument for stabilization policy is in principle also an argument for a change in the benefit system. Of course, if for some reason the benefit system cannot in practice be changed, then stabilization policy is justified on the 'second best' grounds we have described. But this does not imply that one should uncritically accept the system and the costs it incurs, even with stabilization policies to mitigate them.

## The Lucas Critique of Policy Evaluation

It was Lucas (1976) who first pointed out that if expectations are formed rationally, then unless the estimated equations used by model builders to evaluate the consequences of alternative government policies are genuinely structural or behavioural, the implications of such simulations or evaluations may be seriously flawed. The essential insight of Lucas is that, when expectations are formed rationally, agents react to the behaviour of government. Consequently, unless the equations estimated by the model builder are structural, the coefficients in equations which are estimated over one policy regime will implicitly depend on the parameters of the government policy rule in operation. It follows that when alternative government policy rules are stimulated, not only will the government policy rule change, but so also will the parameters in the equations which are not structural. Consequently, the evaluation of alternative policies can be quite misleading.

Let us take as an example the following simple model, with over-lapping contracts (so that stabilization policy is effective), a quantity theory demand for money function and a money supply rule that responds to past output. All the variables are measured in deviations from their normal values.

$$y_t = \beta(p_t - 0.5[E_{t-1}\, p_t + E_{t-2}\, p_t]) \tag{5.1}$$

$$m_t = p_t + y_t \tag{5.2}$$

$$m_t = \mu y_{t-1} + \varepsilon_t \tag{5.3}$$

The solution is

$$y_t = \beta([1 + \beta]^{-1}\varepsilon_t + \tfrac{1}{2}\mu\beta\{(1 + \beta)(1 + \tfrac{1}{2}\beta)\}^{-1}\varepsilon_{t-1}) \tag{5.4}$$

from which it is immediately apparent that the optimal monetary response is nil ($\mu = 0$).

What we have just done is to set out the model in its 'structural' form (that is, in terms of its underlying relationships). But suppose we had written the model in a 'reduced' or solved form, with each variable in terms only of its ultimate determinants after all the model's relationships have worked themselves out in the current period. Equation (5.4) is such a form, but since the error term, $\varepsilon_t$, is not directly observable (it is an implication of equation (5.3), given observations on $m_t$ and $y_{t-1}$, as well as knowledge of $\mu$), we would write (5.4) in terms of observable ultimate determinants (using $\varepsilon_t = m_t - \mu y_{t-1}$ from (5.3)) as:

$$y_t = \sigma_1 m_t + \sigma_2 m_{t-1} + \sigma_3 y_{t-1} + \sigma_4 y_{t-2} \tag{5.5}$$

Having recovered this relationship from the data, we could compute the optimal monetary policy for time $t$, given what has already occurred in $t - 1$ (the planning period). It is obvious that we must set $m_t$ so as to make $y_t = 0$ (we have one instrument, $m_t$, and one target, $y_t$, so the problem here is simple) or:

$$m_t = - (\sigma_2 m_{t-1} + \sigma_3 y_{t-1} + \sigma_4 y_{t-2})/\sigma_1 \tag{5.6}$$

According to our relationship (5.5), this feedback rule for money supply ought to deliver zero fluctuation in output. However, in fact it will deliver fluctuations nearly as large as the feedback rule (5.3) that the central bank was previously following! Actual money supply will be given by (5.6) plus $\varepsilon_t$, which is the unpredictable error in executing monetary intentions. The resulting rule can be written as:

$$m_t = \mu y_{t-1} + \varepsilon_t / \{1 + (\tfrac{1}{2}\mu\beta/1 + \tfrac{1}{2}\beta)L\} \tag{5.7}$$

(using our knowledge of the $\sigma_i$ in terms of the model's structural parameters). When this is substituted into the model, we find the new solution for $y_t$ as

$$y_t = \beta [ (1 + \beta)^{-1} \varepsilon_t + \tfrac{1}{4}\mu\beta\{ (1 + \beta)(1 + \tfrac{1}{2}\beta)^2\}^{-1} \varepsilon_{t-1}] \tag{5.8}$$

This is far from perfectly stabilizing output with respect to past events, though as it happens in this case we have made it more stable.

Where we went wrong was that we used the reduced form to calculate the optimal rule. But that reduced form itself depends on the monetary rule because the rule influences (rational) expectations and so economic behaviour; this problem would not arise in adaptive expectations models, where the effect of money on output does not depend on the rule itself. So the reduced form will not remain constant (as assumed) as we change the rule towards the 'optimum'. Hence we must compute a false optimum.

The policy-maker using these methods of optimal control is doomed to go on recomputing his 'optimal' rule as his 'model' constantly changes: it will never be correct, however, nor is there any guarantee that it will get any better over time. It could get worse, or alternatively better and worse. In general, we cannot say.

The problem we have just described is not too difficult to solve. Once the policy-maker recognizes that the model underlying (5.5) is a rational expectations model consisting of (5.1) to (5.3), he will use the appropriate method and set $\mu = 0$! Estimating the structural parameters of the model is a technical problem not in principle more difficult than estimating the reduced form parameters (we discuss the problem briefly in chapter 13).

We have assumed that (5.1) and (5.2) are truly 'structural', that is, that they are invariant to the policy-maker's rule. However, this may well not be so. People's behaviour is itself the result of optimizing subject to constraints of budgets and technology; policy rules will typically change their budget constraints because expected future prices and incomes will depend in general on the economy's behaviour, which in turn depends on the rules. Equations (5.1) and (5.2) express people's resulting behaviour in demand and supply functions; these may therefore alter as policy rules alter. Rational expectations implies that the vast majority of the economic relationships econometricians typically estimate are not strictly structural.

A simple example of this arose in chapter 4 with the model of (4.22) and (4.23), where we assumed signal extraction from local prices. We saw that output depended on the stabilization parameter, $\mu$:

$$y_t - y^* = [(1 - \phi)/\delta]\{1 + (1 - \phi)/\delta + \alpha\phi$$
$$+ \alpha\mu\phi(1 - \phi)/\delta(1 + \alpha)\}^{-1}\varepsilon_t \tag{5.9}$$

It might seem from this that for maximum stability $\mu$ should be pushed as high as technically feasible (implying dramatic monetary contraction in booms, expansion in recessions). However, this conclusion treats $\phi$ as a structural parameter. It is not since we know that $\phi = 1/(1 + \sigma_v^2/\pi_0^2\sigma_\varepsilon^2)$, the slope of the Phillips curve, depends on the extent to which the variance of local prices reflects local shocks and overall monetary instability. To compute the appropriate value of $\mu$ we must allow for this; as discussed in chapter 4 (p. 65).

Lucas's critique therefore raises deep difficulties for econometricians attempting to recover from the data relationships which are usable for policy-making. One reaction to this problem has been to assert that only the parameters of preferences and technology ('deep structure') will be regime-invariant and that macroeconomists should therefore estimate these. Some early examples are Hansen and Sargent (1980) and Sargent (1978, 1981). A research methodology along these lines is now in full swing. This work models agents at the microeconomic level as intertemporal optimizers subject to the constraints of budget and technology, and attempts to retrieve the parameters of the (aggregated) utility and production functions. These attempts have met with little empirical success to date, and have been too restricted in scope to be usable for macroeconomic policy evaluation. However, it is early days; in a recent book Sargent (1987) has reviewed much of this literature and in chapters 9 and 10 we set out some key features of these 'representative agent' models. A way has been found of embedding sufficient detail into the constraints facing agents to allow these models to confront the data successfully.

One highly promising development is the Prescott 'time-to-build' model of the US business cycle. This model uses estimates of consumption, labour supply and investment functions derived from microeconomic studies (usually of large cross-sectional data sets). Processes for shocks (error terms) to technology and preferences are then estimated from the time series when restricted by the results of these studies. The success of the overall model in predicting the facts of the US business cycle is evaluated by comparing the second and higher moments of the predicted and actual series: techniques of statistical inference from this comparison are not available, at least as yet. Whether such models have sufficient dynamic structure to be useful for evaluating stabilization policy must be doubtful. However, they could be useful for evaluating the longer run effects of supply side policies.

Another reaction has been to model expectations explicitly, but to continue to treat as structural the parameters of such macroeconomic model equations as the consumption and investment functions; this approach has been adopted, for example, in the Liverpool model (chapter 13) and other examples are Blanchard and Wyplosz (1981), Taylor (1979a) and Holly and Zarrop (1983). It is recognized by these authors that the parameters of these equations will change as regimes change, but it is argued that the major impact of regime change will be felt in the expectations variables, while that on the parameters themselves, except for quite violent regime change, may be of second order importance. Again it is too early to pronounce on the relative success of this approach; we discuss the issues further in chapter 13.

It remains possible that a third school of thought referred to in chapter 1, of which a major proponent is Sims (1979), is correct in asserting that there is no practical possibility of policy evaluation and the best we can achieve is the estimation of time-series models whose parameters will shift in an unpredictable way with regime change.

We end this section, therefore, in a cautious vein: policy evaluation is certainly difficult and may even be impossible, but various researches are in hand which may offer scope for better evaluation in the future.

**Optimal Economic Policies and Time-inconsistency**

A crucial feature of an economy with rational expectations is that current outcomes and the movement of the system's state depend in part upon anticipated future policy decisions. This feature is what gives rise to Lucas's critique, just discussed.

The same feature will obviously not occur when expectations are formed in a backward-looking manner, since in these circumstances current outcomes and the movement of the system's state depend only upon current and past policy decisions and upon the current state. In

Lucas's critique, rational expectations causes difficulties for policy-makers in computing optimal policy rules: they need to allow for the full effects on private behaviour of people's expectations about the outcomes of the rules. However, having computed the rules appropriately, policy-makers face a further difficulty – or opportunity – if they are not bound in some way to stick to the rule they so compute but people expect them to stick to it nevertheless. For after one period of operating this rule, people have made certain commitments, expecting the rule to prevail; the policy-maker now faces a new situation, in that he can exploit these commitments in making policy afresh. Such policy behaviour is known as 'time-inconsistency'.

Of course, matters will not rest there, since the people, thus tricked and exploited, will be less willing to believe that the fresh policy rule will prevail without yet further twists. There is also the question of whether people would have been willing to believe the original policy rule in the first place if the policy-makers could wriggle out of it. Finally, we may ask why policy-makers should wish to trick people in this way 'for the social good' – on the face of it, it is peculiar that social good can be achieved by trickery. However, we defer these developments of the argument until after an explanation of the mechanism behind time-inconsistency.

Kydland and Prescott (1977) showed how, in a dynamic economic system in which agents possess rational expectations, the optimal policy at time $t = 0$, which sets future paths for the control variables (taxes, subsidies, monetary growth), implies values of the control variables at some later time $t + i$, that will not be optimal when policy is re-examined at $t + i$, even though the preferences of agents are unchanged. This they called the time-inconsistency of optimal plans.

Two examples (given by Kydland and Prescott, 1977; Fischer, 1980) relate to examinations and patent policy. Optimal policy at the beginning of a course is to plan to have a mid-session exam. However, on the morning of the exam when all student preparation is complete, the optimal policy is to cancel the exam, saving the students the trouble of writing and the lecturer the trouble of grading. Optimal policy may analogously be to withdraw patent protection after resources have been allocated to successful inventive activity on the basis of continued patent protection.

The argument's formal structure can be seen in a simple two-period problem presented by Kydland and Prescott. Let $\pi = (\pi_1, \pi_2)$ be a sequence of policies for periods 1 and 2 and $x = (x_1, x_2)$ be the corresponding sequence for economic agents' decisions. The social objective function is given by

$$S(x_1, x_2, \pi_1, \pi_2) \tag{5.10}$$

Consider first the situation with backward-looking expectations, where no time-inconsistency arises. For simplicity we will assume an absence of stochastic error terms, which does not affect the argument. In this case the model is:

$$x_1 = x_1(\pi_1) \tag{5.11}$$

$$x_2 = x_2(x_1, \pi_2) \tag{5.12}$$

The policy-maker maximizes (5.10) subject to this model, meeting the first order conditions to a maximum (we assume the $S$ function is well-behaved so that second order conditions are met):

$$0 = \frac{\delta S}{\delta \pi_1} = \left( \frac{\delta S}{\delta x_1} + \frac{\delta S}{\delta x_2} \cdot \frac{\delta x_2}{\delta x_1} \right) \delta x_1 / \delta \pi_1 + \frac{\delta S}{\delta \pi_1} \tag{5.13}$$

$$0 = \frac{\delta S}{\delta \pi_2} = \frac{\delta S}{\delta x_2} \cdot \frac{\delta x_2}{\delta \pi_2} + \frac{\delta S}{\delta \pi_2} \tag{5.14}$$

The solution of (5.11) to (5.14) defines the optimal values of $\pi_1$ and $\pi_2$ (and the implied $x_1$ and $x_2$) which the policy-maker chooses at the beginning of period 1. At the end of period 1, $x_1$ and $\pi_1$ have occurred, exactly as the model predicted and the policy-maker intended, respectively. So at this point, were he to recompute his optimal second period policy $\pi_2$, he would simply solve (5.12) and (5.14) for $\pi_2$ and $x_2$. Since $x_1$ and $\pi_1$ are as implied by the complete four-equation solution earlier, the truncated solution for $\pi_2$ and $x_2$ conditional on them will also be the same as before (any reader doubtful of this should check this result with any set of four simultaneous equations). So the policy-maker will automatically continue with his planned policy under the case of backward-looking expectations.

Now consider how rational expectations affect the situation, under the (artificial) assumption that people believe the policy-maker's announced plans. The model now changes because the outcome in period 1 is affected by expectations of period 2 policy

$$x_1 = x_1(\pi_1, \pi_2) \tag{5.15}$$

$$x_2 = x_2(x_1, \pi_2) \tag{5.16}$$

The policy-maker's maximization at the start of period 1 is now given by

$$0 = \frac{\delta S}{\delta \pi_1} = \left( \frac{\delta S}{\delta x_1} + \frac{\delta S}{\delta x_2} \cdot \frac{\delta x_2}{\delta x_1} \right) \frac{\delta x_1}{\delta \pi_1} + \frac{\delta S}{\delta \pi_1} \tag{5.17}$$

$$0 = \frac{\delta S}{\delta \pi_2} = \frac{\delta S}{\delta x_2} \cdot \frac{\delta x_2}{\delta \pi_2} + \frac{\delta S}{\delta \pi_2} + \left( \frac{\delta S}{\delta x_1} + \frac{\delta S}{\delta x_2} \cdot \frac{\delta x_2}{\delta x_1} \right) \frac{\delta x_1}{\delta \pi_2} \tag{5.18}$$

Equation (5.17) is the same as (5.13) under adaptive expectations, but (5.18) adds to (5.14) the last term, which reflects the public's rational anticipation of $\pi_2$ and its effect on period 1 events, $x_1$. The policy-maker obviously wants that effect to be optimal.

At the end of period 1, when $x_1$ and $\pi_1$ have become history, the policy-maker can re-optimize his setting of $\pi_2$ and, if he does so, his appropriate first order condition is:

$$0 = \frac{\delta S}{\delta \pi_2} = \frac{\delta S}{\delta x_2} \cdot \frac{\delta x_2}{\delta \pi_2} + \frac{\delta S}{\delta \pi_2} \tag{5.19}$$

which reverts to (5.14). In other words, having influenced expectations in period 1, he now can neglect any effect of $\pi_2$ on the $x_1$ outcome (just as was the case throughout with adaptive expectations). He solves for $\pi_2$, $x_2$ from (5.16) and (5.19), given $\pi_1$, $x_1$ (and previously planned $\pi_2$, $x_2$) from (5.15) to (5.18).

Obviously the solution for $\pi_2$, $x_2$ will be different from the previous plan (it would be the same if and only if (5.19) were identical to (5.18)). Hence his optimal plan is necessarily time-inconsistent.

In macroeconomic policy time-inconsistency arises because of the desire among policy-makers to exploit the Phillips curve short-run trade-off between output and inflation. If they merely carry forward the money supply plans everyone expects, output will be at the natural rate, $y^*$ (as will unemployment). However, they would ideally prefer higher output (as stressed by Hillier and Malcolmson, 1984) because of the presence of distortions (such as unemployment benefits discussed earlier) which mean that private decisions generate too low an output and employment. So it is optimal to raise money supply growth (and inflation) above its expected level to stimulate output.

Take the following example, using a heavily simplified macromodel; the example originally comes from Barro and Gordon (1983). Let the government set money supply growth, $g_t$, and assume that inflation is equal to this (one can think of this as the government using the money supply to target inflation directly). Output is determined by the Phillips curve:

$$y_t = y^* + \theta (g_t - g_t^e) \tag{5.20}$$

$g_t^e$ is people's rational expectation of money supply growth formed before the $t$-period opens.

The government's (and also the social) utility function is:

$$u_t = - (y_t - ky^*)^2 - s(g_t - g^*)^2 \quad (k > 1) \tag{5.21}$$

$ky^*$ ( $> y^*$) and $g^*$ are the government's ideals for output and inflation, respectively.

Suppose the government announces its planned money growth in $t - 1$; it is believed and therefore equals $g_t^e$. But then it is able to change its mind at the beginning of $t$, after $g_t^e$ has been set, so that a different $g_t$ can be delivered. The set-up is quite artificial, as we pointed out earlier and will shortly discuss.

Before the period the government maximizes $u_t$ with respect to $g_t$, subject to the Phillips curve and $g_t = g_t^e$. In this case $y_t = y^*$ and the maximum is:

$$0 = \delta u_t / \delta g_t = -2s (g_t - g^*) \tag{5.22}$$

whence $g_t = g^*$. However, once period $t$ has begun, the government can re-optimize, maximizing $u_t$ with respect to $g_t$ again subject the Phillips curve, but now given $g_t^e = g^*$. Substituting for $y_t$ from (5.20) in (5.21) gives:

$$u_t = - [ (1 - k) y^* + \theta (g_t - g^*)]^2 - s (g_t - g^*)^2 \tag{5.23}$$

Maximizing this we get:

$$0 = \delta u_t / \delta g_t = -2[ (1 - k) y^* + \theta (g_t - g^*)] (\theta) -2s (g_t - g^*) \tag{5.24}$$

so that

$$g_t = g^* + \frac{\theta (k - 1)}{s + \theta^2} y^* \tag{5.25}$$

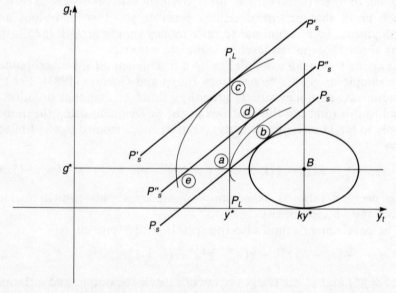

Figure 5.3   Time-inconsistent exploitation of the Phillips curve.

Actual money supply growth is more stimulatory than expected as the government exploits the Phillips curve. Figure 5.3 illustrates this.

The concentric ellipses in figure 5.3 are the government's (society's) indifference curves, with $B$ devoting its 'bliss point'. $P_L P_L$, $P_S P_S$ are respectively the long-run Phillips curve and the short-run, conditional on $g_t^e = g^*$ (we will return to $P_S' P_S'$ and point $c$). Point $a$ is the optimal plan before period $t$ opens. Point $b$ is the optimal action after it opens.

As our heavy earlier hints have indicated, there is an artificiality in the assumptions which permit the government to fool rational private decision-makers in this way. Even though it is for the general good, private individuals will try to avoid being fooled in this way, because as individuals that is their best decision. That is precisely what a distortion involves: the outcome of best private plans does not coincide with the social optimum.

Another way of stating this is to say that individuals will, in forming rational expectations, take account of the government's incentive not to carry through its announced plan. If people know the model, then they know the government's utility function and that it will maximize that. They will be in a position to work out what the government will actually do as opposed to what it says it will do.

In our example, this has radical results. People form their expectations, $g_t^e$, by working back from what the government will do in period $t$ given those expectations. The government will maximize $u_t$ subject to the Phillips curve and $g_t^e$ whatever it is. Substituting (5.20) into (5.21) gives:

$$u_t = -[(1-k)y^* + \theta(g_t - g_t^e)]^2 - s[g_t - g^*]^2 \qquad (5.26)$$

and setting $\delta u_t / \delta g_t = 0$ solves for:

$$g_t = [sg^* + \theta^2 g_t^e + \theta(k-1)y^*]/(s+\theta^2) \qquad (5.27)$$

This is the rule people know the government will actually follow, regardless of its pious intentions. Therefore, to form a rational expectation of $g_t$ for period $t$ in $t-1$, people take expectations of (5.27): in so doing they ensure that $g_t^e = E_{t-1} g_t$. Therefore they solve:

$$E_{t-1} g_t = [sg^* + \theta^2 E_{t-1} g_t + \theta(k-1)y^*]/(s+\theta^2) \qquad (5.28)$$

from which it emerges that:

$$g_t^e = E_{t-1} g_t = g^* + \frac{\theta(k-1)}{s} y^* \qquad (5.29)$$

When the government comes to execute its optimal rule (5.27), whatever it may have announced in advance, it will find that it will generate money supply growth exactly as people expected, $g_t = g_t^e$ as in (5.29). This can be established by substituting (5.29) for $g_t^e$ into (5.27) and solving for $g_t$.

In figure 5.3, this is point $c$, where $y_t = y^*$ on the long-run Phillips curve. Yet the government has reached a tangency point of an indifference curve to the short-run Phillips curve, $P_S' P_S'$, through that point.

What we see here is a combination of two factors. First, rational expectations is ensuring that in the absence of shocks people are not surprised so that their private output plans are not frustrated: $y_t = y^*$ on the long-run Phillips curve and $g_t = E_{t-1} g_t$. This is a restoration of Sargent and Wallace's principle of policy ineffectiveness (in the absence of the various special features in the model which we saw in chapter 4 can restore it).

Secondly, the government is pursuing a particularly destabilizing rule for inflation. Instead of responding to past output, itself a rule that destabilizes money growth and inflation in the presence of shocks (but not here where shocks have been assumed away), it is responding to expectations of inflation in the attempt to stimulate output above its natural (inevitable) level. In other words, whatever money supply growth people may expect it to inject in an attempt to stimulate the economy, it goes one better in its attempt to reach tangency with the short-run Phillips curve. The process is only arrested by the escalating costs of inflation. It can be seen from figure 5.3, where the vertical distance between points $b$ and $c$ is given by $\theta(k-1) [\theta^2/s(s+\theta^2)] y^*$, that as the cost of inflation, $s$, tends to zero, point $c$ tends to infinity.

Consequently, on top of any moderate destabilization of inflation that may occur if it also attempts to respond to past output, the government may produce a very large destabilization of inflation through this type of response. The solution forced by the conflict between the government's determination to reach tangency with the short-run Phillips curve and the people's rational expectations is the point $c$ where both are finally satisfied.

The 'time-inconsistency' of the government's optimal plans has been marginalized by people's rational expectations in this case, because any 'plans' the government may form before period $t$ opens are irrelevant. The only 'plan' of any interest is the computed outcome of the government's true rule. If we refer to this as the government's true plan, then we can say that it is time-consistent, because it will be followed through in period $t$.

Clearly, this time-consistent result of the interaction between the government's rule and people's rational expectations delivers poor social utility. If somehow the government could achieve point $a$ (the result of its original time-inconsistent optimal plan, had it been carried forward), that would be better, since it would achieve lower inflation together with

$y_t = y^*$ as in $c$. Point $b$ is better still but no longer available because of rational expectations.

In terms of the general two-period problem set out in the model of equations (5.10), (5.15) and (5.16), the equivalent of point $a$ is the solution of equations (5.17) and (5.18) together with the model where the policy-maker determines his optimal plan assuming his own credibility. The equivalent of point $b$ is the solution of (5.19) and (5.16) given $x_1$ and $\pi_1$ as determined by this original optimal plan and the full model – here he 'backslides'. The equivalent of point $c$ is given by the joint solution of (5.19) and (5.17) with the model, where his future backsliding is fully taken into account in his decision for first period policy and in the behaviour of private agents.

We have now exposed the artificiality of our original assumption that people automatically believe the plans the government announced at the start of the first period. In fact they will only believe them if the government commits itself in advance to carry them out, on pain of a penalty at least as great as any gain from backsliding. This penalty has to be administered by some agency outside the government's control: otherwise the government could abrogate the penalty. This incidentally creates a difficulty for a sovereign democratic government: if it is sovereign, may it not refuse to submit to any penalty, even one it agreed to? Clearly if it does not surrender its sovereignty over this matter then it cannot enjoy a point such as $a$ in figure 5.3. Without an effective and sufficient penalty, the only possible point is $c$: not only $b$ but also $a$ is ruled out. (Point $c$ is the 'time-consistent' policy case in this literature: in the literature of contracts it would be called the 'self-enforcing' or 'incentive-compatible' case. In effect if no contract can be enforced against the interests of one party, then the only possible contract is one that this party will carry out anyway (Hart, 1983). The parallel here in policy is that no enforceable contract specifying a penalty can be drawn up with the policy-maker.)

Since $a$ is preferable to $c$, it is in the interest of policy-makers to find a mechanism for effective commitment. One such mechanism is a constitutionally independent central bank, such as the Bundesbank (set up after the Second World War) in Germany and the Federal Reserve Board in the USA. Another is to join a currency board system of fixed exchange rates (as in the sterling area) whereby one's money supply is controlled by the dominant currency of the system: the European Monetary System may be evolving in this way. In the case where the government itself controls its own money supply within a floating exchange rate system, the British government between 1972 and 1990 being one, one may seek to create political embarrassment from backsliding.

The Thatcher government's Medium Term Financial Strategy (MTFS) was of this type. It set targets for the money supply and public sector deficit for a rolling four-year period: these targets and the associated commitments to reduce inflation were emphasized by the government as a litmus test of its fitness to govern. The implication was that the public should not re-elect it if it failed: clearly a dangerous commitment to fail on from a political viewpoint.

These mechanisms all have their deficiencies. Democratic governments have the power to change constitutions or to leave currency boards. They can plainly run public sector deficits, which ultimately may drive them to print money to avoid the rising cost of debt finance: central bank obstruction in these circumstances will be over-ruled, with the ultimate threat of removing the bank's independence. The Thatcher MTFS confronted the issue of deficits, and by making the public its judge also avoided the constitutional issue. The question still remained over how far it could get away with backsliding: for example, could it not have tried to persuade the public at an election that somewhat higher inflation then planned was for their good because it allowed lower unemployment (point $b$ in figure 5.3)?

These deficiencies imply that there is with each of these mechanisms some probability of effectiveness, some of backsliding. The resulting solution will reflect these probabilities. Let us pursue this in the context of our inflation–unemployment trade-off example.

Suppose the government commits incompletely to a plan of $g_t = g^*$ so that there is a probability, $\pi$, of its pursuing a backsliding policy $g_t^b$ (that is, maximizing $u_t$ given whatever expectations, $g_t^e$, have been formed on the basis of its 'commitment'). The consequential expectations, $g_t^e$, will be:

$$g_t^e = \pi g_t^b + (1 - \pi)g^* \tag{5.30}$$

To calculate $g_t^b$, we substitute for $g_t^e$ in $u_t$, obtaining

$$u_t = -[(1 - k)y^* + \theta(g_t - \pi g_t^b - (1 - \pi)g^*)]^2 - s(g_t - g^*)^2 \tag{5.31}$$

so that its backsliding strategy is given by setting $o = \delta u_t/\delta g_t$, which yields:

$$g_t^b = g^* + \frac{\theta(k - 1)y^*}{s + \theta^2(1 - \pi)} \tag{5.32}$$

(Our procedure, it will be recalled, is to maximize with respect to $g_t$, given $g_t^b$, then to set $g_t^b = g_t$ in the resulting first order condition and solve for $g_t^b$). It follows that:

$$g_t^e = g^* + \frac{\theta\pi(k - 1)y^*}{s + \theta^2(1 - \pi)} \tag{5.33}$$

The resulting situation is illustrated in figure 5.3 by the Phillips curve $P_S'' P_S''$. The outcome will either be $d$ if the government backslides or $e$ if it does not. Point $d$ is clearly better than $c$ (it may or may not be worse than $a$ depending on the size of $s$, the government's dislike of inflation); backsliding when you have uncertain commitment is better than when you have none, but you might have been better off with totally certain commitment.

Point $e$, following through on uncertain commitment, though clearly worse than $a$ and $d$, may or may not be worse than $c$. For $c$

$$u_t = -y^{*2}(k - 1)^2 [1 + \theta^2/s] \tag{5.34}$$

for $e$

$$u_t = -y^{*2}(k - 1)^2 \{1 + \theta^2\pi/[s + \theta^2(1 - \pi)]\}^2 \tag{5.35}$$

However the expected (probability-weighted) utility of points $d$ and $e$ is better than $c$ and worse than $a$.

It follows that some commitment, however uncertain, is better than no commitment at all, because it gets the government on to a lower Phillips curve, so a better trade-off: expectations of money supply growth $g_t^e$ are reduced.

Uncertainty about whether the government will backslide for some reason is unavoidable given its sovereignty. The essential source of the uncertainty is whether the penalty triggered by backsliding (over-riding the central bank, being politically embarrassed by higher inflation, etc.) will be bigger than the gain from it (lower unemployment, higher output at the expense of somewhat higher inflation).

As we have seen, it pays the government to make a tough commitment to $g^*$. But no government can bind its successor, or even itself at a future date. If its preferences change (a new government or new ministers), or if circumstances change (an unexpected fall in $y$ or rise in unemployment, for example), the penalty may not be sufficient. These elements also qualify the clearcut welfare calculations above; they imply instead some trade-off between credibility and flexibility.

Modelling this uncertainty is clearly difficult. Various attempts have been made. One, initiated by Backus and Driffill (1985), has focused on uncertainty about government preferences. The government may turn out to be 'wet' or 'dry' (in other words, to backslide or not): the probability, $\pi$, of backsliding ('wetness') is constantly re-assessed in the light of policy actions.

Another, initiated by Barro and Gordon (1983), assumes that preferences are known and constant and that the penalty for backsliding is a 'loss of reputation', whereby the public disbelieve the government's announced plans for a certain period of time and assume the government will backslide during this period. The penalty is arbitrary in the Barro and Gordon model but we could reduce the arbitrariness by assuming, for example, that the public's disbelief continues until there is a change of membership in the government (e.g. an election cycle).

During the period of lost reputation, the government is considered to suffer the point $c$. This penalty is in general less than the gain to backsliding on $g^*$ as an announced plan. People work out the announced plan ($g_t^p > g^*$) such that the penalty is just sufficient to offset any gain from backsliding. This is of course the plan that the government will also choose. It produces a point on the vertical Phillips curve between $a$ and $c$.

This idea on its own simply works out what would happen if the penalty for backsliding on a plan were less than the penalty needed to prevent backsliding on $g^*$. The result is a steady $g_t^e = g_t > g^*$. The government would in fact be better off if it could somehow persuade people to disbelieve it for longer!

Uncertainty can be introduced by introducing shocks to the economy which cause the government to choose a $g_t$ different from $g_t^e$. If $g_t > g_t^e$, the government loses credibility: future $g_t$ defaults to point $c$ until credibility is restored. It then reverts to $g_t = g_t^e > g^*$ until the next shock producing $g_t > g_t^e$. One could also introduce the idea of gaining credibility if $g_t < g_t^e$ because of, say, an inflationary shock producing unexpectedly tight policy. A period could ensue in which $g_t^e = g^*$.

The difficulty with this approach is how to define a non-arbitrary strategy on the part of private agents for 'triggering' belief or disbelief – their 'punishment strategy'. On the other hand, if one can motivate (e.g. through political conventions) such a strategy, it is an attractive model of reputation. It can also be refined by recasting it in terms of the probability, $\pi$, of $g_t > g^*$, where $\pi$ depends on the extent to which $g_t$ exceeded $g^*$ in the past.

We have therefore reviewed two approaches to uncertainty – one emphasizes the uncertainty of preferences, the other that of events. The essential point is that the probability of backsliding on announced plans can be assessed rationally on the basis of past revealed preferences and reactions to events. This probability measures the government's 'credibility'. It can also be influenced by the government's own measures to pre-commit itself by closing down or penalizing the options to pursue potentially inflationary policies.

The 'time-inconsistency' problem originally highlighted by Kydland and Prescott (1977) has laid bare an important constraint on policy – its political lack of credibility – and at the same time a major opportunity – the potential building of credibility by policy construction and the delivery of past commitments. However, this building-up may well be costly in lost flexibility, and it is in general preferable, if possible, to reduce the distortion which makes backsliding attractive in the first place. Failing that, it should be possible to design a policy environment in which genuine backsliding is penalized but which does not prevent flexible responses to at least certain sorts of shocks (such as for example an oil crisis).

## Conclusions

'Optimal control' methods of varying sophistication have been used on Keynesian models for much of the post-war period; these have given rise to closed-loop, feedback policies, the so-called 'fine-tuning', 'demand-management' policies of the Keynesian era. One firm conclusion of this chapter is that such methods are dangerously misconceived, both because they do not allow for effects on private behaviour through expectations and because they take a naive view of the social welfare function.

Where conclusions are less firm is about what policies *are* optimal. Two things, however, do stand out. First, government policy should be as *predictable* as possible; higher variance, whether of money supply or fiscal policy, has been shown uniformly to reduce welfare. Secondly, government policy should be as *credible* as possible (i.e. be expected to remain in place as promised for a long period into the future); lack of credibility causes private behaviour to insure against backsliding, which in turn limits policy options, and the overall result is likely to be inferior to that of maintaining policies steadily. On both these counts a fixed rule for the money supply scores well. It also permits reasonable flexibility of interest rates and the exchange rate in response to shocks.

Certainly, the present state of knowledge does not enable policy-makers to choose sophisticated feedback rules with any confidence, even though we could grant that there is likely to be scope in theory for them to be effective and even beneficial in the institutional circumstances of some economies.

## Notes

1  In case it is not already clear, rational expectations implies that agents act at the micro level as if they know the probability distributions over future events (and hence the parameters of the true model); it does *not* imply that governments or other observers of the aggregates, including econometricians, have this knowledge. This distinction is based first on incentive structures. The 'micro-agent' is assumed to face significant costs of expectations errors and the threat of these costs is assumed to force him close enough to 'full knowledge' for this to be a reasonable approximation for aggregate modelling purposes. This is not true in general of government employees or

econometricians when dealing with aggregate data; considerations of power in the first case and of academic prestige in the second are as important as, if not more so than, the need to be *right*. There is more to the distinction. An individual micro-agent may well not know the true model (in fact is unlikely to do so even on an 'as if' basis); but misconceptions of the model across micro-agents should, because of commercial pressures operating symmetrically to weed out poor agents, be randomly distributed around the true model, and on average the misconceptions will cancel out for a large number of agents. A government too may get the model wrong; unfortunately there is only one government at any one time and, if it relies on being right in computing sophisticated policies, it risks egregious error.

2 If output, however, changes for *supply* reasons (e.g. crop failure), this would naturally be added into $y^*$ and the variation computed around this adjusted figure.

3 This situation is not one of full Pareto-optimality, as markets are incomplete and distortions assumed to exist; however, it is a situation of restricted Pareto-optimality, under the provisos given.

4 This has particular relevance in the UK (see Minford et al., 1985).

# 6

# Budget Deficits and Their Financing

---

In this chapter we consider the link between fiscal and monetary policy. We begin with a model with wealth effects. These provide a compelling logic binding fiscal and monetary policy; later we shall discuss what links survive if there are no wealth effects and we shall argue that there are still important ones. (In an appendix to this chapter we review the theory concerning the existence of wealth effects, and conclude that they are likely to exist.) Finally, we ask what size of budget deficit is desirable.

**A Convenient Representation of the Government Budget Constraint**

Private sector net financial wealth consists, in a closed economy (which we continue to assume), of government bonds and high-powered money (the 'monetary base', consisting of the notes and coins issue plus commercial banks' deposits with the central bank), i.e. government net financial liabilities. These are recognizable as the 'outside money' of an earlier literature (Patinkin, 1965; Metzler, 1951; Gurley and Shaw, 1960). Bank deposits are 'inside money' in that banks are a private sector institution; their deposits are therefore both assets and liabilities of the private sector, cancelling out in net terms.

Let $f$ be the stock of government net financial liabilities (hence government debt) in real terms (i.e. deflated by the consumer price index). $f$ will rise for two reasons: first, a government deficit will create new liabilities, and second, the existing stock of liabilities will be subject to capital gains, as the price of bonds rises or the consumer price index falls. We write:

$$\Delta f_t = f_{t-1}\pi d_t - f_{t-1}(q\ \Delta R_t + \Delta p_t) \tag{6.1}$$

where $d$ is government deficit as a fraction of GDP, $\pi$ is the inverse of the ratio of government debt to GDP, $q$ is the proportionate response of long-term bond prices to the long-term interest rate $(R)$. The unit coefficient on $\Delta p_t$ reflects our assumption that all government liabilities are denominated in money terms. We will view (6.1) with $\pi$, $q$ held constant at some average value as an appropriate approximation. Hence:

$$\Delta\theta_t = \pi d_t - q \, \Delta R_t - \Delta p_t \tag{6.2}$$

where $\theta = \log f$. Equation (6.2) will be the form in which we represent the government budget constraint in what follows.

To (6.2) we add a relationship determining the supply of high-powered money (in logs), which we shall write as $m$, the same as total money, reflecting the convenient and conventional assumption that there is a fixed 'money multiplier' between the two. We write:

$$\Delta m_t = \Phi\pi(d_t - \bar{d}) + \Delta\bar{m} + \varepsilon_t \tag{6.3}$$

where $\bar{d}$ is the equilibrium government deficit as a fraction of GDP, $\varepsilon$ is an error term, and $\Delta\bar{m}$ is the equilibrium rate of growth of money. Equation (6.3) states that out-of-equilibrium money supply will have an independent random component (to which we could add other independent temporary determinants of money if we wished) as well as a component responding to the temporary component of the deficit. Given (6.2), (6.3) implicitly also determines the supply of nominal bonds as the difference between nominal financial assets and the monetary base.

Equation (6.3) focuses on two aspects of monetary policy with which we shall proceed to deal. First, how far does the equilibrium growth rate of money reflect the government deficit? Secondly, how far is money supply growth rate varied (over the 'cycle') as budgetary financing needs change? In other words, what are the links between fiscal and monetary policy, first in, and second out, of steady state? This distinction is an important one in rational expectations models, as we shall see.

We begin with behaviour out of steady state.

## Stability and Bond-financed Deficits Out of Steady State

One issue that has been given great prominence since the early 1970s is the possibility of instability in models with wealth effects, if budget deficits are bond-financed. This can be illustrated in a simple fixed-price IS/LM model without rational expectations (a log linear adaptation of Blinder and Solow's 1973 model). We use non-stochastic continuous time and abstract from the steady state relationship between money and deficits by setting $\bar{d} = \Delta\bar{m} = 0$:

$$y_t = k\theta_t - \alpha r_t + \phi d_t \tag{6.4}$$

$$m_t = \bar{p} + \delta y_t - \beta r_t + \mu\theta_t \tag{6.5}$$

$$\dot{\theta}_t = \pi d_t - q\dot{r}_t \tag{6.6}$$

$$d_t = \bar{g} - ty_t \tag{6.7}$$

$$\dot{m}_t = \Phi \pi d_t \tag{6.8}$$

$\bar{g}$, government expenditure as a fraction of GDP, includes debt interest: this formulation assumes that other expenditure is reduced as debt interest rises. If it were not, the instability under bond finance discussed below would be worsened severely. $ty_t$ measures marginal tax receipts as a fraction of GDP and hence $t$ is the income elasticity of taxation minus one (initial average tax receipts are netted out of $\bar{g}$) and a dot denotes the time derivatives. Because prices are fixed at $\bar{p}$, $r_t$ is both the nominal and real interest rates. Equations (6.4) and (6.5) are the IS and LM curves with wealth effects; (6.6) and (6.8) are the budget constraint and money supply relationship for this model.

The model solves for $y_t$ and $r_t$ given $\theta_t$. Using (6.8) and (6.6) gives $\dot{m}_t = \Phi(\dot{\theta}_t + q\dot{r}_t)$ so that $m_t = \Phi(\theta_t + qr_t) + K_m$, where $K_m$ is an arbitrary constant. Substituting for $m_t$ from this into (6.5) and for $d_t$ from (6.7) into (6.4) yields the equations for $y_t$ and $r_t$. Substituting the solution of them for $y_t$ and $\dot{r}_t$ into (6.6) yields the equation of motion for $\theta_t$ as:

$$\dot{\theta}_t = \frac{-\pi t (k\beta - \alpha\mu + \Phi kq + \Phi\alpha)}{[(1 + \phi t)(\beta + q\mu) + \delta(\alpha + qk)]} \theta_t \tag{6.9}$$

For stability we require $(k\beta \dots + \Phi\alpha) > 0$. Clearly if money supply is held constant regardless of the deficit, i.e. $\Phi = 0$ (bond financed deficits), then we must have $k\beta > \alpha\mu$, which raises the possibility of instability if there are relatively strong wealth effects in the LM curve. $\Phi > 0$ reduces the possibility; Blinder and Solow and others have accordingly advocated money-financed deficits as a means of avoiding possible instability.

This instability is illustrated in figure 6.1. In addition to the *IS* and *LM* curves we have drawn in a '*WW*' curve, which is the equation of the budget constraint (6.6), showing the level of output where $\dot{\theta}_t = 0$, that is there are no changes in wealth. For $\dot{\theta}_t = 0$, we must have both $d_t = 0$ and $\dot{r}_t = 0$; $\dot{r}_t = 0$ automatically when $\dot{\theta}_t = 0$ because, as we have seen, $r_t$ and $y_t$ (the intersection of the IS and LM curves) depend on $\theta_t$ and cease to move when $\theta_t$ stops moving. This level is $\bar{y} = \bar{g}/t$ since from (6.7) $d_t = 0$ at this point. To the right of the *WW* curve, $\theta_t$ is falling (and rising to the left). The *IS* curve shifts leftward as $\theta_t$ falls but the *LM* curve shifts rightwards. Instability under bond-financing ($\Phi = 0$) occurs when the intersection moves rightwards (and down), i.e. $k\beta < \alpha\mu$, as the effect of $\theta_t$ on $y_t$ (from equations (6.4) and (6.5)) is

$$\frac{k\beta - \alpha\mu}{\beta + \alpha\delta}$$

This can be seen diagramatically by noting that the rightward shift of

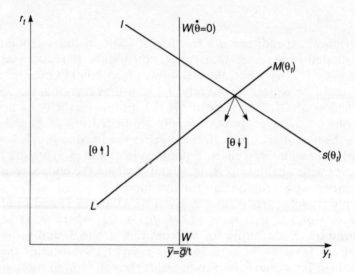

Figure 6.1   Instability with bond-financed deficits.

the $LM$ is $\mu\theta$, the leftward shift of the $IS$ is $k\theta$; but the flatter the IS curve (the higher $\alpha$) the more the $LM$ curve shift dominates the output movement, and vice versa the flatter the $LM$ curve (the higher $\beta$).

We pointed out that there is additional instability if one assumes government expenditure is fixed and does not fall to offset debt interest. The interested reader can work this case out, using in place of (6.7):

$$d_t = \bar{g} - ty_t + \bar{r}/\pi\ \theta_t + 1/\pi\ r_t \qquad (6.7)'$$

where the last two terms approximate debt interest around some average interest rate, $\bar{r}$, and an average financial asset to GDP ratio, $1/\pi$. The reader will find that the equivalent of (6.9) contains a number of extra positive terms in the numerator, increasing the chances of instability.

Under rational expectations, however, this Blinder–Solow argument carries less force. To convert their model into a rational expectations form, it is sufficient to recognize that the valuation of financial assets is forward-looking, i.e. it depends on expectations of future interest rates; for convenience, now use discrete time. Returning, for example, to the model given by (6.4) to (6.8), replace (6.6) and (6.8) by:

$$\Delta\theta_t = \pi d_t - q(\mathrm{E}_t\ r_{t+1} - \mathrm{E}_{t-1}\ r_t) \qquad (6.6)'$$

$$\Delta m_t = \Phi\pi d_t \qquad (6.8)'$$

If the model is now solved by the methods of chapter 2, we obtain a second order characteristic equation in which one of the roots should be unstable for a unique stable (saddlepath) solution. The roots involve all the coefficients and there is no general condition to ensure the saddlepath property.

If $\Phi = 0$, the characteristic equation $x_t + ax_{t-1} + bx_{t-2} = 0$ with roots $\sigma_1, \sigma_2$ has:

$$a = -(\sigma_1 + \sigma_2) = -1 + [D + \pi t(k\beta - \alpha\mu)]/$$

$$\{q[\delta k + (1 + \phi t)\mu]\}$$

$$b = \sigma_1\sigma_2 = -D/\{q[\delta k + (1 + \phi t)\mu]\} \tag{6.10}$$

where $D = (1 + \phi t)\beta + \delta\alpha$.

Since $b < 0$, the roots cannot be complex, and at least one of the roots must be $< 0$ (alternating motion) and the other positive (monotonic motion), which is consistent with a saddlepath. For example, take the following parameter values, which approximate those of the Liverpool model of the UK:

$$\beta = 2, \phi = k = \delta = 1, t = 0.3, \alpha = 0.5, q = 3, \mu = 0, \pi = 2$$

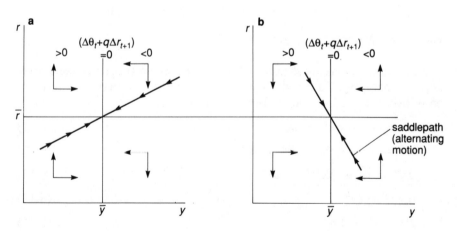

Figure 6.2 Two possible stable types of motion under rational expectations.

a, Monotonic saddlepath with $k\beta > \alpha\mu \left( \dfrac{\partial y}{\partial \theta} > 0, \dfrac{\partial r}{\partial \theta} > 0 \right)$; $\Delta\theta_t, \Delta r_{t+1}$ have same sign.

b, Alternating saddlepath with $k\beta < \alpha\mu \left( \dfrac{\partial y}{\partial \theta} < 0, \dfrac{\partial r}{\partial \theta} > 0 \right)$; $\Delta\theta_t, \Delta r_{t+1}$ have opposite signs.

These give $b = -1.03$, $a = -0.43$. Hence the roots are $\sigma_1, \sigma_2 = 0.82$, $-1.25$: the monotonic saddlepath (figure 6.2a). Had we found by contrast $\mu = 5$ so that $k\beta < \alpha\mu$, we would have had $\sigma_1, \sigma_2 = 1.015$, $-0.135$; again a saddlepath, but this time with alternating motion (figure 6.2b).

Interestingly, in the particular example here, the $k\beta < \alpha\mu$ ($\mu = 5$) is actually more stable in that, although it is alternating, the absolute value of the stable root is much lower than in the case of $\mu = 0$. Computer examination of a wide range of values for the parameters suggests that problems with saddlepath stability arise whether $k\beta >$ or $< \alpha\mu$.

If $k\beta > \alpha\mu$, there is saddlepath stability when $q$ or $\mu$ are low (otherwise the roots have a tendency to be both less than unity in absolute value: a 'non-uniqueness' problem). If $k\beta < \alpha\mu$, there is saddlepath stability when $q$ or $\mu$ are high; otherwise the roots tend to be both greater than unity. The two typical cases of saddlepath stability are shown in figure 6.2.

We conclude this section negatively: there is no compelling reason within rational expectations models why the cyclical or short-run component of monetary policy should be influenced by fiscal policy. The decision, for example, whether to pursue a constant money supply growth rate through the cycle even though the budget deficit will be moving cyclically, can be taken on other grounds, notably those appropriate to stabilization policy. We now turn to the steady state component of the money supply rule, where the situation is quite different.

## Long-term Monetary Targets

We now take the previous model, but abstract from short-run behaviour while reinstating the possibility of steady state inflation. We have in equilibrium (* values are equilibrium ones):

$$y^* = k\theta^* - \alpha r^* + \phi \bar{d} \tag{6.11}$$

$$m^* = p^* + \delta y^* - \beta R^* + \mu \theta^* \tag{6.12}$$

$$\Delta \theta^* = \pi \bar{d} - q\Delta R^* - \Delta p^* \tag{6.13}$$

$$\bar{d} = \bar{g} - ty^* \tag{6.14}$$

$$R^* = r^* + \Delta p^* \tag{6.15}$$

$$\Delta m^* = \Delta \bar{m} \tag{6.16}$$

The question we wish to ask is: can $\Delta \bar{m}$ be chosen independently of $\bar{d}$? For simplicity assume a steady state growth rate of zero ($\Delta y^* = 0$), although this does not affect the argument. Assume also that $\bar{d}$ and $\Delta \bar{m}$ are chosen to be constants.

The first thing to notice is that, if in steady state both real interest rates and inflation are constant, then at once we have $\Delta R^* = 0$ from (6.15), $\Delta\theta^* = (\alpha/k)\,\Delta r^* = 0$ from (6.11); then from (6.12) and (6.16) we have $\Delta\bar{m} = \Delta m^* = \Delta p^*$, while from (6.13) we have $\pi\bar{d} = \Delta p^*$. It then follows that $\pi\bar{d} = \Delta\bar{m}$; monetary and fiscal policy have to be 'consistent', that is the rate of money supply growth has to be equal to the deficit as a fraction of financial assets, $\pi\bar{d}$. This in turn is equal to the rate at which *nominal* financial assets are growing ($\Delta\theta^* + \Delta p^*$); hence if money is growing at this rate, so also are bonds. Consistent monetary and fiscal policy hence implies that money and nominal bonds must be growing at the same rate.

Clearly we would like to ensure – as would any sensible government – that in equilibrium neither real interest rates nor inflation are moving. We have already imposed a terminal condition on inflation as part of our general solution procedure; therefore by imposition this will be constant in steady state. Assuming this, we may then derive by a similar procedure to the one already used:

$$\Delta r^* = \frac{k}{k(\beta + q) + \alpha(-\mu)}\,(\pi\bar{d} - \Delta\bar{m}) \qquad (6.17)$$

In other words, if the government wishes (given its terminal condition on inflation) to avoid steadily rising or falling real interest rates, then it must pursue consistent fiscal and monetary policy. This has to happen at some stage; otherwise eventually either (rising $r^*$) government expenditure would have to contract to zero (taxes rise to absorb the whole of GNP) or (falling $r^*$) real interest rates would become negative – neither of which is possible. Of course a sensible government will wish to stop any such tendency well before any such stage is threatened.

This argument has been conducted on the assumption that $\bar{d}$ is set, with changing interest payments on debt being offset by changes in government spending or taxes; if one assumes instead that government spending and tax rates are unaltered, then the steady state inflation rate, $\pi\bar{d} = \Delta\bar{m}$, depends on the level of government spending and taxes chosen; the algebra of this is more complex (see Minford et al., 1980), and the inflation resulting from any initial rise in the deficit is much greater than in the analysis above, because the eventual deficit is compounded by the rise in interest payments, but the essential message remains that there must be consistency between fiscal and monetary policy in steady state.

To conclude, wealth effects imply a constraint across the steady state components of fiscal and monetary policy, though not the short-run components. Hence in (6.3) $\Delta\bar{m} = \pi\bar{d}$, whereas we are free to write any short-run response function or error process besides.

## Are Wealth Effects Crucial to a Fiscal–Monetary Link?

We have stressed the role of wealth effects in forming a steady state fiscal–monetary link. However, even if there are no wealth effects, there are still limits to the possible divergence of fiscal and monetary policy within rational expectations models.

Such limits are placed by ceilings on the stock of government debt that the private sector will hold. In a world with no wealth effects, rising debt implies no change in real interest rates; in effect, future taxes being substituted for current taxes leaves everyone's wealth, savings and investment unaltered, and so requires no change in interest rates. Nevertheless, there are a number of natural ceilings on the debt the private sector will hold.

Debt is raised from *one* group of citizens, in order to avoid taxing *another* group (probably the majority) now; in effect the second group promise to pay off the first (or their inheritors) with future taxes. Therefore public debt is a form of contract between two sets of citizens, the terms of which depend for their enforcement on the honesty of government (the contract broker). If the debt is in money terms, then there are two ways of defaulting: explicit default, where the money amounts are not delivered; and implicit default, where the anticipated real amounts are not delivered because inflation is higher than anticipated.

One way of looking at wealth effects is therefore as proxying the increasing risk-premium required by the risk-adverse lending group as government debt rises. In that model, as debt rises, the marginal utility both of consumption and of real money balances rise, and real interest rates are forced up, as we saw above.

If wealth effects are ruled out, it is still plausible to assume some upper limit to the debt holding of the lending group, if only their total net worth. Such a limit has been suggested by Sargent and Wallace (1981) in a paper designed to investigate the upper limit on deficits when money supply growth is being held down by 'monetarist' policies.

In their overlapping-generations model, debt is held by the young, to be redeemed from them when old (the old will only wish to consume, in the absence of heirs). In such a model the government clearly cannot borrow more from the young than their current income. We will consider below (chapter 9) the detailed workings of such a model; in particular we will find that there are some circumstances when the issue of bonds does 'create wealth' by making possible certain inter-generational exchanges. But in most the issue of bonds in place of tax does not have wealth effects.

Now consider how the ceiling on debt would affect a simple macro model. Suppose that GDP, $N$ (also standing for the population by an appropriate choice of indices), grows at the rate $n$ and that the real rate of interest, $r$, is constant and greater than $n$. Let $* =$ rate of growth, $' =$ per capita value, $\pi =$ rate of inflation, $p =$ price level. Write the demand for high-powered money, $H$, in the quantity theory manner as:

$$H_t = hP_tN_t \qquad (6.18)$$

so that $H_t^* = \pi_t + n$. Suppose now that at time $t = 1$ new intentions are announced and carried out, for future fiscal and monetary policy; the announcement (fully believed) changes the present real value of bonds to $b_1$ as prices and interest rates react. There are then two phases of policy: 'transition' from $t = 2, \ldots, T - 1$, and 'terminal' from $t = T, \ldots, \infty$. During the transition phase policies may be different from their terminal phase when they must be in steady state. The government budget constraint is from $t = 2$ onwards:

$$b_t - b_{t-1} = d_t + rb_{t-1} - (H_t - H_{t-1})/P_t \qquad (6.19)$$

Here $b =$ real bonds and $d =$ real deficit *excluding* debt interest, i.e. the change in real bonds equals the deficit including real debt interest less money financing (notice that on our assumption of no further policy change there are no unanticipated capital gains from $t = 2$ and anticipated capital losses from inflation are deducted implicitly by using the real interest rate).

Expressing (6.18) in per capita terms, dividing all through by $N_t$, gives:

$$b_t/N_t = d_t/N_t - [H_{t-1}/P_tN_t] \, [(H_t - H_{t-1})/H_{t-1}])$$
$$+ (1 + r)b_{t-1}/(1 + n)N_{t-1} \qquad (6.20)$$

Using $P_tN_t = (1 + H_t^*)P_{t-1} \, N_{t-1}$, this becomes

$$b_t' = d_t' - hH_t^*/(1 + H_t^*) + (1 + r - n)b_{t-1}' \qquad (6.21)$$

Since $r > n$ this is an explosive difference equation if interest-exclusive deficits and monetary targets are pursued independently. Suppose that during transition a constant $H^*$ and $d'$ are chosen: these policies are monetarist so that $H^*$ is 'low' but fiscal policy is 'expansionary', so that $d' > hH^*/(1 + H^*)$. The set limit on this per capita stock of debt $b'$, discussed above, is now bound to be reached at some point. At the date when this occurs, then policies have to change so as to ensure:

$$0 = b_{t+1}' - b_t' = d' - hH^*/(1 + H^*) + (r - n)b_t' \qquad (6.22)$$

i.e. that real bonds do not change any more. However, the policies could have been chosen so as to change *before* this, so that $b_t' < b'$ at this point. In general, the terminal date, $T$, for the switch to a sustainable policy with unchanging per capita debt can be chosen freely from $t = 2$ onwards, so that $H_T$ and $d_T$, the terminal or steady state policies, are governed by:

$$0 = b'_T - b'_{T-1} = d'_T - hH^*_T/(1 + H^*_T) + (r - n)b'_{T-1} \quad (b'_T \leqslant b')$$
(6.23)

The point is that there is a trade-off between the transitional policies (including the length of time they are pursued) and the terminal policies because the transitional policies affect the terminal stock of debt:

$$b'_{T-1} = (1 + r - n)^{T-2}b'_1 + \sum_{i=2}^{T-1} (1 + r - n)^{i-2}(d' - hH^*/1 + H^*)$$
(6.24)

The trade-off implies each of the following:

1  If the government wishes to maintain a constant interest-exclusive deficit $d' = d'_T$, then the smaller is current (transitional) money supply growth, the larger will *future* money supply growth $H^*_T$ have to be. Given fiscal 'profligacy', there is therefore a trade-off between current and future inflation.

2  If the government wishes to maintain constant money supply growth $H^*$, then the higher are the transitional deficits the larger are the future *surpluses* that will be required. Given monetary discipline, there is therefore a trade-off between current and future fiscal discipline.

The message is, in short, that tough monetary policies require tough fiscal policies.

### The Role of Long-dated Nominal Bonds

We have so far neglected the term in $b'_1$, the value of real bonds after the policies are announced; implicitly we have suggested that $b'_1$ was quite small. This then allows scope for policy-makers to choose between trade-offs 1 and 2 above. If, however, $b'_1$, is large, and close to $b'$, then there is little scope for choice; the policy-makers are forced to go rapidly to steady state fiscal–monetary policies, hard as these must be.

If the government bonds are short-dated, then the revaluation due to policies of lower inflation will be small unless the change is drastic; hence, for example, on a one-year nominal bond $b_0$ the change in value will be $-b_0(H^* - H_0^{*e})$ where $H_0^{*e}$ is the money supply growth expected before the policy change. If the bonds are indexed, then the revaluation will be nil (given the fixed real interest rate assumption).

If the bonds are long-dated, the revaluation effect can be very large. For example, take a bond paying a fixed money amount, $M_K$, on maturity at $t = K$. The present value of this at $t = 1$ expected at $t = 0$ was $b_0 = M_K / [(1 + R_0)^{K-1}]$ where $R_0 = H_0^{*e} + r - n$ was the nominal interest rate at $t = 0$; the actual present value at $t = 1$ is then $M_K / [(1 + R_1)^{K-1}]$. Hence the unanticipated capital revaluation on such a bond is $-b_0(K - 1)(H_K^* - H_0^{*e})$ where $H_k^* = [(T - 1)/(K - 1)] H^* + [(K - T)/(K - 1)] H_T^*$ (i.e. a weighted average of the transitional and the terminal $H^*$). For a credible anti-inflation policy where $H_K^* = H_T^* = n$, this revaluation will be a $K - 1$ multiple of the one-year bond revaluation, and create the necessity for harsh fiscal discipline with much greater rapidity.

## A Digression on Definitions of the 'Deficit'

Several definitions of the government 'deficit' are in use: inclusive or exclusive of debt interest, and if inclusive, inclusive of either nominal or real debt interest. We have used all of these definitions at different stages in the preceding analysis; all are useful in focusing on different aspects of the problem. However, it is obvious that a *definition* as such imparts no information. The information is of course in the *model*. We have looked at two models: one with wealth effects and one without wealth effects but with a ceiling on real government debt per capita. From the viewpoint of controlling inflation permanently, both have told essentially the same story: that both fiscal and monetary discipline are required on average, though with the possibility of varying time paths.

To show this, consider a continuous time version of the government budget constraint expressed in nominal terms in the steady state:

$$\dot{H} + \dot{B} = Pg - tPN + RB \tag{6.25}$$

where $B$ is the nominal market value of bonds (in steady state interest rates will not be changing), $R$ is the market nominal interest rate, $t$ the tax rate, $g$ government spending, $H, P, N$ money supply, prices and GNP as before: $\cdot$ denotes the instantaneous rate of change.

From our previous analysis, with or without wealth effects, we constrain the ratio of debt to GDP to a constant in steady state so that:

$$\frac{\dot{B}}{B} = \pi + n \text{ (the growth of nominal GNP)} \tag{6.26}$$

Equation (6.25) can be written as:

$$\frac{\dot{H}}{H} \cdot \frac{H}{PN} + \frac{\dot{B}}{B} \frac{B}{PN} = \frac{g}{N} - t + \frac{B}{PN} R \tag{6.27}$$

So that using (6.26):

$$\frac{\dot{H}}{H} = \bar{v}\left(\frac{g}{N} - t + \bar{b}(r - n)\right) \tag{6.28}$$

where $\bar{v}$ is the equilibrium velocity of money and $\bar{b}$ the equilibrium ratio of debt to GNP.

Equation (6.28) says that the steady state growth rate of money depends upon the ratio to GDP of the steady state deficit inclusive of real debt interest (sometimes called the 'inflation-adjusted real deficit'), minus an allowance for growth, $\bar{b}n$. We can also note that since in equilibrium $(\dot{H}/H) = \pi + n$,

$$(\pi + n)(H + B) = Pg + RB - tPN \tag{6.29}$$

or

$$(\dot{H}/H) = \pi + n = [Pg + RB - tPN]/\{H + B\}$$
$$= (PSBR/PN)\{PN/(H + B)\} \tag{6.30}$$

which says that money growth equals the public sector borrowing requirement to GDP ratio times the 'velocity' of 'outside money'.

Equations (6.28) and (6.30) are of course exactly equivalent, although one uses the inflation-adjusted deficit while the other uses the unadjusted deficit. However, when (6.28) is used to assess what fiscal policy must be used to validate a certain counter-inflationary monetary policy (e.g one to reduce $\dot{H}/H$ to $n$ from some high level), great care must be taken to include in $\bar{b}$ the effects of falling inflation and interest rates on the value of outstanding bonds; this adjustment can be very large, as we saw above, when a large proportion of these bonds are non-indexed and of long maturity, so that large cuts in the government deficit excluding interest may be necessary. When (6.30) is used, the implications are more transparent since nominal debt interest will not change except for short maturity stocks, which are rolled over before inflation comes down. These remarks are relevant to the debate on the Thatcher government's Medium Term Financial Strategy, which did not always carefully observe this point (e.g. Buiter and Miller (1981) incorrectly argue that the fiscal policies were 'unnecessarily' restrictive using a crude adjustment for current inflation on debt at current market value).

Given the overall policy requirement of fiscal–monetary consistency, the application in any situation will be largely a question of what is politically feasible. This is particularly true of the short-run time path immediately on announcement. It may well be wise, for example, to cut public spending rapidly as money supply growth is cut, even though this implies a 'real' budget surplus (i.e. inclusive of real debt interest) in the first few years because during this period debt interest on long-dated stock is still offset by high inflation. This real surplus will disappear as soon as inflation comes down, because the debt interest on long-dated stock will fall away only very slowly. Then, with the spending cuts done, the budget deficit will be at steady state levels and some of the debt revaluation (on the long-dated stock) will have been worked off by the previous real surpluses; this is an illustration of the previous section's discussion.

## What Is the Optimal Budget Deficit and Financing Pattern?

We have seen that if a government wishes to achieve a certain money supply growth rate (to reach a desired inflation rate), then it is limited in the steady state (or 'average') deficit it can pursue at the same time. Nevertheless, provided it is willing to make up temporary deficits in excess of this with future deficits that fall short of it (even running into surpluses), then as we have seen it can still achieve its monetary objectives. The question we now ask is: what is a desirable pattern of such temporary deficits and surpluses?

In chapter 4 we looked at this issue from the point of view of stabilization policy ('demand management'). We concluded, first, that tax rates acted as an effective automatic stabilizer and that this was desirable, if the tax rates were an unavoidable microeconomic distortion and if unemployment was distorted upwards in cyclical troughs by the benefit system; secondly, that activist, 'feedback', fiscal policy was also effective and could also be beneficial on similar grounds. But we now consider the issue from the viewpoint of optimal public finance alone; that is, we consider the distortionary costs of taxation. In order to do this, we shall drop the hitherto harmless fiction that taxes are lump sum, and assume instead that each period there is an average ($=$ marginal) tax rate, $T_t$.

Let output, $N$, be (apart from tax effects) at $\bar{N}$, so that stabilization is not of interest, and for simplicity suppose further that $\bar{N}$ is constant, real government spending is constant at $\bar{G}$, and money supply growth is constant at $\mu$. As in the Sargent–Wallace example, let the demand for money be given by the quantity theory as:

$$H_t = hP_t\bar{N} \tag{6.31}$$

and the budget constraint be given by:

$$b_t - b_{t-1} = G - T_t\bar{N} + rb_{t-1} - \frac{H_t - H_{t-1}}{P_t} \tag{6.32}$$

where $b_t$ are indexed one-period bonds with a constant real interest rate, $r$ (e.g. someone holding $b_t = 1$ is able to claim $1 + r$ units of commodities next period from the government). We can rewrite the budget constraint as:

$$b_{t-1} = (T_t\bar{N} - \bar{G} + h\bar{N}\mu/(1 + \mu) + b_t)/(1 + r) \tag{6.33}$$

remembering that

$$(H_t - H_{t-1})/P_t = H_t - H_{t-1}/[H_{t-1}(1 + \mu)/h\bar{N}] = h\bar{N}\mu/(1 + \mu).$$

This equation states that the present value of next period's net revenues plus bonds issued must be equal to the value of bonds outstanding.

But since $b_t$, next period's bond issue, must equal the following period's net revenues plus bonds issued then, $b_{t+1}$, similarly $b_{t+1}$ in terms of $t + 2$ net revenues and $b_{t+2}$, and so on, we can successively substitute out $b_t, b_{t+1}, b_{t+2}, \ldots$, in terms of the net revenues to come. If we assume that as $i \to \infty$, $(1/1 + r)^i b_{t+i} \to 0$ (in other words that the government's debt is expected to grow more slowly than the rate of interest, so that its present value is diminishing), then we obtain

$$b_{t-1} = 1/1 + r \left[ \sum_{i=0}^{\infty} (1/1 + r)^i \left( T_{t+i}\bar{N} - \bar{G} + \frac{h\bar{N}\mu}{1 + \mu} \right) \right]$$

$$= \left( \frac{h\bar{N}\mu}{1 + \mu} - \bar{G} \right) \Big/ r + \left[ \sum_{i=0}^{\infty} (1/1 + r)^{i+1} T_{t+i}\bar{N} \right] \tag{6.34}$$

This says that the outstanding value of bonds must be equal to the present value of future taxation less the present value of government spending (net of inflation tax revenue). This is the constraint on the pattern and total of taxation.

Now examine the distortions costs of taxation. By the usual consumer surplus triangle analysis, we can write the present value of these costs at the end of $t - 1$, $C_{t-1}$, as:

$$C_{t-1} = \sum_{i=0}^{\infty} 1/2\, T_{t+i}^2\, \varepsilon\, \bar{N}(1/1 + r)^{i+1} \tag{6.35}$$

where we have assumed the elasticity of output to the tax rate is constant at $\varepsilon$.

The optimal tax rates are discovered by minimizing $C_{t-1}$ subject to the tax constraint. Form the Lagrangean:

$$L = C_{t-1} - m \left( K - \sum_{i=0}^{\infty} (1/1 + r)^{i+1} T_{t+i}\, \bar{N} \right) \tag{6.36}$$

where $K = b_{t-1} + \left( \bar{G} - \frac{h\bar{N}\mu}{1 + \mu} \right) \Big/ r$

$$0 = \frac{\delta L}{\delta T_{t+i}} = T_{t+i}\varepsilon + m \tag{6.37}$$

(together with the taxation constraint). Since $\varepsilon$ and $m$ are fixed constants, this yields

$$T_{t+i} = T = \frac{m}{\varepsilon}$$

This result, due to Lucas and Stokey (1983), extends Ramsey's (1927) rule that commodity tax rates should be inversely proportional to their demand elasticities. In other words, the optimal tax rate, $T$, is a constant. We can work out what it must be by solving for $T_{t+i} = T$ in the taxation constraint as:

$$T = rb_{t-1}/\bar{N} + \bar{G}/\bar{N} - h\mu/(1 + \mu) \tag{6.38}$$

The constant tax rate is that which will pay the interest on the outstanding stock of debt plus the government spending bill net of the inflation tax. Hence the stock of debt is held constant by optimal taxation. (If GDP was growing and government spending constant as a fraction of it, then the constant tax rate formula would imply that debt would also be constant as a fraction of GDP. The reader may like to rework the optimal tax rate problem with GDP growing at the rate $n$, using the budget constraint formulation of equation (6.21). He or she should find that the steps are identical, except that $r - n$ is substituted for $r$ and bonds and government spending are expressed as fractions of GDP; the optimal tax rate remains constant.)

To put optimal tax rates another way, remember that optimality requires the intertemporal rate of transformation between revenues to equal that between welfare costs; that is,

$$\left(\frac{\delta C_{t-1}}{\delta T_{t+i}}\right) \bigg/ \left(\frac{\delta R_{t-1}}{\delta T_{t+i}}\right) = \left(\frac{\delta C_{t-1}}{\delta T_{t+i+1}}\right) \bigg/ \left(\frac{\delta R_{t-1}}{\delta T_{t+i+1}}\right) \tag{6.39}$$

where $R_{t-1} = \sum_{i=0}^{\infty} (1/1 + r)^{i+1} T_{t+i} \bar{N}$

is the present value of revenues. In words this states that the marginal cost per unit of revenue gained from raising the tax rate in period $t + i$ must equal that from raising the tax rate in period $t + i + 1$. The former (LHS) is $T_{t+i}$ $\varepsilon$, the latter (RHS) is $T_{t+i+1}$ $\varepsilon$ (both equal the $m$ of our Lagrangean, the 'shadow cost' of raising revenue).

Figure 6.3 illustrates this. It is assumed that workers have a constant marginal product $MPL$. The supply curve, $SS$, shows the output they produce as their marginal real wage, $w$, rises, increasing their hours input into the overall production function. The tax rate, $T$, depresses their marginal take-home pay by $Tw$. The triangles of consumer surplus are minimized in total area when they are equal: as one increases from this point, the other decreases by less because their area depends on the square of the tax rate. The height of the triangle is measured by $T_{t+i}$, which is also a measure of the loss per unit of extra revenue raised.

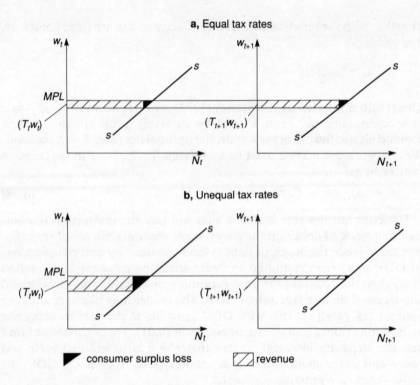

Figure 6.3   The optimality of a constant tax rate.

## Conclusions

We have seen that there are important links between fiscal and monetary policy with rational expectations. These links do not involve short-run behaviour, i.e. over the economic cycle; independent fiscal and monetary responses to the cycle do not in general cause instability (or non-uniqueness), even with wealth effects. By contrast, with adaptive expectations and wealth effects, coordination may be necessary even in the short run to avoid instability.

It is in steady state that fiscal and monetary policy must be 'consistent', i.e. the growth rate of real government bonds must be reduced to the rate of growth of GDP (assuming this is the rate at which the demand for bonds will grow in steady state at constant real interest rates). This condition is enforced in a wide spectrum of circumstances by a ceiling on the stock of debt that can be absorbed by lenders. The key implication is that budget deficits must generally at some point be brought down in line with money supply growth if counter-inflation policies are to be sustained.

## Appendix: The Theory of Wealth Effects

There are two components in our measure of 'outside money' or 'financial wealth of the private sector': high-powered money and government bonds.

Take high-powered (or 'base') money first. This liability of government in principle creates an obligation of repayment. In a convertible 'fiat' money system, the paper says 'Pay the Bearer £1', which now means that the bearer is entitled to exchange it for whatever quantity of goods or gold it is worth in the market; the central bank in principle will produce this amount but of course in practice it refers any such bearer directly to the market (it would otherwise accept the money and take it to the market itself, which comes to the same thing). The central bank may also fix the rate at which it will redeem its notes, as under fixed exchange rates.

The government is under no obligation to underwrite its currency value at any particular rate, however. Hence it need not raise any further taxes in order to pay off the currency liability; it could simply decide to leave the currency outstanding as it is (letting the market value it as it will). This will be contrasted with the need to pay off interest and principal on bonds via higher taxes. From the private sector's viewpoint, there is therefore no countervailing tax liability associated with their money asset. Its present value is its face value.

How issuing money affects the economy, prices and real money balances is the main topic of this book. Clearly the fact that for consumers money is wealth plays a key part in these effects. But what of government bonds, the vast bulk of financial wealth?

The argument here turns on the present value of the stream of taxes required to pay off bond interest and principal. It is clear that in a world of lump-sum taxes, no uncertainty and infinitely lived individuals, a government transfer to individuals today financed by bonds, which will be paid off tomorrow from lump-sum taxes on those individuals with the same incidence as the transfer, leaves everything unchanged. Each individual obtains a transfer, held in the form of bonds, whose value is offset exactly by his future tax liability; his wealth remaining the same, he will wish to consume the same and will therefore lend the government the amount of the transfer (i.e. continue to hold the bonds). Consumption and investment will be unchanged, and therefore so will the rate of interest.

The question naturally arises: why should the government bother to carry out this operation if it affects nothing and nobody? Barro (1974) has suggested that the reason is the transactions costs of changing tax rates when there are transitory shifts in public expenditure (such as for wars); a temporary rise in tax rates would require more resources to implement (e.g. more inspectors, notification to the populace) than making a bond issue (to the same people who would otherwise be taxed). Yet this seems tenuous; bond issuing and servicing carries a transactions cost which might be greater.

This answer also does not fit the case of sustained bond issue to finance a sustained rise in public expenditure; a case that has been exemplified frequently by post-war Western governments. Many governments have appeared in these cases to have viewed borrowing as a more attractive option politically than current taxation (and of course some have also viewed the printing of high-powered money as a still more attractive option, at least within some limit set by the inflation consequence). Governments of 'conservatives' by contrast have typically proclaimed the aim of 'sound finance', i.e. budgets balanced except for 'below-the-line' capital expenditure on revenue-generating projects.

With this in mind, we may consider possible relaxations of the strong assumptions set out earlier. First, we already saw that if taxes are not lump-sum, then a change in their intertemporal pattern will cause distortions, which will have real effects. Secondly, there may be distribution effects between recipients of current transfers and the payers of future taxes; these too would obviously have real effects. Neither of these two effects, however, appears to imply any systematic direction of 'wealth effect', whereas we want a reason for a positive wealth effect of issuing bonds (cutting taxes).

Thirdly and more interestingly, we must drop the assumption of infinite life. But Barro (1974) has shown in a model of overlapping generations that, if each person leaves a bequest, then everyone acts as if he is infinitely lived. The reason is that the transfer he receives diminishes the utility of his heirs while raising his current resources. Yet he has already decided, having left them a bequest, that his optimal course is to give them their previous utility at the expense of his current resources; therefore he will raise his bequest in order to offset the government's action, in effect saving the whole of the transfer for his heirs. The transfer, by not changing his opportunity set, leaves his net wealth and behaviour unchanged.

If he has not planned a bequest, then the level of utility he desires for his heirs cannot be established; the transfer may or may not push their utility below his desired level. Hence we cannot establish how much, if at all, he will offset the transfer by saving.

It is of interest that, if the law provided for heirs to pay off their parents' debts, then this would not matter, because bequest could be negative (parents could borrow against the collateral of their children) or positive, a continuous variable; hence the transfer would always be offset. However, the law prevents this in most societies, no doubt mainly because the rights of children require protection from selfish parents.

This suggests that the issue of whether *planned* bequests are general is non-trivial (accidental bequests, e.g. because death comes unexpectedly early, are beside the point).

The key assumption, however, is that of no uncertainty. If we drop this, we are faced with two types of uncertainty: first, about the *aggregate* flow of future interest and principal, and the tax levies necessary to fund them – uncertainties such as those about formal default by the government and unexpected monetarization (we might term this informal default); secondly, uncertainty about the individual *incidence* of future taxes.

With aggregate uncertainty, whatever the shape of the probability distribution over future interest and principal payments, it is the same distribution (by definition) as that over future tax levies. Therefore, with rational expectations everyone's expectation of the mean and variance of both streams will be the same. It follows that each person can leave himself with exactly the same risk–return combination on his portfolio of physical, human and financial assets by investing his transfer in government bonds; this is a perfectly hedged operation and without a change in other risks or returns, he would do just this. Hence, as before, nothing would change.

When we turn to individual incidence, the picture changes. Suppose for simplicity that there is now no aggreagate uncertainty. Yet each individual faces considerable uncertainty about how much tax he and his heirs will pay; he does not know future income, future family size, the possibility of emigration, etc. Let us ignore emigration, in which case the change in tax prospects will have no impact on him; this no doubt affects only a minority. Let us assume that the tax system, as is typically the case in Western economies, is progressive; also assume that people are identical and risk averse. Suppose everyone receives the same transfer and holds it in the form of bonds. Then the individual will perceive his and his heirs' potential net income after tax as follows: at the one extreme they will be poor, receive the bond interest, but pay little tax, from there progressing with higher income towards the other extreme where they will be rich, receive the bond interest, and pay a lot of tax. If taxes are raised they will pay little more if poor, but significantly more if rich. This effect of a high covariance between tax and income is illustrated in figure 6.A.1 (for a simplified distribution with only 'poor' and 'rich' states of equal probability).

We are interested in the change in the 'certainty equivalent' of each man's future net income after tax; by this we mean the sure income that would yield him the same utility as the income possibilities he actually faces. Before the bond transfer and consequent future tax liability, let him have an expected net income of $E\,y$, the average of his 'poor' and 'rich' states; the expected utility of this is $E\,U_0$ and the certainty equivalent is $\bar{y}_0$. After the bond transfer, everyone's expected net

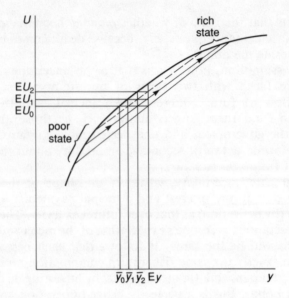

Figure 6.A.1   Certainty equivalent and expected net income after tax.

income remains the same because the tax payments averaged across the two states must equal the bond interest receipts for the government's budget to balance in the future. But now each person will be better off than before when poor (he received the bond interest but his extra tax burden is less than this), and worse off than before when rich (his extra tax burden exceeds the bond interest); the arrowed line on figure 6.A.1 joins these two states, and, because of the insurance he receives in effect, his expected utility rises to $EU_1$ and his certainty equivalent to $\bar{y}_1$ so that the bond transfer increases private wealth. Barro (1974) has further pointed out that if the tax rate is raised when taxes go up to pay for the bond interest, then this increases the progressiveness of the tax system and this insurance effect is enhanced, as illustrated by the dashed line with higher expected utility $EU_2$ and certainty equivalent income $\bar{y}_2$.

Clearly this insurance effect of bond issue would be eliminated if the private insurance market already provided full insurance. However, this is unlikely because of incentive incompatibility (see e.g. Hart, 1983); full insurance gives the insured person an incentive to lie about his poverty or fraudulently to avoid trying to be rich. Of course, the bond issue may be incentive-incompatible at the margin, given existing private insurance; this, however, is relevant to the optimality of the bond issue, not to its net wealth effect (except in so far as it changes the probabilities of being poor and rich, which we ignore).

# 7

# The Political Economy of Democracy

One of the major developments in the public choice literature in the past two decades has been the construction and empirical testing of models that consider the interaction of the preferences of government and electors and the behaviour of the economy.

Important early examples of this work are the papers by Nordhaus (1975), MacRae (1977) and Frey and Schneider (1978a, b). A key assumption of this work is that expectations are formed in an error-learning or adaptive manner. The purpose of this chapter is to consider the implications that the rational expectations hypothesis has for the behaviour or role of the authorities. Clearly in a world of rational expectations, the authorities, as well as voters, have by assumption an unbiased and efficient forecast of the outcomes of different policy rules. This raises the interesting issues of whether there is scope for differences in economic policy between different political parties and of how voters will react to differences in policy and economic performance.

We begin by outlining the early work in the public choice literature, which is based on adaptive expectations. We then consider the rational expectations alternative.

## The Nordhaus Model

Perhaps the most interesting model of an adaptive expectations vintage which stresses the interaction of the preferences of the government and the elector is the model of Nordhaus (1975). The Nordhaus model is based on the Downs (1957) hypothesis that governments have an over-riding goal of winning the next election. Hence they obey the 'median voter theorem' (namely, that their policies will be designed with maximum appeal to the floating voter who will decide the election) and are consequently concerned to maximize their popularity over the period of office. This has the implication that both parties will offer identical policies, since they will be driven by competition for the median voter to offer a policy which will win him or her over: identical policy will give each party an equal chance of winning, which is the equilibrium.

Their popularity is assumed to depend on a number of key economic variables, notably the rate of inflation and unemployment. It is further assumed that voters are myopic, which implies that they give highest weight in voting to the current rates of inflation and unemployment, without consideration to their future values. The government is assumed to maximize its popularity subject to the constraint that the rate of inflation, the rate of unemployment and the expected rate of inflation are linked via an expectations-augmented Phillips curve. Finally it is assumed that price expectations are formed adaptively. The Nordhaus model thus has the following mathematical structure (in continuous time).

$$\text{Maximize } P = \int_0^T G(u,p)(1+r)^t \tag{7.1}$$

subject to the constraints:

$$p = g(u) + p^e \tag{7.2}$$

$$Dp^e = \phi(p - p^e) \tag{7.3}$$

where $p$ is the rate of inflation ($p^e$ the expected rate), $u$ is the rate of unemployment, $r$ is the discount rate (*positive* to reflect voter myopia), $G$, $g$ are functions, $\phi$ is a positive constant, and D is the differential (rate of change) operator such that, e.g. $Dx = dx/dt$. Equation (7.1) is the government's objective function.

Popularity, $P$, is maximized between the time of arrival in office (0) and the time of the next election ($T$). Equation (7.2) is the augmented Phillips curve and equation (7.3) the adaptive expectations mechanism.

Clearly the optimal paths of unemployment and inflation will depend on the precise choice of functions $G(\ )$ and $g(\ )$. Nordhaus specifies an objective function:

$$G(\ ) = -\alpha p - \frac{\beta}{2}u^2 \tag{7.4}$$

and a linear augmented Phillips curve:

$$g(u) = a - bu \tag{7.5}$$

where $\alpha$, $\beta$, $a$, $b$ are positive constants.

The mathematics required to solve this problem is outside the scope of this book (see e.g. Cass and Shell, 1976). It turns out that the path of the unemployment rate between elections implied by its solution has the form shown in figure 7.1.

The essential implication, then, of this work is that governments deliberately cause a business cycle so that, at the date of election, they are in the most favourable position *vis-á-vis* voters' preferences; hence on arriving in office, they raise unemployment to initiate a reduction in inflation, then after two years or so they stimulate the economy to reduce

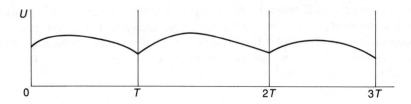

Figure 7.1   The path of the unemployment rate between elections.

unemployment in time for the election date, leaving their successor to cope with the rise in inflation that is the lagged result of this policy.

While the optimal pattern of inflation or unemployment does depend on the precise choice of functional forms, the essential insight of Nordhaus, that governments may have a vested interest in creating business cycles, will survive these and other changes (such as the length of the electoral period $T$; see Chappell and Peel, 1979). The assumption that government popularity depends on variables such as the rate of inflation or unemployment has received some empirical support. In particular Frey and Schneider (1978a, b) have reported empirical work for a variety of different countries, such as the United Kingdom, USA and West Germany, in which a measure of government popularity, typically based on opinion polls, is found to be significantly related to such economic variables.

More recent work (e.g. Borooah and Van der Ploeg, 1982; Chrystal and Alt, 1981; Minford and Peel 1982; Harte et al., 1983), shows that the work of Frey and Schneider is not statistically robust with respect to changes in the sample period or the economic variables chosen. This is perhaps not too surprising. Economists, when analysing agents' choice between alternatives, are concerned to stress the appropriate relative prices. This point has typically been neglected in the empirical work on government popularity. The alternative hypothesis is best outlined by Tullock (1976), who writes:

> Voters and customers are essentially the same people. Mr Smith buys and votes; he is the same man in the supermarket and in the voting booth. There is no strong reason to believe his behaviour is radically different in the two environments. We assume that in both he will choose the product or candidate he thinks is the best bargain for him.

When we also recognize that voters are expressing preferences for different policies over the life-time of a government, it is clear that the relevant choice should reflect expectations of future policy differences between parties. From this perspective the most charitable interpretation of the conventional work is that the future paths of economic variables under the party in power are formed adaptively and that the paths of economic variables under the alternative parties are considered by electors as fixed. We now consider how rational expectations affect the possibility of a political business cycle.

## Rational Expectations and Reputation

It is possible to motivate a political business cycle by reference to the new literature on reputation and partial information, discussed in earlier chapters. Suppose that before the run-up to the election, the government has acquired a good reputation for monetary prudence and that there is partial information about current events, with people observing current economic activity but not observing current policy variables, such as the money supply and government spending. Votes are cast according to people's assessment of the equilibrium levels of output and inflation as rationally expected, but they have a signal extraction problem.

In this vein, let election popularity (the voting balance) be given by:

$$P_t = -(E\,\bar{y}_t - k\,\bar{y}_{t-1})^2 - f(E\,g_t - \pi^*)^2 \tag{7.6}$$

where $\bar{y}$ is equilibrium output ($k > 1$ reflects the people's desire for a better supply side), and $g$ is the equilibrium level of inflation and also of policy levers (money supply growth and the fiscal deficit behind it).

$$\text{Let } \bar{y}_t = \bar{y}_{t-1} + \varepsilon_t \tag{7.7}$$

$\varepsilon_t$ is random, partly the result of past policies whose fruits cannot be accurately forecast. Actual output (observed) is given by a Phillips curve where $g_t^e$ is the people's expectations of government policy based on its reputation:

$$y_t = \bar{y}_t + \theta(g_t - g_t^e) \tag{7.8}$$

$$\text{But } g_t = g_t^e + m_t \tag{7.9}$$

where $m_t$ is the unforeseen policy change unobserved by the public but known by government.

The public's signal extraction gives

$$E\,\bar{y}_t = \bar{y}_{t-1} + \phi(y_t - \bar{y}_{t-1}) = \bar{y}_{t-1} + \phi(\varepsilon_t + \theta(g_t - g_t^e)) \tag{7.10}$$

$$E\,g_t = g_t^e + E\,m_t = g_t^e + (1 - \phi)(y_t - \bar{y}_{t-1})/\theta$$

$$= g_t^e + \frac{(1 - \phi)}{\theta}(\varepsilon_t + \theta(g_t - g_t^e)) \tag{7.11}$$

The government now maximizes $P_t$ (subject to $g_t^e$, $\varepsilon_t$, $\bar{y}_{t-1}$ given) with respect to $g_t$ in the election run-up by setting $0 = \delta P_t / \delta g_t$, and this first order condition yields

$$
g_t = \frac{\left\{ \phi(k-1)\theta\bar{y}_{t-1} - (1-\phi)\, f(g_t^e - \pi^*) - \left[ \phi^2\theta + f\frac{(1-\phi)^2}{\theta} \right]\varepsilon_t \right\}}{\left\{ \phi^2\theta^2 + f(1-\phi)^2 \right\}} + g_t^e
$$

(7.12)

$g$ responds positively to target output ($k\bar{y}_{t-1}$) and positively to a bad supply shock (negative $\varepsilon_t$), although it is restrained by 'bad reputation', high $g_t^e$. So there is a tendency for monetary policy to expand pre-election, especially if the supply side is bad.

The government would in this model aim to build up its reputation after an election; then in the run-up it would 'use up' some of this reputation. Clearly there are strict limits to the policy boost that can be delivered in this way; these fall far short of the crude swings in policy optimal under the Nordhaus model. Nevertheless, there is still a basis here for a political business cycle under rational expectations. Models of a similar structure are to be found in Cukierman and Meltzer (1986) and Alesina and Sachs (1988), for example.

The intuition behind this and other such models can be appreciated if one asks: would any government like to go into an election during a recession? Clearly no one can be sure of what is truly the reason for the economy's bad performance; and some blame is bound to rub off on the government. Yet the very transparency of this motivation could undermine even this limited political business cycle model. Suppose that everyone knows the government will maximize $P_t$ in the run up to an election. Then reputation-building is useless and the policy unravels.

First, take the model as at present set up. People would form their expectation $g_t^e$ not by observing past actions but by taking expectations of (7.12) and setting $E_{t-1}\, g_t = g_t^e$. The result is

$$
g_t^e = \pi^* + \frac{\phi(k-1)\theta}{(1-\phi)f}\bar{y}_{t-1}
$$

(7.13)

When the government comes to maximize (7.6) knowing $\varepsilon_t$ but initially supposing the public does not know it, it would choose some function:

$$
g_t = g_t^e + q\,\varepsilon_t
$$

(7.14)

But the public will know that this is the government's current policy because it knows the government's preferences. Therefore it will know that

$$
y_t = \bar{y}_{t-1} + (1 + \theta q)\varepsilon_t
$$

(7.15)

where $q$ is the government's known response to $\varepsilon_t$. So the public will in fact be able to infer the value of $\varepsilon_t$ and so $E\, g_t = g_t$, $E\, \bar{y}_t = \bar{y}_t$. This being so, the whole problem changes. Now there is no signal extraction problem; instead,

$$P_t = -(\bar{y}_t - k\bar{y}_{t-1})^2 - f(g_t - \pi^*)^2 \tag{7.16}$$

The government's maximizing strategy is simple: $g_t = \pi^*$. There is no political business cycle again: straightforward honesty is the best policy.[2]

Clearly this argument implies an extraordinarily perceptive voting public and clear knowledge of the government's motivation. Both must be in doubt. Given the paradox of voting, let alone of investing in good information extraction as a voter, there are reasons to doubt such rationality. Government motives may be obscure, given the ideological factor; or they may deliberately be obscured as in the Backus and Driffill (1985) model.

Nevertheless, this case of unravelling at least serves to show that full rational expectations with known government objectives does remove the political business cycle. It provides a useful benchmark, and cautions that the political business cycle, at least if practised too vigorously, is likely to self-destruct.

We now turn to the central issues of what might determine voting and party policies if voters have this full (benchmark) rationality.

## A Rational Expectations Model of Voters and Parties

An alternative model is proposed by Minford and Peel (1982a) in which the expectations of both voters and the authorities are assumed to be formed rationally. We argue that the marginal costs of information-gathering can be regarded as sufficiently low for the representative voter to develop an informed opinion of the future path of economic variables. One simple mechanism (and there are probably some others) by which this can occur is via public forecasts. Forecasts of inflation and output from major forecasting institutions (for instance, in the UK the Treasury, the London Business School, the National Institute and Liverpool) will represent informed opinion and are given widespread publicity by newspapers and television, which the voters obtain at negligible marginal costs. While these public forecasts will differ to some extent, they will tend to be correlated and voters' expectations, as conditioned by them, will more closely approximate rational expectations than some mechanistic adaptive alternative.

Although the typical voter may face low costs of gathering information and opinions this does not explain why he or she votes. The direct marginal benefits of voting, in the sense that an individual vote will influence the electoral outcome, appear *a priori* to be less than the marginal costs of voting. Indeed, the 'paradox of voting' is that, because the effect of one vote on the election outcome is negligible, the voter obtains no expected marginal gain from voting. However, the most attractive rationale for rational voting is the 'civic' recognition by voters that democracy cannot function unless many people vote (see Mueller (1979) for a fuller discussion of these issues). In game-theoretic terms, democratic behaviour is a game with rules, one set of which governs voting; such games evolve from social discovery processes (for a discussion of such evolutionary processes see Sugden, 1986). Voters are expected to vote according to their own preferences; since the normal voter has only the vaguest idea of the 'nation's good' and little ability to evaluate it, he or she is expected to evaluate the effect of party policies on his or her individual or household interests, where they should have a keen and accurate perception. Then the electoral process aggregates these votes into a popular preference for one party's policies. A number of authors (e.g. Meltzer and Richard, 1981, 1983) have emphasized that such 'voting one's pocket' opens up the possibility of 'rent-seeking' by voter coalitions with a vested interest: politicians then have to weigh up their ability to attract (organized) votes from vested interests against their chance of appealing to the (disorganized) votes of the ordinary voters. We return below to the effects this choice may have on party platforms.

Controversy, into which we cannot enter here, surrounds what sort of process delivers the better results. Anglo-Saxon systems of first-past-the-post deliver strong mandates, which notably Popper (1988, 1945/1966) has defended as providing a strong capacity of electorates to get rid of governments. Continental systems of proportional representation deliver governments which can only survive by consensus between coalition partners. The Anglo-Saxon systems have produced large-scale swings of policy, with 'experiments' on a grand scale. The continental have produced a slowly changing compromise set of policies, which never became as socialist as, say, the UK when socialism was fashionable in the 1960s but neither moved so rapidly towards deregulation and free markets as the socialist tide receded in the 1980s.

Given our assumptions about the information set of agents, we follow a number of different authors in supposing that political parties in part pursue. economic policies which are broadly in accordance with the objective economic interests and subjective preferences of their 'class', defined as their core political constituency. For instance, Johnson (1968) writes:

> From one important view, indeed, the avoidance of inflation and the maintenance of full employment can most usefully be regarded as conflicting class interests of the bourgeois and proletariat, respectively, the conflict being resolvable only by the test of relative political power in the society.

Robinson (1937) also writes:

> In so far as stable prices are regarded as desirable for their own sake, as contributing to social justice, it must be recognized that justice to the rentier can be achieved only by means of the injustice to the rest of the community of maintaining a lower level of effective demand than might otherwise be achieved. We are here presented with a conflict of interests . . . and actual policies are largely governed by the rival influences of the interests involved.

(Clearly we do not accept the assumption made in both these comments that output is demand determined.)

## Voters

We assume that there are three relevant sets of voters: Labour (Democrats), Conservatives (Republicans) and floating voters. The supporters of each party come from different parts of the electorate (for example, 'labourers' and 'capitalists'; see Hibbs, 1978). The stylized assumption is that Labour voters primarily hold human capital and the Conservatives primarily financial capital.

The current utility function of the voters is written in quadratic form as:

$$C_t = c_1 p_t + c_2 p_t^2 + c_0 \tag{7.17}$$

$$V_t = v_1 p_t + v_2 p_t^2 + v_3 y + v_4 y^2 + v_0 \tag{7.18}$$

$$L_t = l_1 y_t + l_2 y_t^2 \tag{7.19}$$

where $c_1$, $c_2$, $v_1$, $v_2$, $v_4$, $l_2$ are negative and $c_0$, $v_0$, $v_3$, $l_1$ positive constants; $y$ is disposable labour income.

The floating voter who determines the election outcome is assumed to express his voting intentions (up to and including the time he votes in the election) according to which party is expected to give him greater utility from the time of the next election onwards. Formally he takes the expectation $E_t V_T$ (which is taken as a proxy for his expected utility for all time beyond the election) conditional on each party's policies in turn, $E_t V_T^L$, $E_t V_T^C$ (Labour and Conservative respectively); he casts his vote for Labour if $E_t V_T^L > E_t V_T^C$ and vice versa. In aggregate it is assumed that voters are distributed around the typical floating voters, yielding a cumulative voters' balance function of the form:

$$B_t = b(E_t V_T^G - E_t V_T^O) + h_t \tag{7.20}$$

where $G$ denotes 'government' and $O$ 'opposition'; $h_t$ is an error process for non-economic omitted variables. Taking expectations of (7.18) for the government yields:

$$E_t V_t^G = v_1 E_t p_t + v_2 E_t p_t^2 + v_3 E_t y_t + v_4 E_t y_t^2 \tag{7.21}$$

these being the expected outcomes (i.e. under the current government).

Doing the same (a 'counterfactual' expectation) for the opposition and subtracting from (7.21) gives:

$$E_t V_t^G - E_t V_t^O = \beta_1 (E_t p_t - \bar{p}) + \beta_2 (\text{var}_t p - \overline{\text{var} p})$$

$$+ \beta_3 (E_t y - \bar{y}) + \beta_4 (\text{var}_t y - \overline{\text{var} y}) \tag{7.22}$$

where $\text{var} p$, $\text{var} y$ are the variances of $p$ and $y$ around their expected values and $\bar{p}$, $\bar{y}$, $\overline{\text{var} p}$, $\overline{\text{var} y}$ reflect the relevant expectation and variances of the opposition.

Unlike previous voting functions, this formulation is explicitly forward-looking in inflation and income and it includes variances of the relevant economic variables. In their related empirical work, Minford and Peel (1982, *q.v.* for details) use the perhaps unsatisfactory proxy of time trends for the opposition party's policies and there is clearly scope for the use of more subtle alternatives. Using Gallup data for the United Kingdom over the period 1959–75, they produce evidence that (7.22) performs in a more satisfactory manner than the conventional Frey-Schneider alternative. However, in later empirical work on the UK, West Germany and Sweden, Harte (1986) finds that these voting functions are as unstable as their non-rational predecessors. Similar instability is found, with alternative functions under rational expectations, by Borooah and Van der Ploeg (1982). This instability is not difficult to explain, in terms of Lucas's (1976) critique. These voting functions are, in spite of their forward-looking terms, 'reduced-form' expressions in which the effects of voter preferences, the model and the exogenous processes driving policy (in each party) as well as the economic environment, are jointly solved out. Even if preferences are unchanged, then other elements will change and shift the voting functions. The instability does not necessarily invalidate the theory but it should make us modest in our expectations of estimating it.

A side implication of this approach is that voter preferences will gradually change with their economic interests. For example, *embourgeoisement*, carrying with it the wider accumulation of non-human capital (including home and share-ownership), will increase the size of the 'capitalist' class relative to the 'labour' class. Strong evidence of this change has been produced for the UK (Crewe, 1988). There is also evidence from opinion poll data from 1987, at a time when Labour policies were still designed to appeal to traditional Labour voters, that share ownership was significantly correlated with voting Tory; with privatization having greatly extended share ownership (from 8 to 25 per cent of the population), this could have been an important electoral factor.

Another possible implication is suggested by Hall's (1978) approach to testing the consumption function. Just as consumers may consume according to their view of permanent income, so voters may vote according to their perceived 'permanent' interests as delivered by either party, including non-economic interests, which are not captured in our functions. We take a brief diversion to explain Hall's idea.

According to the permanent income hypothesis of consumer behaviour (Friedman, 1957):

$$C_t = kY_t^p \tag{7.23}$$

where $C$ is real consumer expenditure and $Y^p$ is permanent income. Permanent income is defined as the discounted value of the stream of all current and future real income, $Y$ (including income from assets); therefore:

$$Y_t^p = \sum_{i=0}^{\infty} E_t \ Y_{t+i}/(1 + r)^i \tag{7.24}$$

where $r$ is the constant real rate of interest at which agents are assumed to be able to lend and borrow.

From the definition of permanent income, and independently of the question of how expectations are formed:

$$E_{t-1} \ Y_t^p = Y_{t-1}^p \tag{7.25}$$

Equation (7.25) follows because, from the very definition of permanent income, agents do not expect it to change, for it is the constant stream of income which they envisage over an infinite planning horizon.[1]

Taking expectations of (7.23) conditional on the information set at E at $t - 1$ and subtracting from (7.24) we obtain:

$$Y_t^p - E_{t-1} \ Y_t^p = \sum_{i=0}^{\infty} (E_t \ Y_{t+i} - E_{t-1} \ Y_{t+i})/(1 + r)^i \tag{7.26}$$

Since, given the assumption of rational expectations, all the right-hand side variables in (7.26) are innovations (or news), we have:

$$Y_t^p - E_{t-1} \ Y_t^p = \varepsilon_t = \text{news} \tag{7.27}$$

Consequently, from (7.25):

$$Y_t^p - Y_{t-1}^p = \varepsilon_t \tag{7.28}$$

The above argument is simple to understand. If expectations are rational, then, given the definition of permanent income, the only reason

agents will revise their view of their permanent income is new information or news. If this were not the case it would imply that expectations were not rational since agents should have revised their permanent incomes
in previous periods.

Equation (7.28) in conjunction with (7.23) implies that:

$$C_t = C_{t-1} + k\varepsilon_t \tag{7.29}$$

In other words, real consumer expenditures follow a random walk.

Equation (7.29) has the testable implication that all previous information, as embodied, for example, in lagged values of consumption, inflation or indeed any variable, should not add any significant explanatory power to (7.29). This is the result first discovered by Hall (1978). Allowance for factors such as growth in incomes over time or the seasonal pattern of consumption does imply slight modification to (7.29) but allowing for this the empirical results have been impressive (see e.g. Bilson, 1980; for an alternative view see Davidson and Hendry, 1981).

The idea that 'permanent' variables under rational expectations will follow a random walk forms the basis for an alternative model of voting intentions.

Assume that voters' evaluation of parties is based on their judgement of the difference in their permanent income (or utility) between parties. This judgement can be based on non-economic as well as economic variables. It follows that under rational expectations the popularity of parties should follow a random walk. Consequently, appropriate testing of voting models under rational expectations will involve relating changes in popularity to innovations or news.

As with the consumption function, past rates of inflation or unemployment or economic variables in general should not have explanatory power. There is some weak evidence for this hypothesis. The problem is the low power of tests of the random walk against models in which there is merely a degree of voter persistence.

Voting responses are unstable and possibly, as the random walk model suggests, quite unpredictable. Yet one extraordinary regularity survives in all models: the mid-term swing of polled opinion away from the governing party, and back again as the election approaches. This quasi-seasonal effect is routinely incorporated into voting functions, but no explanation for it exists. The usual rationalization is in terms of a 'costless protest': the electorate use polls (and by-elections) to signal their preferences for modifications of government policy. This does not amount to a desire to change the government, so that as the election approaches, true preferences re-emerge.

## Explaining Party Policy

With respect to party policy, we assume that the authorities are faced with an economy in which there is no long-run trade-off between inflation and output, but where, in the short run, fiscal and monetary policy can stabilize the economy by appropriate choice of feedback rules; these are assumed to be effective on the grounds of, for example, contracts, as discussed in chapter 3. The absence of a long-run trade-off does not, however, avoid a choice of the long-run budget deficit and, of course, the implied monetary growth rate. It might seem that all parties would have as their long-run target zero inflation, and hence choose targets for the budget deficit and money supply growth to go with this. This is clearly not the case, however, once we recognize that a budget deficit with inflation implies a different incidence of the existing tax burden from one with zero inflation, since an unanticipated shift to high inflation on the accession of a new government will lower the capital value of nominal government debt. This will expropriate debt holders to the advantage of the general taxpayer, who now pays less tax.

We assume for formal purposes, very simply, that each party maximizes the expected value at the next election date of a weighted average of the utility of its own supporters and that of the floating voter. The expectation is formed at time $t = 0$, the time of strategy choice, and it is supposed that this choice occurs only once in each period between elections and then cannot effectively be changed. We suppose that a party has had its 'honeymoon' period, has had to react to the pressures of office and after about half a year of its term has settled down and then chooses its strategy. The other party has by this time settled in opposition and also chooses its strategy. Once chosen, the parties cannot with credibility change them.

Formally then, for example, the Conservative Party maximizes:

$$\mu \, E_0 \, C_T + (1 - \mu)E_0 \, V_T \tag{7.30}$$

where $\mu$ is the weight given to its own supporters. The function will be expected to be maximized at time $T$, the time of the election. In principle it ought to be expected utility from this date onwards, with a suitable discount factor, but for empirical purposes this is considered needlessly complicated, given that we have ruled out expected future changes in policy programmes.

Equation (7.30) is maximized subject to the voters' preferences and their model of the economy. The formal mathematics of this is somewhat complicated (see Minford and Peel, 1982a). However, the implication of the analysis is important. This is that different political parties, who represent different class interests, will pursue different policies. In particular party policies will differ significantly, not only in budget and money supply targets but also in feedback coefficients according to the interaction between voter preferences and the model structure. Labour reaction functions will, relative to Conservative reaction functions, embody a higher steady state budget deficit and be more responsive to real rather than nominal shocks.

Quite clearly the precise form of reaction function will be dependent on the true model of the economy and the nature of voter preferences (which may not be constant). However, the main point of this work is robust, namely that in an economy with rational expectations on the part of both government and voters, there is scope for systematic policy differences between different political parties.

Empirical results on UK reaction functions for the period 1959–75 support the model in that signifcant differences between the political parties were discovered. Harte et al. (1983) also confirmed the fruitfulness of the approach, and found significant statistical differences in reaction functions between the parties in the UK, Sweden and West Germany.

These ideas are to be contrasted with the results of the median voter theorem, which predicts the same policies for each party. This theorem is therefore rejected by the data for first-past-the-post democracies, for which it was constructed. For proportional representation systems, the theorem could apply to the parliamentary parties closest to holding the balance of power; for these democracies, there is stronger evidence of party policy convergence, with the differences in Sweden and Germany appearing less marked than in the UK and USA.

Although there are party differences in policy, nevertheless the median voter (or party) theorem embodies an important principle: of policy convergence towards the centre. This principle has inspired a number of studies investigating how far the interests of this median or 'swing' group of voters (or their party) influence particular, as opposed to general economic, policies. Are particular taxes designed to shift the tax burden away from these voters? Are government expenditures fixed to benefit them? Models which answer 'yes' include that of Meltzer and Richard (1981, 1983), who also find evidence for these forces.

At this point a conflict arises with another strand of the public choice literature: this considers the power of vested interests, distinguished by their high motivation and efficient organization. Olson (1965, 1982) argues that they are more effective than ordinary voters, including median or floating ones, whose interests are less intensely affected by general tax or expenditure changes; hence ordinary voters devote less attention (costly information-gathering and assessment) to the issues and vested interests prevail over policy.

## Related Issues and Current Research

Political economy, the topic of this chapter, is a burgeoning area of research, for two reasons. First, the government is an agent with object-ives, whose actions are of obvious importance: modelling them should be superior to treating policy as exogenous or a fixed feedback rule. Secondly, analytical and computational tools have improved to the point where it is feasible to compute the equilibria in games between govern-ments and the public or other governments.

Much of this research has already been discussed. But two topics deserve emphasis.

In chapter 5, we discussed the issue of time-inconsistency and the incentives both to cheat on promises if believed and, once people realize this incentive, to find a mechanism which ensures promises are carried out. Models of reputation under imperfect information are attempts to explain variations in credibility between the total public gullibility of the first and the total cynicism of the second; such models can produce a political business cycle, as we have seen.

They may also produce strategies to bind successor governments into policies which benefit the current government. A high inherited level of public debt, for example, may constrain a future socialist government (when it comes to re-optimize) from increasing public expenditure; a conservative government might then push tax cuts further than otherwise in order to reduce tax rates and public spending long term, should it lose power. Models supporting such strategies are to be found in Alesina and Tabellini (1989, 1990).

The question of how policy promises can be enforced, by voting behaviour or by other parties or by constitutional structures, is also important, since good policies typically involve making promises which are then kept. Rogoff and Sibert (1988) consider voters punishing the government, although this involves the difficulty of why individual voters should bother, given their lack of power to influence anything individually (as in the voting paradox above). Alesina (1987) considers strategies where the other party deters promise-breaking in an inter-party pact (or 'bipartisan policy'): this may not apply well to controversial policy areas, such as public spending and inflation. Tabellini (1987) considers the role of independent, overlapping governors in an indepen-dent central bank. A good survey of all these issues is to be found in Alesina (1989).

The second topic concerns the source of inflation itself. Much existing literature assumes inflation is motivated by governments needing infla-tion revenue (seigniorage) to finance exogenous public spending, with the extent of the inflation tax being determined by an optimizing choice across tax patterns, to minimize the welfare and collection costs of taxation. Yet this approach is at variance with the considerations of political economy suggested in this chapter. Instead, inflation may serve the interests of the dominant voter and the party that represents him – as explored in Minford and Peel (1982) and Minford (1988). On this view, inflation, and its associated high interest rates, high inflation variance and expansionary public spending-cum-deficit programmes, is not an accident or the result of Keynesianism, but a deliberate strategy. The elimination of these policies will occur, not through better understanding nor through constitutional devices (which can always be over-ridden by a democratic majority) but through the formation of a new dominant voter coalition with different interests. This effect on macroeconomic policies parallels the effects explored by Meltzer and Richard (1981, 1983) and Olson (1965, 1982) on distributional and micro policies.

## Conclusions

Recent work in the public choice literature has considered the interaction of the preferences of the government and electors and the behaviour of the economy. This early work assumed that expectations are formed adaptively and generated one key conclusion, namely that the authorities may deliberately create a business cycle. When expectations are formed rationally, the authorities may still be able to generate a political business cycle, provided there is imperfect information and uncertainty about their objectives; however, the scope is more limited and can disappear altogether as information improves.

Another key result of the public choice literature is the median voter theorem, according to which party policies should be essentially the same, because they are designed to capture the floating voter. However, there is more empirical support for an alternative theory in which parties attempt to maximize the expected future utility, not only of floating voters but also of their own class-based supporters. This will give rise to systematic differences in the parties' reaction functions.

We also considered the way in which government popularity and voting behaviour has been modelled. We suggested that the conventional approach based on past economic indicators was deficient in ignoring expectations of future economic variables and the behaviour of the opposition. However, because of the importance of non-economic factors, it is unlikely that functions based solely on economic variables will generate statistically robust results; the evidence to date confirms this lack of robustness.

Finally, we considered research on how vested interests and voter coalitions may influence the strategies of political parties towards a whole range of variables – inflation, public spending, public debt and subsidies, to name but a few. Modern analytical and computational tools offer us the chance of a better understanding of the causes of government strategy.

## Note

1 This assumes that there is no systematic growth in $Y$. But allowing for a growth trend does not alter the essential point of the argument that follows. It adds a constant into (7.25). Equation (7.29) would then become a random walk 'with drift' (i.e. with a constant anticipated growth component).
2 There is one curious possibility: the government sets $q = -\theta^{-1}$, in which case the public cannot work out $\varepsilon_t$ since $y_t = \bar{y}_{t-1}$, and consequently $E\bar{y}_t = \bar{y}_{t-1}$, $Eg_t = g_t^e$. However, $P_t$ is almost certain to be worse in this case than for other values of $q$ where complete information prevails, because in it the public will expect discretion whereas otherwise $g_t = g_t^e = \pi^*$. To rule this odd case out completely we may appeal to voter disgust at being denied current information.

# 8

# The Macroeconomics of an Open Economy

All economies are of course open to trade and capital transactions with others; only the world economy is not. So in principle, the models we have dealt with to this point are all to be considered as models of the world economy. Even the United States, once blithely treated as 'closed' by the majority of macroeconomists, has been recognized in the past decade at least to be importantly affected by international influences.

These influences are transmitted through the balance of payments, which records the transactions of a country's residents with residents elsewhere. The current account records all transactions with non-residents which alter the net assets of residents, that is, transactions that require payment. Exports of goods and services and receipts of factor income from abroad (interest, profits and dividends, and remitted rents or wages) increase residents' net worth: if residents do not receive direct payment by cash or cheque, then they receive IOUs in some form. Imports decrease residents' net worth. Exports net of imports, the current account balance, therefore measures the change in residents' net worth as a result of transactions with 'foreigners', non-residents. This implies that movements in the current account have net wealth effects wherever in the domestic economy wealth matters – notably spending, possibly the demand for money and the supply of labour.

The capital account of the balance of payments records all transactions with non-residents which do not alter net assets of residents but rather re-shuffle them: for example, borrowing from or lending to them (a swap of a loan liability for cash), equity issues (a swap of the ownership of physical assets for cash), direct purchase of physical assets, 'direct investment' (a swap of physical assets for cash) or combinations of these (like equity purchase financed by borrowing).

Within the capital account, transactions with the central bank are singled out. The central bank's net foreign assets, the 'foreign exchange reserves', can finance purchases and sales of the domestic currency, usually for reasons of exchange rate policy. Apart from net interest earned or capital gains, which are typically small enough to neglect, the reserves will only rise or fall because of these sales or purchases, i.e. foreign exchange intervention.

The reserves have monetary significance. If we think of the central bank as the monetary arm of the government, issuing money and holding reserves for it, then we can write the consolidated bank/government balance sheet as:

| *Assets* | *Liabilities* |
|---|---|
| 1  Physical capital | 4  Government bonds (incl. |
| 2  Value of cumulated current | Treasury Bills) |
| deficits | 5  Currency in the hands of |
| 3  Reserves | banks and public |

Items 1 and 2 are the result of the government's past decisions to invest (1) and to consume more than its revenue (2). These are financed by borrowing (item 4) or currency issue (5). Changes in item 3, the acquisition of foreign assets (net), must be similarly financed by new borrowing or currency issue, given the inherited items 1 and 2. In change terms we can write:

$$\Delta M = \Delta R + DEF - \Delta B \tag{8.1}$$

where $M$ = currency issue, $R$ = reserves, $DEF$ = the government's investment and consumption less revenue ('total' deficit, or 'borrowing requirement'), $B$ = bonds outstanding. $DEF$ and $B$ can be computed either inclusive or exclusive of capital gains or losses. The essential point of (8.1) is that if there is foreign exchange intervention, $\Delta R$, to sell the domestic currency, this will increase the money supply, $\Delta M$, unless there is an offsetting open market operation, in this case the sale of bonds, $\Delta B$, for currency.

We can immediately link this to the exchange rate regime. Under fixed exchange rates, the central bank stands ready to maintain the exchange rate with whatever intervention is needed. At this exchange rate, the economy will throw up a current account, $CURBOP$, and a balance, $CAPBOP$, on all capital transactions not involving the central bank (or 'capital balance' for short). By definition the current account balance, being the net acquisition of foreign assets, must of course be equal to the balance of net foreign asset transactions recorded in the capital account, including transactions in the foreign exchange reserves. By balance of payments convention (an application of double-entry book-keeping), assets acquired are recorded with a negative sign in the capital account, liabilities with a positive sign. This implies that all non-reserve transactions which would increase the reserves, by requiring payments from foreigners, are positive, and vice versa.

Hence

$$CURBOP + CAPBOP \equiv \Delta R \tag{8.2}$$

It follows that the supply of money is affected through (8.1) by whatever reserves movements are thrown up at the fixed exchange rate.

A floating exchange rate is defined by the absence of foreign exchange intervention: $\Delta R = 0$. Hence the rate has to move to whatever level will continuously force the current and capital accounts together to zero.

A useful way to approach the open economy aspects then is to set up models of the current and capital account respectively.

## The Current Account – Two Models

There are two main models of trade flows in the short or medium run. The first assumes that products are non-homogeneous and produced under imperfect competition: the products of British firms differ from those of German firms, say, even in the same market. The second assumes that products are homogeneous and produced under perfect competition: prices for British and German output of the same product are equalized across all world markets (that is, in any given market they will be equal, though transport costs will cause prices of both to differ between markets).

Let us take each model in turn, in each case treating home costs and prices as given: we will revert to this 'supply' aspect shortly.

### Imperfect Competition

The imperfect competition model is illustrated in figure 8.1. $XX$ shows the demand for exports by non-residents (shifted by world trade, $WT$), $MM$ that for imports by residents (shifted by domestic demand, $D$). The $\phi M$ curve shows the real value of imports as $P_H/P_F( = 1/\phi)$ varies.

This is the familiar model of import and export demand, encountered in the majority of macro models. The resulting current account equation is:

$$CURBOP = P_H X(WT, P_H/P_F) - P_F M(D, P_H/P_F) \qquad (8.3)$$

In real terms

$$\frac{CURBOP}{P_H} = X - \phi M \qquad (8.4)$$

where $\phi = P_F/P_H$ is the inverse of the terms of trade. It is usually found in empirical work (e.g. by Stern et al., 1976) that the current account improves after a few years when the terms of trade worsen (as could occur with a devaluation that is not fully offset by a rise in home prices), although in the short run because of lags in the response of trade volumes

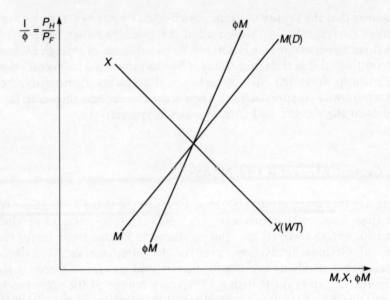

**Figure 8.1**   Imperfect competition model of the current account.

Normalization of $\phi$ so that $\phi = 1$ when $X = M$.

the current account may worsen (the 'J-curve'). The condition for improvement (the Marshall–Lerner condition) can be written in terms of elasticities as:

$$\varepsilon_x + \varepsilon_m - 1 > 0 \tag{8.5}$$

This applies exactly when trade is initially in balance $(X = \phi M)$ and is derived straightforwardly from:

$$0 < [\delta(CURBOP/P_H)/\delta\phi] \cdot \phi/X = \frac{\delta X}{\delta\phi} \cdot \frac{\phi}{X} -$$

$$\phi \cdot \frac{\delta M}{\delta\phi} \cdot \frac{\phi}{\phi M} - M \cdot \phi/\phi M$$

$$= \varepsilon_x + \varepsilon_m - 1 \tag{8.6}$$

remembering that

$$\varepsilon_m = - \frac{\delta M}{\delta\phi} \cdot \frac{\phi}{M}$$

is positive by the elasticity convention.

## Perfect Competition

The perfect competition model is illustrated in figure 8.2. We take non-traded goods ('home') prices, $P_{NT}$, as given in this case; traded prices, $P_T$, are of course set by world market conditions. A devaluation, not offset fully by a rise in home prices, will raise $P_T$ relative to $P_{NT}$. Domestic demand, $D$, depending overall on output, $y$, and wealth, $\theta$, is split between traded and non-traded goods by relative prices, $P_{NT}/P_T$. The supply of non-traded goods, at given $P_{NT}$, rises or falls to meet demand for them (in practice market-clearing will require that $P_{NT}$ move to equilibrate the two). The supply of traded goods will depend on traded prices relative to home prices (and costs): we will assume throughout that capital stocks are fixed (although this can easily be varied to obtain long run solutions; see appendix).

The current account equation we obtain is:

$$\text{CURBOP} = P_T(Q_T[P_{NT}/P_T] - D_T[D, P_{NT}/P_T]) \qquad (8.7)$$

where we have aggregated over exported and imported products; in fact $P_T Q_T = P_{XT}Q_{XT} + P_{MT}Q_{MT}$ (similarly $P_T D_T$), so if there is an improvement in the terms of trade, $P_{XT}/P_{MT}$, the current account would improve, with no consequence for trade volumes provided $P_{NT}/P_T$ remained constant – unlike the imperfect competition model. A fall in

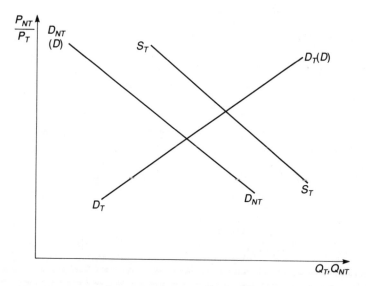

Figure 8.2   Perfect competition model of the current account.

$P_{NT}/P_T$ (due, say, to a devaluation not fully offset by a rise in $P_{NT}$) will unambiguously improve the current account in both the short and the long run – unlike the effects of the analogue, a terms of trade change in the imperfect competition model.

### Home Prices – the Supply Side

We held home prices constant to study the partial equilibrium determination of the current account, largely from the demand side. We now discuss how home prices in the two models are determined, and also the general demand–supply equilibrium of the model.

### Imperfect Competition

Figure 8.3 illustrates this in the imperfect competition model (it is a diagram adapted from the earlier Parkin–Bade diagram of figure 3.2). In the bottom left hand quadrant, the labour supply curve slopes upward as the real consumer wage, $W$, deflated by the consumer price index,

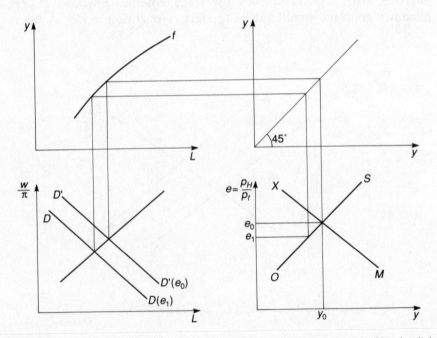

Figure 8.3 Supply and demand in the open economy under imperfect competition (capital stock fixed).

$\pi$, rises. $\pi = P_H^\alpha P_F^{1-\alpha}$; that is, it is a weighted average of home goods prices and import prices. The demand for labour, however, reacts to the real producer wage,

$$\frac{W}{P_H} = \frac{W}{\pi} \cdot \frac{\pi}{P_H} = \frac{W}{\pi} \cdot (P_F/P_H)^{1-\alpha}$$

so as $(P_H/P_F) = e$ rises, the real producer wage falls relative to the real consumer wage and the demand for labour rises, shifting $DD$ rightwards. The higher employment is translated, by the production function and the 45° line in the top two quadrants, into an open economy supply curve, $OS$ in the bottom right hand quadrant. Finally, we use figure 8.1 to derive a curve showing combinations of $e$ and $D$ that give current account equilibrium: that is, where the $XX$ and $\phi M$ curves cross each other as $D$ is varied. The resulting curve is the $XM$ in the bottom right quadrant of figure 8.3: note that since along it $D = y$ (implied by current account equiilibrium), we can draw it in $e$, $y$ space.

When these relationships are put together, we can see in figure 8.3 that $e_0$, $y_0$, $L_0$, $(W/\pi)_0$ are the general equilibrium, conditional on the capital stock. (We can also let this vary: for this long run case, see appendix.)

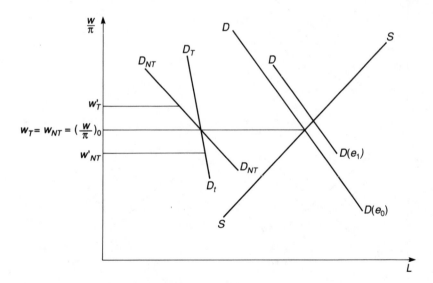

Figure 8.4   The labour market under perfect competition (capital stock fixed).

$w_T'$, $w_{NT}'$ show the producer real wage facing traded and non-traded goods producers respectively as $e$ rises from $e_0$ to $e_1$, $(W/\pi)_0$ remaining unchanged.

### Perfect Competition

Figures 8.4 and 8.5 explain how the perfect competition open economy supply curve is derived. Figure 8.4 shows the demand for labour by traded and non-traded goods industries: the non-traded demand is assumed to be more elastic that the traded, because factor proportions are more malleable, given the capital stock, than in manufacturing (hotel porters versus machine operatives). Since $\pi = P_{NT}^{1-\alpha} P_T^{\alpha}$,

$$W/\pi = (W/P_{NT})(P_{NT}/P_T)^{\alpha} \text{ but also}$$

$$W/\pi = (W/P_T)(P_{NT}/P_T)^{-(1-\alpha)}$$

this implies that if $(P_{NT}/P_T)$ (which now becomes the real exchange rate, $e$), rises, producer real wages, at a given $(W/\pi)$, rise for the traded goods sector, to $w_T'$, but fall for the non-traded sector, to $w_{NT}'$. Overall, under our assumption, the demand for labour rises, just as in figure 8.3.

Figure 8.5 then takes up the rest of the story, as in figure 8.3. In the top left hand quadrant is shown the production function in the whole economy ($f$) as well as those for traded and non-traded goods: clearly

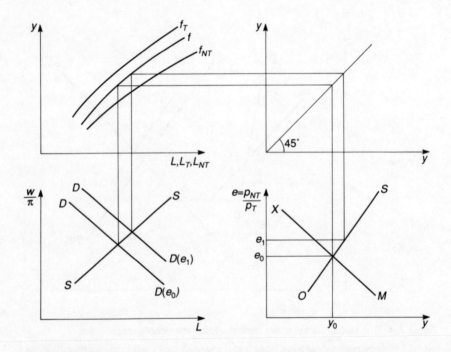

Figure 8.5 Supply and demand under perfect competition (capital stock fixed).

one can trace out production in each of these two sectors as well, from their demands for labour in figure 8.4.

The *XM* curve in figure 8.5 is derived from figure 8.2 by varying $D$ and tracing out the $P_{NT}/P_T$ values for which there is intersection between demand and supply for traded goods (current account equilibrium). As with the derivation of the *XM* in figure 8.3, $D = y$ at these values so that we can draw the relationship as between $P_{NT}/P_T$ and $y$. General equilibrium is at the intersection of the *XM* and *OS* curves, at $e_0, y_0,$ $L_0, (W/\pi)_0$

## The Open Economy Supply Curve (OS) and the Effect of Prices

The OS curve we have just derived can be thought of as the equivalent of $y^*$ in the closed economy Phillips curve; that is, it is the state of the economy when there are no price surprises (including prices different from those built into wage contracts, for the New Keynesian case).

The analysis when there are price surprises is the same as in the closed economy case, only here the *OS* curve shifts in *e, y* space – a

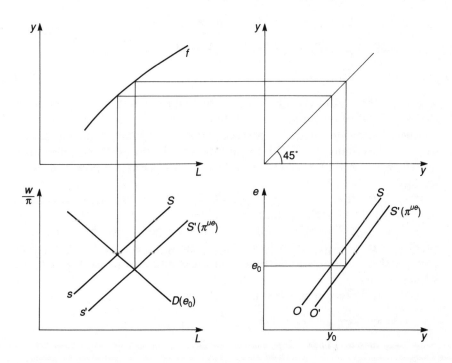

Figure 8.6  A price surprise shifts the *OS* curve – the open economy Phillips curve effect.

presentational difference only. Figure 8.6 illustrates the resulting open economy 'Phillips curve' effect.

## The Capital Account and the Rest of the Open Economy Model

We shall see in chapter 11 (where we deal with efficient markets) that, as a result of portfolio diversification, the equilibrium price or return on an internationally traded asset is (possibly totally) insensitive to variations in its supply. In the case of interest rates, this gives rise to the uncovered interest parity condition ($S$ = price of home currency):

$$R_t = R_{F,t} - (\mathrm{E}_t\, S_{t+1} - S_t) \tag{8.8}$$

This safe return on one-period bonds (in domestic currency terms) is the benchmark for all other domestic asset returns: if the yield is sensitive to the supply of available assets, one can add to (8.8) an extra term in the stock of net foreign assets, and possibly also total assets, inclusive too of the physical capital stock. However, empirically such terms are rarely significant and we ignore them here.

It is useful to rewrite (8.8) in real terms:

$$r_t = R_t - \mathrm{E}_t\, \pi_{t+1} + \pi_t = R_{F,t} - \mathrm{E}_t\, \pi_{F,t+1} + \pi_{F,t}$$
$$- (\mathrm{E}_t\, S_{t+1} + \mathrm{E}_t\, \pi_{t+1} - \mathrm{E}_t\, \pi_{F,t+1}) + (S_t + \pi_t - \pi_{F,t})$$
$$= r_{f,t} - \mathrm{E}_t\, e_{t+1} + e_t \tag{8.9}$$

where $r$ is the real interest rate and $e$ the real exchange rate expressed as the (log) ratio of consumer price deflators. Whether we have the perfect competition model or the imperfect competition model, this definition of the real exchange rate will do equally well. In the perfect competition model, $\pi - \pi_F = (1 - \alpha)P_{NT} + \alpha P_T - \pi_F$ (all prices are now expressed in logs).

If $\pi_F = P_T$, then $\pi - \pi_F = (1 - \alpha)(P_{NT} - P_T) = (1 - \alpha)e$. In general $\pi_F = \delta P_T + (1 - \delta)P_{F,NT}$ and $\pi - \pi_F = (1 - \alpha)P_{NT} - \{(\delta - \alpha)P_T + (1 - \delta)P_{F,NT}\}$. Clearly in all cases $\pi - \pi_F$ picks up the movement of domestic non-traded prices relative to some set of foreign prices converted into domestic currency: in most circumstances it will move with $e$.

In the imperfect competition model,

$$\pi - \pi_F = \alpha P_H + (1 - \alpha)P_F - \delta P_F - (1 - \delta)P_H =$$
$$(\alpha + \delta - 1)(P_H - P_F)$$

where $\alpha > 0.5 < \delta$. Here $\pi - \pi_F$ is a transform of the terms of trade, the real exchange rate in this model.

If we now turn to the rest of the model, we can modify the *IS* curve as:

$$y_t = -\alpha r_t - \delta e_t + k\theta_t + \bar{d} \qquad (8.10)$$

where $\theta$ = net nominal wealth, including now net foreign assets, and $e$ enters because of the effect on demand of the current account. The *LM* curve becomes:

$$m_t = \pi_t + ny_t - \beta R_t \qquad (8.11)$$

Now let us ignore government bonds as net wealth; we can then write the current account as

$$\Delta\theta_t = -qe_t - \mu y_t \qquad (8.12)$$

Add the definition

$$e_t = \pi_t + S_t - \pi_{F,t} \qquad (8.13)$$

the open economy supply curve:

$$y_t = \sigma e_t + p(\pi_t - E_{t-1}\pi_t) \qquad (8.14)$$

and the definition of real interest rates:

$$r_t = R_t - (E_t \pi_{t+1} - \pi_t) \qquad (8.15)$$

Equations (8.9) to (8.15) make up a seven equation model determining $y, e, r, \theta, \pi, R$ and either $m$ ($S$ fixed: fixed rates) or $S$ ($m$ fixed: floating rates). The solution can be found by the methods in chapter 2: it turns out that the characteristic equation is second order, and for a saddlepath solution one root should be unstable and the other stable.

Here we use a graphical method (figs. 8.7–8). We can note (setting constants = 0) that $E_t\, e_{t+1} = je_t + \varepsilon_t$, where $\varepsilon_t$ is a combination of the current shocks to the model and $j$ is the stable root. Now using (8.9) eliminate $r_t$ in favour of $e_t$ throughout the model. Since (8.9) is the '*BB* curve' (as in Parkin and Bade) along which the foreign exchange market is always clearing, when we do this substitution in the *IS* curve we are obtaining Parkin and Bade's *ISBB* curve, the *IS* curve when the foreign exchange market is cleared. Notice that this *ISBB* curve shifts with $\theta_{t-1}$, the previous stock of net foreign assets (we eliminate $\theta_t$ in terms of $e_t, y_t$ and $\theta_{t-1}$ in 8.12).

The *XM* and *OS* curves have been derived earlier. This leaves the determination of prices in the right hand quadrant. Under fixed exchange rates ($S = \bar{S}$) we can use (8.13) to obtain prices along the 45° line, *FX*. Under floating, prices are determined by (8.11), (8.9) and (8.15) as:

$$\pi_t = m_t - ny_t + \beta(r_{F,t} + E_t \pi_{t+1} - \pi_t + (1-j)e_t - \varepsilon_t) \qquad (8.16)$$

So the slope of the *FL* curve is (given by the saddlepath solution, $E_t\pi_{t+1} = j\pi_t + \eta_t$, $\eta_t$ being a combination of shocks, like $E_t$)

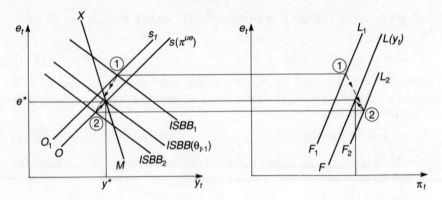

Figure 8.7　The full open economy model and a fiscal shock under floating rates.

$$\frac{\delta e_t}{\delta \pi_t} = \frac{1 + \beta(1-j)}{\beta(1-j)} > 1$$

Finally we can illustrate how the model works, with a fiscal shock, shifting the *ISBB* curve temporarily to the right. This is shown under floating in figure 8.7 by the dashed lines. The *ISBB* shifts out the $ISBB_1$. This raises output, shifting the *FL* curve to $F_1L_1$, lowering prices and so shifting the *OS* curve left to $O_1S_1$. This creates a current account deficit (equilibrium in period 1 is to the right of the *XM* curve) and $\theta$ falls so that next period, the *ISBB* shifts leftwards to $ISBB_2$. Also in period 2, the *OS* curve returns to *OS* ($\pi^{ue}$ now being zero), while the *FL* curve shifts to the right with falling output.

The same fiscal shock is shown for fixed rates in figure 8.8. It can be seen that apart from the effect on prices, which may fall under floating but must rise under fixed, the effects are quite similar. The real exchange rate, real interest rates and output rise; and these rises are later reversed.

Needless to say, this model represents just the barest bones of a fully specified open economy model. But it should clarify the key elements, before the encrustation of complications from adjustment lags, contracts and the rest.

## Conclusions

The open economy model is of key importance in applied macro-economics, since all economies (except the world) are open! This chapter has extended the earlier analysis to capture the main essentials of openness.

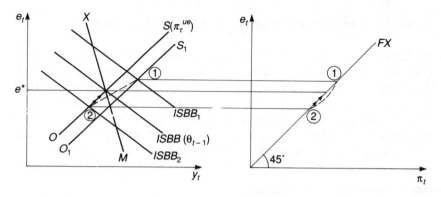

Figure 8.8   A fiscal shock under fixed rates.

The current account determines movements in net foreign assets, a key element of national wealth; these impact on spending. The current account depends on demand and relative prices; either relative home/foreign prices (under imperfect competition) or relative traded/non-traded prices (perfect competition). These relative prices are in turn determined by supply conditions interacting with demand: the open economy supply curve is derived analogously to the Phillips curve in the closed economy, but wages react additionally to the changing relative foreign prices.

The capital account (excluding the central bank's operations) has monetary importance: together with the current account it determines the demand for and supply of money. If the central bank does not intervene in the foreign exchange market, then demand must equal supply: the exchange rate moves to ensure this – floating rates. Consumer prices are then determined by the domestically set money supply, interacting with the demand for money. If the central bank intervenes, to hold the exchange rate – fixed rates – the reserves will adjust to equal the gap between demand and supply: but changes in the reserves will change the money supply through the central bank's balance sheet. With market efficiency, the reserves will adjust so rapidly, as capital flows to take immediate advantage of any uncovered interest differential, that the central bank loses all, even short-term, control of the money supply. When all these factors are put together, the open economy model shows how the economy can be stimulated temporarily, with the real exchange rate and real interest rates moving in sympathy with output and the price level, but that losses of net foreign assets cause it to reverse this stimulus in order to restore the economy's original wealth.

## Appendix: Long-run Equilibrium in the Open Economy

In the long run, the capital stock is variable. It is natural to assume
constant returns to scale, since there is a tendency for industries to be
driven to operate at their lowest cost level by the processes of international competition: if there were decreasing returns to scale, industries
would contract, and if increasing, they would expand until constant
returns were achieved. As for external returns to scale, there is pressure
to internalize these externalities and similarly to drive industry operations to the minimum cost point: even if the externalities are at the
national level, forces operate to internalize them through national
policy.

### Imperfect Competition

Assuming constant returns to scale and mobile international capital,
figure 8.3 is redrawn for the long run as figure 8.A.1. Now in the labour
market there is a unique feasible real consumer wage that can be paid

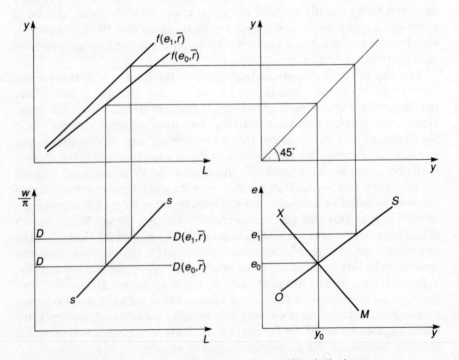

Figure 8.A.1   The open economy under imperfect competition in the long run.

given the terms of trade and the international cost of capital ($\bar{r}$): $P_H = W^\beta (\bar{r}P_F)^{1-\beta}$ and $\pi = P_H^\alpha P_F^{1-\alpha}$,

$$\text{so } W/\pi = W/P_H^\alpha P_F^{1-\alpha} = P_H^{1/\beta} (\bar{r}P_F)^{-(1-\beta)/\beta}/(P_H^\alpha P_F^{1-\alpha})$$

$$= (P_H/P_F)^{(1/\beta-\alpha)} \bar{r}^{(1-1/\beta)}$$

(note that $1/\beta > 1 > \alpha$; capital goods are assumed to be imported but this does not affect the essential argument).

As $e$ rises from $e_0$ to $e_1$, so the feasible real consumer wage rises; labour supply increases. $W/P_H = [P_H/\bar{r}P_F]^{(1/\beta-1)}$ also rises, so that labour input per unit of output is reduced and the production function shifts upwards. The open economy supply curve is accordingly flatter in the long run than in the short.

## Perfect Competition

Figures 8.A.2 and 8.A.3 show the long-run equilibrium of the perfect competition model. As in the short run we have $\pi = P_{NT}^{1-\alpha} P_T^\alpha$. But in the long run under constant returns we also have

$$P_T = W^\delta (\bar{r}P_T)^{1-\delta} \tag{8.A.1}$$

$$P_{NT} = W^\beta (\bar{r}P_T)^{1-\beta} \tag{8.A.2}$$

Together these two imply that $e = P_{NT}/P_T = \bar{r}^{1-\beta/\delta}$. Using the definition of $\pi$, they also imply that

$$W/\pi = \bar{r}^{-\{1-\beta+\alpha[\beta-\delta]\}/\delta} \tag{8.A.3}$$

So assuming that $\pi$ is set by domestic monetary conditions, these three equations determine $W, P_T, P_{NT}$ as functions of $\pi$ and $\bar{r}$; in other words, $\bar{r}$ determines real consumer wages ($W/\pi$), the real exchange rate, $e (= P_{NT}/P_T)$, and real product wages ($W/P_T, W/P_{NT}$).

Figure 8.A.2 shows how from $e^*$ (given by $\bar{r}$), any slight rise in $e$ would lead to an infinite expansion of the traded goods industry, and vice versa; assume for these purposes that labour is in infinitely elastic supply at some $W$ and that $P_{NT}$ is given by (8.A.2) so that non-traded industry expands to whatever is required by demand. As demand is varied, traded goods are made available by this process ($P_T$ rising or falling) to keep the current account in balance. This yields the flat $XM$ curve in figure 8.A.3.

Turning now to constraints on labour supply, we see in Figure 8.A.3 how at each $e^*$ (corresponding to a certain $\bar{r}$) there is a unique real consumer wage, $(W/\pi)^*$; any rise of $W/\pi^*$ above this reduces the output of both industries, and also their demand for labour, to zero, since it exceeds labour's long-run unique marginal product. At this

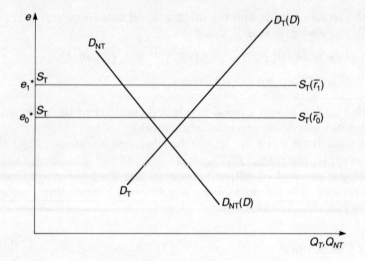

Figure 8.A.2   The perfect competition model of the current account in the long run.
As $\bar{r}_0$ falls to $\bar{r}_1$, $e_0^*$ rises to $e_1^*$ if NT is labour-intensive.

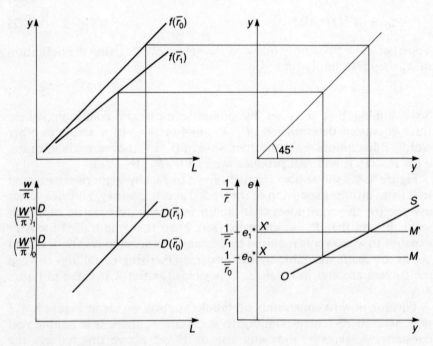

Figure 8.A.3   Supply and demand under perfect competition in the long run.
As $F_0$ falls to $F_1$, $e_0^*$ rises to $e_1^*$ (assumes NT labour-intensive).

$(W/\pi)^*$ there is a particular labour supply which defines the level of employment and output.

If we assume that the non-traded sector is labour-intensive ($\beta$ is larger than $\delta$), then as $\bar{r}$ rises, both $e$ and $W/\pi$ fall. This is the assumption made in figures 8.A.2 and 8.A.3, giving an upward-sloping long-run $OS$ curve (otherwise it would slope downwards). As in figure 8.A.1 under imperfect competition, the production function shifts upwards in the long run as labour-intensiveness falls in both sectors.

# 9

# Representative Agent Models in Cashless Economies

Macroeconomic models have traditionally been constructed from aggregate demand and supply relationships. These relationships are in turn justified by 'micro-foundations': that is to say, it is shown that people or firms (agents) maximizing their utility or expected utility would on average behave according to these relationships. To obtain average aggregate from individual behaviour, assumptions have been made about the distribution of preferences and technological idiosyncracies: often, appeal can be made to the central limit theorem, which says that the mean of many independent random variables has a normal distribution.

Nevertheless, the parameters of these relationships are only loosely tied to the parameters of the preferences and technology of individual agents. We saw this earlier when discussing Lucas's critique (Lucas, 1976) of econometric models: certain of the model's parameters will shift under changes of policy regime or other exogenous variable processes. Yet we would like to have models which can be used to evaluate the effects of just such changes. This argues the need for models whose parameters are solely those of preferences and technology, so-called 'deep structure'.

In response to this need, a variety of models have been produced which make dramatically simple assumptions about preferences and technology, in order to make a complete treatment practicable. Often technology is reduced to stochastic per capita endowments of a single consumption good and consumers are treated as identical representative agents.

These models are obviously no use for traditional forecasting and policy analysis where we try to predict and control particular sequences of events. But this is not the use for which they are intended. Rather it is to model an economy in the sense of mimicking and so understanding its (average) time-series properties when shocked; from a policy viewpoint, this should guide us towards policies which improve those properties. This is a long-term perspective. With it tends to go the view that economists and policy-makers should only be concerned with these average properties over the long term and not with short-term sequences of events.

There are horses for courses. In practice, whether they ought to be or not, economists are called upon to help in both the short- and the long-term aspects of problems. Provided they are honest about the short-comings of the tools they use in both contexts, I can see no objection to them earning their living doing both. For this reason, I have presented the more traditional models already and now proceed to give an account of these deep structure models. Inevitably, it is too short to be more than an introduction: for a fuller treatment the reader is referred to Sargent (1987), whose approach we follow closely in this chapter and the next.

## The Basic Structure of a Representative Agent Model

In these models the representative consumer maximizes expected utility subject to his or her budget constraint; the government spends, levies taxes and prints money subject to its budget constraint; and markets clear, imposing general equilibrium. From this structure it is possible to derive relationships between the stochastic shocks and macroeconomic outcomes such as consumption, prices and interest rates.

### Consumer Maximization

Take first the consumer decision. In a non-stochastic world he would typically be assumed to maximize a time-additive utility function:

$$U = \sum_{t=0}^{\infty} \beta^t \, u(c_t) \tag{9.1}$$

$c_t$ is consumption, and $u$ is a well-behaved utility function with positive and diminishing marginal utility of consumption. Let his budget constraint be:

$$A_{t+1} = R_t (A_t + y_t - c_t) \tag{9.2}$$

where $A_t$ is wealth at the beginning of period $t$, $R_t$ is the interest rate (gross, inclusive of capital repayment) and $y_t$ is income. $A_0$ and $y_t$ are given.

Using the Lagrangean method, we can write the maximand as:

$$L = u(c_0) + \beta u(c_1) + \beta^2 u(c_2) + \dots$$
$$+ \mu_0 [A_1 - R_0 (A_0 + y_0 - c_0)] + \mu_1 [A_2 - R_1 (A_1 + y_1 - c_1)]$$
$$+ \mu_2 [A_3 - R_2 (A_2 + y_2 - c_2)] + \dots \tag{9.3}$$

yielding the first order conditions with respect to the consumer's choice variables $c_0, c_1, \dots, A_1, A_2, \dots$ as:

$$0 = \frac{\delta L}{\delta c_0} = u'(c_0) + \mu_0 R_0 \quad 0 = \frac{\delta L}{\delta A_1} = \mu_0 - \mu_1 R_1$$

$$0 = \frac{\delta L}{\delta c_1} = \beta u'(c_1) + \mu_1 R_1 \quad 0 = \frac{\delta L}{\delta A_2} = \mu_1 - \mu_2 R_2 \tag{9.4}$$

where $u' = \dfrac{\delta u}{\delta c}$.

Equation (9.4) yields a string of relationships between the marginal utility of consumption in one period and the next:

$$u'(c_t) = \beta R_t u'(c_{t+1}) \tag{9.5}$$

The consumer equates his marginal rate of transformation $u'(c_t)/\beta u'(c_{t+1})$, with the gross rate of interest, a result illustrated in figure 9.1.

As figure 9.1 and equation (9.5) suggest, one can split up the consumer's problem into a sequence of two-period decisions. Given $(A_t + y_t)$, he decides $c_{t+1}$ relative to $c_t$: that is, he can either decide $c_{t+1}$ if he has already decided on $c_t$ or $c_t$ if he must consume $c_{t+1}$. This splitting up

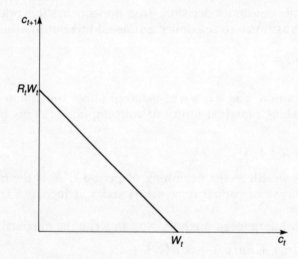

Figure 9.1   Intertemporal consumer choice.

$$W_t = A_t + y_t + \sum_{i=1}^{\infty} \prod_{j=1}^{i} R_{t+j-1}^{-1} y_{t+i}.$$

current ($t$) assets plus the present value of current and future income stream.

of the decision problem is known as dynamic programming. In dynamic programming, each period's consumption is first solved given the last period's consumption, wealth and income; finally the initial consumption level is set so that all assets are ultimately consumed.

For many purposes we shall only need to consider the first stage of the decision process. Occasionally, dynamic programming solutions are presented backwards from the future (i.e. consumption in one period is solved given consumption in the next period): this method is convenient if there is some fixed terminal point from which one can work back (at which, for example, the consumer dies, leaving a fixed or no bequest). But it is obviously only a presentational matter whether one period's consumption is seen as depending on last period's or next period's.

The consumer decides what to do one period at a time, and in principle he can recompute his decision for the next period when it comes: he decides $c_0$ this period (with a plan for $c_1, c_2, \ldots$), next period he decides $c_1$ (given $c_0$, then in the past, and with a plan for $c_2, c_3, \ldots$). Of course in this problem with no stochastic shocks he will always stick to his original plan (this is not to be confused with the time-inconsistency of policy-makers who can influence *other* people's decisions and then recompute: our consumer only affects himself). He might as well decide at the start on his consumption plan and just carry it out without further thought.

We now turn to a stochastic environment, where in each period a particular shock is realized. The consumer will have decided on consumption in the previous period based on his expectation across all possible shocks. He will also have a plan for his consumption in future periods; this will be a contingency plan, in which his consumption will depend on which shocks occur. Since he does not actually have to decide irrevocably on future consumption until the period involved, this contingency approach is the optimal one: he maintains his flexibility until the last possible moment. Then as the shocks are realized, he picks the relevant branch of his contingency plan. Figure 9.2 illustrates.

We can think of this equivalently as the consumer either recomputing his best expected plan each period or as computing at the start a total contingency plan and carrying it out as the shocks are realized: the point is that the consumer is making use of his potential flexibility in the face of shocks by deferring decisions on actual consumption until he has to take them.

The consumer is assumed to maximize expected utility in this environment, or

$$U_0 = E_0 \sum_{t=0}^{\infty} \beta^t u(c_t),$$

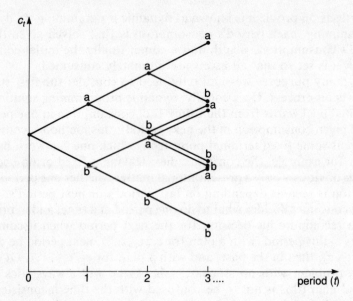

Figure 9.2 Contingency plan for consumption, with the shock each period taking two values (a, b).

subject to $A_{t+1} = R_t(A_t + y_t - c_t)$, where $R_t = R(1 + \varepsilon_t)$, for example, but $y_t$ is a known series. We can now use the principle of dynamic programming and take each period's decision separately.

We can write $U_0$, substituting $c_1$ out from the constraints, as:

$$U_0 = u(c_0) + E_0\, \beta u\left(R_0\,[A_0 + y_0 - c_0] + y_1 - A_2/R_1\right)$$
$$+ E_0\, \beta^2 u(c_2) + \ldots \tag{9.6}$$

Maximizing this with respect to $c_0$ ($A_0$ given) gives:

$$0 = \frac{\delta U_0}{\delta c_0} = u'(c_0) + E_0\, \beta u'(c_1)(-R_0)$$

or $u'(c_0) = E_0\, \beta R_0 u'(c_1)$ $\hspace{2cm}$ (9.7)

Analogously at $t = 1$, the consumer maximizes $U_1$ ($A_1$ given) to obtain:

$$u'(c_1) = E_1\, \beta R_1 u'(c_2) \tag{9.8}$$

and in general:

$$u'(c_t) = E_t\, \beta R_t u'(c_{t+1}) \tag{9.9}$$

which is the expected analogue of (9.5).

By the law of iterated expectations it follows that:

$$E_0 \, u'(c_t) = \beta E_0 R_t u'(c_{t+1}) \tag{9.10}$$

We can reach this general result more compactly by using expected Lagrangeans, taking the expectations operator through the Lagrangean multipliers.

Let the consumer be faced with a given realization $A_t$; then he can choose $c_t, c_{t+1}, A_{t+1}$ to maximize (at $t$) $U_t$ subject to the constraint, or the expected Lagrangean,

$$L = U_t + E_t \{ \mu_t (A_{t+1} - R_t [A_t + y_t - c_t]) $$
$$ + \mu_{t+1} (A_{t+2} - R_{t+1} [A_{t+1} + y_{t+1} - c_{t+1}]) + \ldots \} \tag{9.11}$$

$$0 = \frac{\delta L}{\delta c_t} = \beta^t u'(c_t) + E_t \, \mu_t R_t \tag{9.12}$$

$$0 = \frac{\delta L}{\delta A_{t+1}} = E_t \, \mu_t - E_t \, \mu_{t+1} R_{t+1} \tag{9.13}$$

$$0 = \frac{\delta L}{\delta c_{t+1}} = E_t \, \beta^{t+1} u'(c_{t+1}) + E_t \, \mu_{t+1} R_{t+1} \tag{9.14}$$

Equation (9.9) follows by substitution.

## General Equilibrium

Equation (9.9) can be turned into a pricing formula for an asset. Suppose the asset yields an uncertain dividend, $d_{t+1}$, and has a current price, $p_t$, so that $R_t = (p_{t+1} + d_{t+1})/p_t$. Then

$$u'(c_t) = E_t \, \beta (p_{t+1} + d_{t+1})/p_t u'(c_{t+1})$$

$$\text{or} \quad p_t = \frac{\beta}{u'(c_t)} E_t \, u'(c_{t+1}) (p_{t+1} + d_{t+1}) \tag{9.15}$$

Since all consumers are identical, the only way this asset will be held (by anyone and everyone) is for (9.15) to hold.

One way to create a simple economy with an asset market is to follow Lucas's tree model (Lucas, 1978). Let the only asset be an identical tree, one belonging to each consumer, who has no other source of income. Let each tree produce non-storable fruit, an all-purpose consumption good, in the quantity $d_t$.

Fruit can be exchanged for trees at the price $p_t$ (units of fruit per tree). But Walras's Law implies that if the fruit market is in excess demand, the tree market is in excess supply. Therefore market-clearing across the whole economy (trees and fruit) implies that

$$c_t = d_t \tag{9.16}$$

Equations (9.15) and (9.16) therefore constitute our model of the economy, yielding the compact form:

$$p_t = \{\beta/u'(d_t)\} E_t \, u'(d_{t+1})(p_{t+1} + d_{t+1}) \tag{9.17}$$

Substituting successively for $E_t \, p_{t+1}, E_{t+1} \, p_{t+2}, \ldots$ and using the law of iterated expectations ($E_t \, E_{t+i} = E_t$), yields:

$$p_t = E_t \left[ \beta \frac{u'(d_{t+1})}{u'(d_t)} d_{t+1} + \beta^2 \frac{u'(d_{t+1})}{u'(d_t)} \frac{u'(d_{t+2})}{u'(d_{t+1})} d_{t+2} + \cdots \right]$$

$$= E_t \sum_{j=1}^{\infty} \beta^j \frac{u'(d_{t+j})}{u'(d_t)} d_{t+j} \tag{9.18}$$

Depending on the form of the utility function, one can solve for $p_t$ as a function of the current and expected $d$. One convenient case is where $u(c_t) = \ln c_t$ so that $u'(c_t) = 1/c_t$, in which case

$$p_t = E_t \sum_{j=1}^{\infty} \beta^j d_t = \frac{\beta}{1 - \beta} d_t \tag{9.19}$$

In this case the asset price varies with whatever stochastic process drives the harvest of fruit.

### The Government Budget Constraint

In this general equilibrium framework with no money, let us introduce a government issuing debt, bonds, each of which pays next period one unit of the fruit, regardless; $b_{t+1}$ is the number of such bonds per capita issued in $t$ ($b_t$ the number issued in $t - 1$). Its budget constraint will be

$$g_t - T_t + b_t = b_{t+1}/R_{1t} \tag{9.20}$$

where $g_t$ = government spending per capita, $T_t$ = taxes per capita (an equal poll tax), $R_{1t}$ = the one-period-ahead rate of return on debt ($R_{jt}$ = the $j$-period-ahead rate of return).

For this debt to be held, it must be as with trees that

$$u'(c_t) = \beta \, E_t \, R_{1t} u'(c_{t+1}) \tag{9.21}$$

Since $R_{1t}$ is certain, this implies

$$R_{1t}^{-1} = \beta \, E_t \, u'(c_{t+1})/u'(c_t) \tag{9.22}$$

Now market-clearing of the fruit market implies:

$$c_t + g_t = d_t \tag{9.23}$$

The consumer's budget constraint is

$$d_t - c_t - T_t + b_t + p_t S_t = b_{t+1}^d/R_{1t} + p_t S_{t+1}^d \tag{9.24}$$

where $S_t$ is his existing holding of trees and $S^d_{t+1}$ is his desired holding of trees for next period.

Using the two budget constraints, (9.20) and (9.24), and fruit market-clearing, (9.23), Walras's Law reappears for debt and trees together:

$$b_{t+1}/R_{1t} + p_t S_t = b^d_{t+1}/R_{1t} + p_t S^d_{t+1} \tag{9.25}$$

Since debt and trees are perfect substitutes at the $R_{1t}$ given by (9.22) and $p_t$ given by (9.18), any excess supply of debt (excess demand for trees) is eliminated by an infinitesimal movement in either $p_t$ or $R_{1t}$.

The Ricardian equivalence result immediately follows in this model, that taxes are irrelevant, to consumption from (9.23), and to interest rates and asset prices:

$$R^{-1}_{1t} = \beta \, E_t \, u'(d_{t+1} - g_{t+1})/u'(d_t - g_t) \tag{9.26}$$

$$p_t = \sum_{j=1}^{\infty} \beta^j \, E_t \, u'(d_{t+j} - g_{t+j})d_{t+j}/u'(d_t - g_t) \tag{9.27}$$

Only the path of GDP and government spending matters.

### Government Solvency: Are There Limits on Government Borrowing?

In chapter 6 we considered how limits on steady state debt, arising either from wealth effects of government bonds or from a maximum lending capacity of private agents, forced governments to avoid extra debt in steady state (by printing money at a rate 'consistent' with the fiscal deficit). Here we have no such limits: there are no wealth effects of debt (there is Ricardian equivalence) and private agents will take up as much debt as the government issues. So can the government issue debt without constraint?

The answer is that it can only issue debt that is 'backed' by future surpluses exactly sufficient to pay it off with its interest. If its debt is so backed, then it is said to be solvent. Solvency is guaranteed if the government budget constraint is met at all times.

This can be seen by repeated forward substitution for $b_{t+i}$ in (9.20). So

$$b_t = T_t - g_t + [T_{t+1} - g_{t+1} + b_{t+2}/R^t_{1t+1}]/R_{1t} \tag{9.28}$$

where $R^t_{1t+1}$ is the one period interest rate at $t + 1$, expected at $t$.

Continuing and using the arbitrage condition that

$$R_{jt} = \prod_{i=0}^{j-1} R^t_{1t+i}$$

we obtain:

$$b_t = T_t - g_t + \sum_{j=1}^{N} (T_{t+j} - g_{t+j})/R_{jt} + b_{t+N+1}/R_{N+1,t} \qquad (9.29)$$

Provided $b_{t+N+1}$ is increasing at a rate less than $R_{N+1,t}$ the last term $\to 0$ as $N \to \infty$, yielding:

$$b_t = T_t - g_t + \sum_{j=1}^{\infty} (T_{t+j} - g_{t+j})/R_{jt} \qquad (9.30)$$

which is the solvency condition, also called the transversality condition. This condition is equivalent to the proviso that debt must rise at a rate less than the rate of interest, as (9.29) reveals.

It may be useful to illustrate this point with an example where the net rate of interest, $r$, is constant at all times. Consider three cases.

First, let debt be increasing faster than the rate of interest. By definition (9.20):

$$\Delta b_t = r b_{t-1} + (1 + r) d_{t-1} \qquad (9.31)$$

where $d_t$ is the primary (exclusive of interest) deficit. Because $\Delta b_t/b_{t-1} > r$, $d_{t-1}$ must be positive. This is the case of Ponzi finance, where debt is run up to pay off interest and pay for extra net spending.

Suppose this situation prevails from time $N + 1$, where the remainder term of (9.29) cuts in, and let $\bar{d}$ be constant. Then the remainder can be written (using (9.29) in repeated substitution):

$$b_{t+N+1}/(1 + r)^{N+1} = -\bar{d}/(1 + r)^{N+1}[1 + (1 + r)^{-1}$$
$$+ \ldots + (1 + r)^{-N+1} + \ldots] = -\bar{d}/r(1 + r)^N \qquad (9.32)$$

More generally, let debt be growing at the constant rate $g(> r)$, so that $\Delta b_t/b_{t-1} = r + (1 + r)(d_{t-1}/b_{t-1}) = g$ and $(d_{t-1}/b_{t-1}) = (g - r)/(1 + r)$ is constant. Then the remainder term becomes:[2]

$$-\frac{1}{(1 + r)^{N+2}}[(g - r)b_{t+N+1}] \sum_{i=0}^{\infty} \frac{(1 + g)^i}{(1 + r)^i} = -\infty \qquad (9.33)$$

The present value of the government's future cash flow in (9.32) is negative and in (9.33) is infinitely negative; in both cases its debt at $t + N$, $b_{t+N}$, is valueless. In other words it will be impossible to issue debt for $t + N + 1$, $b_{t+N+1}$, to pay off $b_{t+N}$; it follows that $b_{t+N}$ itself could not have been issued, given that this was known. And so on, back down the chain to the present time, $t$. In period $t$ the government will be unable to issue any more debt, $b_{t+1}$, will therefore default on its current debt, $b_t$.

Secondly, consider the case where $g = r$. Then (9.33) becomes 0. There are neither primary deficits nor surpluses from $t + N$. The accumulated debt, $b_{t+N+1}$, is equal to the previous deficits cumulated at the rate of interest or

$$b_{t+N+1} = \sum_{i=0}^{N+1} (1+r)^i (T_{t+i} - g_{t+i}) + (1+r)^{N+1} b_t \qquad (9.34)$$

This, however, has no value, as there is no future cash flow to service it; hence there is also insufficient cash flow from $t$ onwards to pay off the current debt, $b_t$. The government is not therefore solvent; it will again be unable to issue new debt and will default on $b_t$.

Thirdly and finally, consider the case where $g < r$. Then (9.33) becomes finite and equal to

$$[\{-1/(1+r)^{N+2}\}(g-r)b_{t+N+1}(1+r)/(r-g)]$$
$$= b_{t+N+1}/(1+r)^{N+1}.$$

Hence the present value at $t$ of future surpluses from $t + N + 1$ onwards in this case is equal to that of the debt which will have been accumulated up to that point by previous deficits, $b_{t+N+1}$. The government's outstanding debt is therefore 'backed': the government could pay off its debt at any time (by just surrendering its cash flow to creditors). The essential point is that with $g < r$, there are primary surpluses from $t + N + 1$.

The government's solvency or transversality condition can therefore be seen to be the commonsense condition that after *some* date it must generate *primary surpluses*: these allow the debt to be paid off.

It may seem puzzling that even so debt can go on rising for ever, never actually being paid off. Yet this is just a trick of infinite time: if time were finite, then of course the solvency condition would force the government to produce enough primary surplus in the last period to pay off its debt. Because time is infinite, people are happy to hold the debt provided the present value of primary surpluses backs it, postponing (possibly for ever) actual repayment, knowing they can claim their money back at any time.

## The Pricing of Contingent Claims

We saw earlier that the price of an asset paying a stochastic dividend, $d_t$, was:

$$p_t = \beta \, E_t \left[ \frac{u'(c_{t+1})}{u'(c_t)} (p_{t+1} + d_t) \right] \qquad (9.35)$$

The price and the dividend is in units of the consumption good, 'fruit' or whatever. Now consider a claim which pays out one unit of the consumption good in $t + 1$ when the state of the economy, some vector $x_{t+1}$, has a value between $x_0$ and $x_1$. By extension of (9.15) its value will be:

$$q_t [x_0 \leqslant x_{t+1} \leqslant x_1] = \beta \; E_t \left\{ \frac{u'(c_{t+1})}{u'(c_t)} \, | x_0 \leqslant x_{t+1} \leqslant x_1 \right\}$$

$$= \beta \int_{x_0}^{x_1} \frac{u'(c[x_{t+1}])}{u'(c_t)} f(x_{t+1}, x_t) \; dx_{t+1} \tag{9.36}$$

$f(x_{t+1}, x_t)$ is the probability density function over $x_{t+1}$ (given that $x_t$ has occurred); integrating the area under this function gives the probability of $x_{t+1}$ lying in the range $x_0$ to $x_1$. Equation (9.36) says that the price of a contingent claim is the marginal utility of one unit next period (relative to this period's marginal utility), if $x_{t+1}$ lies in the range, times the probability of its lying in that range.

Equation (9.36) allows any contingent claim to be priced. One simply specifies the range of contingency, evaluates the marginal utility of consumption in that contingency, multiplies by the pay-off in units of the consumption good, and weights each part of the range by its probability. Equation (9.36) can also be derived directly from the consumer's maximum problem subject to a budget constraint containing the contingent claim: this is left as an exercise for the interested reader.

Contingent claims which nest other contingent claims within them (for example, a claim on two-period-ahead consumption given $x_{t+2}$ and $x_t$) must be consistent with the claims nested within them (otherwise arbitrage opportunities occur).[2] Hence, for example, a claim on consumption two periods ahead must have the same price today as the current price of a one-period-ahead claim on consumption two periods ahead times the current price of a claim on consumption one period ahead. This is exactly analogous to the arbitraging of interest rates of $n$-period-ahead maturity with the $n$ one-period interest rates for the intervening periods.

### Government Bonds as Net Wealth: Models with Intertemporal and Geographic Constraints

We saw above that, subject to the solvency condition, a government could borrow as much or as little as it liked with no effect on the economy, assuming its taxes were lump sum (distortionary taxes are another matter as we showed in an earlier chapter, where we discussed the Lucas–Stokey optimal tax-smoothing proposition) – this is Ricardian equivalence. Yet a number of authors have been impressed with the role that a government issued liability could perform by intermediating between people who may not be willing to lend directly to each other for some reason: they will still be willing to lend to a government which in turn may transfer, or lend, to others. Of course, such government bonds will generally affect economic outcomes and be net wealth.

Two main sets of reasons have been advanced why people would be unwilling to lend to some other people: one is death (the young will not lend to the old because the old have no incentive to pay it back after death), the other is geographic isolation (members of one tribe will not lend to members of another if they cannot see them again to reclaim the debt).

## Overlapping Generations Models

Samuelson's overlapping generations model, used (see chapter 6) by Barro (1974) with a bequest motive in order to re-establish Ricardian equivalence, has been used extensively by Neil Wallace and his colleagues under the assumption of inter-generational indifference (no bequests) to establish a role for government liabilities.

Suppose all generations are made up of $N$ identical agents, whose income stream in perishable consumption units is $y - \varepsilon$ and $\varepsilon$ in their youth and old age respectively: $0 < \varepsilon < y/2$ so that they obtain more income when young than old. Consumption when young and old is respectively $c_t^h(t)$ and $c_t^h(t+1)$ for the $h$th agent of generation $t$. Assume there is no investment opportunity other than a loan market, but that the government has no borrowing, tax or spending programme initially. Then we can easily show that there will be no lending by agents when young, $l_t^h$, at all: the old will not lend (because they will not be alive to be paid back) or borrow (because they cannot pay back when dead).

Assume the consumer maximizes a logarithmic utility function

$$U_t^h(c_t^h(t), c_t^h(t+1)) = \ln c_t^h(t) + \ln c_t^h(t+1)$$

subject to $y - \varepsilon - c_t^h(t) = l_t^h$ and $\varepsilon + [1 + r(t)]l_t^h = c_t^h(t+1)$

where $r(t)$ is the net rate of interest, to be determined by the clearing of the loan market (this by Walras's Law also clears the goods market). His Lagrangean is therefore:

$$J = \ln c_t^h(t) + \ln c_t^h(t+1) + \mu_t^h(t) [y - \varepsilon - c_t^h(t) - l_t^h]$$
$$+ \mu_t^h(t+1) \{ \varepsilon + [(1 + r(t)]l_t^h - c_t^h(t+1) \} \tag{9.37}$$

The first order conditions yield:

$$c_t^h(t) = c_t^h(t+1)/[1 + r(t)] \tag{9.38}$$

The consumer's life-time constraint is:

$$c_t^h(t) + c_t^h(t+1)/[1 + r(t)] = (y - \varepsilon) + \varepsilon/[1 + r(t)] \quad (9.39)$$

so that

$$c_t^h(t) = \frac{y - \varepsilon}{2} + \frac{\varepsilon}{2(1 + r(t))} \quad\quad\quad (9.40)$$

and $l_t^h = \dfrac{y - \varepsilon}{2} - \dfrac{\varepsilon/2}{1 + r(t)}$ $\quad\quad\quad (9.41)$

Market-clearing requires that

$$\sum_h l_t^h = 0$$

and hence $l_t^h = 0$ since all agents are identical. Consequently:

$$1 + r(t) = \varepsilon/(y - \varepsilon) < 1 \quad\quad\quad (9.42)$$

Negative interest rates are required to induce people to consume all of their youthful income, since no one is available to make a loan to.

Now let the government borrow (a one-period loan) to spend in the first period only, the sum $G(1) = N[(y/2) - \varepsilon]$; it pays off its debt from taxes $(\tau)$ on the young in period $T$. Its budget constraint is:

$$G(t) + L^g(t) = \sum \tau_{t-1}^h(t) + \sum \tau_t^h(t) + [1 + r(t-1)]L^g(t-1) \quad\quad (9.43)$$

where $L^g(t)$ is the loan it takes out in $t$ and it starts with $L^g(0) = 0$. In this case, this implies

$$G(1) = -L^g(1) = N[(y/2) - \varepsilon];$$

$$L^g(t) = [1 + r(t-1)]L^g(t-1); \quad T > t \geqslant 2$$

and $\sum_h l_T^h = [1 + r(T-1)]L^g(T-1)$, setting $L^g(T) = 0$ $\quad$ (9.44)

The loan market equilibrium in period 1 is now:

$$O = L^g(1) + \sum_h l_1^h = -N[(y/2) - \varepsilon] + N\left[\frac{y - \varepsilon}{2} - \frac{\varepsilon/2}{1 + r(1)}\right]$$

$$(9.45)$$

which is only satisfied if $r(1) = 0$. This government intervention has therefore raised interest rates by siphoning off the young's expenditure into loans. Subsequently, the government debt remains constant: $L^g(2) = L_g(1)$, which implies that $r(2) = 0$; and so on until $T$, when $L^g(T) = 0$ but the tax bill reduces the income of the young, and

$$0 = \sum_h l_t^h \text{ gives } r(T) = 0.$$

Thereafter, of course, the equilibrium gives $r(t) = \varepsilon/(y - \varepsilon)$ $(t > T)$, as in (9.42).

The implications for consumption patterns of this intervention are beneficial to every generation except the $T$th and beyond. Generations less than $T$ now consume:

$$c_t^h(t) = y/2 = c_t^h(t + 1) \tag{9.46}$$

whereas previously they consumed $y - \varepsilon$ and $\varepsilon$ respectively in $t$ and $t + 1$. Figure 9.3 illustrates the improvement in their welfare. The 45° line $yy$ shows each generation's consumption possibilities when young and old, provided there is some mechanism (like the government loan sequence above) to ensure that when it transfers resources to the old, the same will be done by the next generation to it. Clearly the optimal point is along the 45° line from the origin.

The $T$th generation is worse off, as its consumption pattern becomes $y/2$ in youth (because of the tax bill) and $\varepsilon$ in old age. The following generations are of course unaffected.

This would therefore appear not to be a Pareto-improving policy across all generations. However, in an economy with an infinite life, it

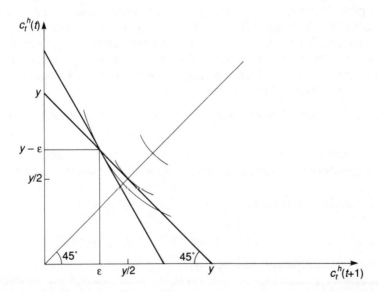

Figure 9.3   The welfare effect of consumption-smoothing in the overlapping generations model.

can be made so by deferring repayment of the government debt indefinitely: the $T$th generation then never arrives! In this case the government bond issue is a source of net wealth to the country, even if the initial output diverted to government spending, $G(1)$, is thrown away!

The gain, to repeat, lies in the ability of government bonds to effect loans from the young generation to the old. The young invest in government debt, the old pay it off; but they do not have to deal with each other directly.

### Geography: the Bewley–Townsend Model

Exactly the same point can be made about two communities, each with uneven income patterns over time, but which are separated in space rather than by time as the above generations are.

Let community A people have an income stream in perishable consumption units of $y - \varepsilon$ and $\varepsilon$ (a variable harvest say) while community B people have the stream $\varepsilon$ and $y - \varepsilon$, in even and odd periods respectively. All A and B people share identical preferences. But the A people will not lend to the B people, or vice versa, because the two groups rarely meet (they may trade but one group having traded, their next trading session is with another group); Bewley (1980) and Townsend (1980) suggest a 'turnpike' with A and B people passing each other in opposite directions, meeting once but never again. The A and B people both live for $T + 1$ periods (where we can allow $T \to \infty$); assume there are $N$ each. It is obvious that A people will consume in even and odd periods $y - \varepsilon$ and $\varepsilon$ respectively, B people $\varepsilon$ and $y - \varepsilon$; their consumption pattern will be as uneven as their income pattern. As with our overlapping generations model, a government which borrows can smooth their consumption.

Write its budget constraint per capita as:

$$g_t + l_t^g = \tau_t + (1 + r(t - 1))l_{t-1}^g \quad (T \geqslant t \geqslant 0, \text{ given } l_{-1}^g = 0)$$
$$(9.47)$$

The government levies the same tax, $\tau_t$ on everyone; $g_t$ and $l_t^g$ are per capita spending and one-period loans. Each $h$th consumer maximizes

$$\sum_{t=0}^{T} \beta^t u(c_t^h) \text{ subject to}$$

$$c_t^h + l_t^h \leqslant y_t^h + (1 + r(t - 1))l_{t-1}^h \, (T \geqslant t \geqslant 0, \text{ given } l_{-1}^h = 0).$$

The market equilibrium in loans is:

$$\tfrac{1}{2} l_t^A + \tfrac{1}{2} l_t^B + l_t^g = 0 \tag{9.48}$$

Let us for maximum simplicity assume the government merely acts as a lender and borrower, and does not use its tax or spending powers. Then $l_t^g = 0$ (net) for all $t$ and it follows from market equilibrium that

$$c_t^A + c_t^B = y \qquad (9.49)$$

The consumer's optimum in the usual way yields:

$$\frac{u'(c_t^h)}{u'(c_{t+1}^h)} = \beta(1 + r(t)) \qquad (9.50)$$

Hence, since from (9.49) $c_t^B = y - c_t^A$,

$$\frac{u'(c_t^A)}{u'(c_{t+1}^A)} = \frac{u'(y - c_t^A)}{u'(y - c_{t+1}^A)} = \beta(1 + r(t)) \qquad (9.51)$$

It follows that $c_t^A = c_{t+1}^A$ and $1 + r(t) = 1/\beta$: full consumption smoothing with the rate of interest equal to the rate of time preference. Imposing the terminal condition that all loans must be paid off (so that the present values of consumption and income are equal), and letting $T \rightarrow \infty$, yields

$$c^A[1/(1 - \beta)] = [y - \varepsilon(1 - \beta)]1/(1 - \beta^2) \qquad (9.52)$$

This is the result of equating the present values of A's constant infinite consumption stream and of A's alternating infinite income stream, starting $y - \varepsilon$. Hence

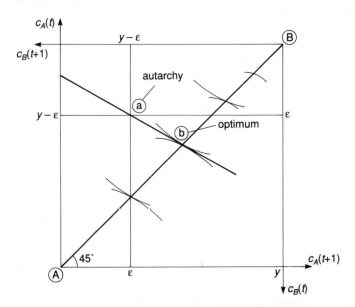

Figure 9.4  Optimal lending between coeval groups – the Bewley–Townsend model.

The 45° line in the contract curve. b is the optimal feasible point, given endowments.

$$c^A = [y - \varepsilon(1 - \beta)]/1 + \beta$$

$$\text{and } c^B = [\beta y + \varepsilon(1 - \beta)]/1 + \beta \tag{9.53}$$

This outcome is illustrated in figure 9.4, a box diagram with A's preferences running from the bottom left hand corner and B's from the top right. Because of positive time-preference, their indifference curves have a slope of $-\beta$ along the 45° line between these two corners (compare figure 9.1 where the slope is $-1$); A and B agents being identical, their contract curve lies along this 45° line. The autarchic point is at $a$; the optimum at $b$ is where the budget line going through $a$ with the slope $-(1 + r)^{-1} = -\beta$ cuts the contract curve.

## Conclusions

In this chapter we have examined the behaviour of representative agent models in a cashless society. We have seen that where loan and other contingent claim markets are complete, these claims are priced so that the expected future discounted marginal utility of consumption equals its current marginal utility. Since all agents are identical, consumption must equal (perishable) output in every period. If a government enters the market, then Ricardian equivalence holds: only government spending affects consumption and asset yields. The government's solvency condition implies that it must have enough prospective net revenue to equal in present value its outstanding debt.

Ricardian equivalence is removed if some constraint on market completeness prevents optimal loan trades being made between agents. Two such constraints were considered: overlapping generations without a bequest motive where the young will not lend to the old; and communities which are spatially separated so that loans cannot be reliably recovered. In both cases a government which borrows to finance a deficit can achieve intermediation between surplus and deficit agents.

## Notes

1 This is obtained by writing the remainder term (using (9.29) in repeated substitution) as:

$$\frac{1}{(1 + r)^{N+1}} [-d_{t+N+1} - d_{t+N+2}/(1 + r) - \dots$$

$$- d_{t+N+K}/(1 + r)^{K-1} - \dots]$$

$$= -1/(1+r)^{N+1} \left[ \frac{d_{t+N+1}}{b_{t+N+1}} \cdot b_{t+N+1} + \frac{d_{t+N+2}}{b_{t+N+2}} \cdot \frac{b_{t+N+2}}{1+r} + \dots \right]$$

$$= -\frac{(g-r)b_{t+N+1}}{(1+r)^{N+2}} \left[ 1 + \frac{1+g}{1+r} + \frac{(1+g)^2}{(1+r)^2} + \dots \right]$$

2 If this were not satisfied, agents would become infinitely wealthy by issuing debt at one maturity and buying it at another in infinite offsetting quantities.

# 10

# Money in Representative Agent Models

Representative agent models face a fundamental difficulty: money, defined as a non-interest-bearing means of payment, has no role to play unless one is created for it by an artificial constraint. Consider the models of chapter 9. In models, like Lucas's, with infinitely lived agents, there is nothing to stop trades in fruit (different sorts presumably) being paid for by an interest-bearing claim on fruit-in-general. In the Bewley–Townsend model, with parallel communities, government bonds can be used in payment. In the overlapping generations (OLG) models, again government bonds can be used. Money is inferior to interest-bearing claims precisely because it pays no interest. Nor is it persuasive to argue that to be used in transactions it cannot pay interest: bearer bonds, whose interest is written on the certificate, could be used, if not some clearing system for credit balances. The transactions costs of these methods are not generally thought to be large, certainly not relative to the rate of interest.

Accordingly, these models have a problem. On the one hand they seek to explain the economy's institutions and behaviour as the result of optimizing voluntary trading. On the other hand, one major institution – money – is ruled out by such trading.

To resolve this problem, a constraint on this trading must be assumed, which justifies the use of money. One such is Lucas's 'cash-in-advance' constraint (following Clower, 1965), whereby it is assumed that spending can only be carried out with money, which must therefore be accumulated in advance (Lucas, 1980).

Similar to this is the assumption that money 'has utility' and is an argument of the consumer's utility function. Effectively, this is being justified by the Clower constraint, and is merely an alternative way of expressing it, implying a degree of substitutability of money in transactions, whereas the cash-in-advance model assumes none.

In the Bewley–Townsend model, government bonds are assumed away, leaving only money as an exchangeable item (possibly a government liability). But why it carries no interest is not explained.

OLG models are the only ones to attempt an optimizing-agent explanation. They accept that money must offer a yield equal to that of bonds, or it cannot be held (will become valueless, with the 'price level' in terms of it becoming infinite). Then equilibrium must involve a rate of inflation (or equivalent money creation and distribution to existing holders) equal to the rate of interest.

It should not perhaps surprise us that a theory of money as the result of optimizing trades has proved so elusive. Hayek (1988) has drawn attention to the evolutionary nature of economic (and other) institutions: money precedes governments, and so also their bonds. The traditional theory of money in this vein has it that monetary tokens or generally used but easily transportable commodities were the first, primitive financial instrument available for avoiding the double coincidence of wants in exchange: these then acquired the public good characteristic of being generally acceptable, being 'money'. Other financial instruments and claims only gradually acquired the same acceptability in exchange: the modern financial system exhibits a vast spectrum that can be used in settlement via credit-balance clearing systems and permanently open markets, but this system is well up the scale of evolutionary achievement.

The Bewley–Townsend model can be thought of as examining how a primitive monetary economy behaves and values money. The models of cash-in-advance and cash-in-the-utility-function examine the behaviour of a modern monetary economy, with a spectrum of financial instruments but where money is still the only acceptable means of payment in every part of the economy: we envisage the corner shops and suchlike insisting on cash payment.

This leaves the OLG models as a case apart. They examine how money can coexist with other assets as a store of value. (Implicitly, any asset can be used for transactions; or else money's use for this gives it no advantage.)

It is not obvious what application these models have. The OLG assumption (with no bequests) breaks up inter-generational links and opens up a role for government as an inter-generational intermediary, as we saw in chapter 9 with government bonds. It is frankly difficult to see why a government would print money in such a world when bonds can be issued. (A competitive banking system paying interest on money would be a different matter.) However, a number of these models have grafted on to the OLG constraint additional constraints: that only money (not bonds) exists, and that there are regulatory requirements to use it (e.g. to pay taxes). (Incidentally, this regulatory theory of money, presumably motivated by the government's desire for revenue, is the nearest any of these models gets to an optimizing theory of why money exists.) Constraints place such OLG models alongside the Bewley–Townsend ones as examinations of economies at a rather early stage of monetary evolution.

In short, these models do not tell us *why* money exists (apart, possibly, from a regulatory theory); but they may tell us how economies with money behave. In the rest of this chapter we look at a sample of these monetary models, and consider what insights we obtain from them about the operation of a monetary economy.

## The Cash-in-advance Model

If money has no use, it becomes valueless. This is obvious enough. Consider some cowrie shells which are stated by some village chieftain to be currency: if no one needs them in order to exchange goods (and they are useless for any other purpose), then there are two possibilities. One is that they have a value in exchange: but if so, they will be spent in order to obtain that value from the goods for which they can be exchanged. Since everyone will get rid of them in this way, they fall in value until they are worthless – the other possibility.

This is worth briefly demonstrating. Suppose the chieftain (government) issues currency of $M$ per capita and will spend $M/p_0 = g_0$ where $p_t$ = the price level, $g_0$ = government spending in period 0: the government spends no more, $g_t = 0$ ($t \geqslant 1$). If there exist other assets with a gross return $R_t$, then for currency to be held it must have an equal return so that

$$p_t/p_{t+1} = R_t = (q_{t+1} + d_{t+1})/q_t \tag{10.1}$$

where $q_t$ is the price of the assets (trees) and $d_t$ their dividend (fruit). Now consider the consumer's budget constraint when the market equilibrium holds:

$$q_t \bar{s} + M/p_t + d_t = c_t + q_t \bar{s} + m_{t+1}/p_t \quad (t \geqslant 1) \tag{10.2}$$

where $\bar{s}$ = the number of trees per capita and $m_{t+1}$ = the number of currency units held for period $t + 1$.

Since $c_t = d_t$ by goods market equilibrium, it follows that

$$M/p_t = m_{t+1}/p_t;$$

that is, $M_t/p_t$ is never spent, but it grows at the rate $(R_t - 1)$ each period, so that its present discounted value is $M/p_t$, of course.

It follows that if there is market equilibrium the consumer can only spend $d_t$ in every period; and yet if $M/p_t > 0$, he will fail to spend all his wealth over his infinite lifetime; that is, he will spend all except $M/p_t$ (in present value). This is sub-optimal. The consumer will therefore attempt to spend more than $d_t$, which will drive the price level to infinity. Since $1/p_1 = 0$, money will not be held in period 0, so that $1/p_0 = 0$, and the government will be unable to spend anything

$(g_0 = 0)$.

In order to give money value, it must be given a source of usefulness. As we have seen, one way to provide this is through the Clower constraint, revived by Lucas (1980).

In Lucas's model each household has to acquire money *before* going to buy goods for consumption. Then while one member is shopping for consumption, the other householder is selling the household product for money, which is taken into the next period. Then that part of it not needed for shopping is exchanged for income-yielding assets; and the whole sequence is repeated, starting again with shopping/selling later in that period.

Begin at the start of a period, where the household has money, $M_t/p_t$, and assets: one tree, $s_{t-1} = 1$, whose price is $r_t(x_t)$, and government nominal debt, $l_t(x_t)/p_t$, where $x_t$ is the 'state' of the economy (the vector of exogenous variables). All quantities are measured per capita: everyone now goes into a securities-trading session where assets are acquired and taxes are paid. The market-clearing conditions for this are:

$$m_t^p + m_t^g = M_{t+1} \tag{10.3}$$

$$s_t = 1 \tag{10.4}$$

$$l_{t+1}^p(x_{t+1}) = l_{t+1}(x_{t+1}) \tag{10.5}$$

where $M_{t+1}$ and $l_{t+1}(x_{t+1})$ are respectively the money supply and government claims issued by the government and $m_t^p$, $l_{t+1}^p(x_{t+1})$ the private sector's demand for these; $m_t^g$ is the government's demand for money.

Having acquired money, government and private agents go into a goods trading session in which household products are sold for money to government and household consumers:

$$p_t d_t = m_{t+1} \tag{10.6}$$

is the household income carried into the next period in the form of a money holding. $d_t$ is the harvest per tree.

$$p_t g_t = m_t^g \tag{10.7}$$

$$p_t c_t \leqslant m_t^p \tag{10.8}$$

are the government's and household's consumption respectively.

Walras's Law (i.e. the government and household budget constraints together with the market clearing conditions (10.3 to 10.5)) imply that the goods market clears:

$$p_t c_t + p_t g_t = p_t d_t \tag{10.9}$$

Now consider the household's consumption decision in this framework. It maximizes

$$E_{t=0} \sum_{t=0}^{\infty} \beta^t u(c_t) \text{ subject to}$$

$$\theta_t(x_t) \geq m_t^p/p_t + \tau_t + r_t(x_t)s_t$$

$$+ 1/p_t \int l_{t+1}^p(x_{t+1}) \, n(x_{t+1}, x_t) \, dx_{t+1}$$

$$m_t^p \geq p_t c_t$$

$$\theta_{t+1}(x_{t+1}) = (p_t d_t s_t)/p_{t+1} + r_{t+1}(x_{t+1})s_t + l_{t+1}^p(x_{t+1})/p_{t+1}$$

$$+ (m_t^p - p_t c_t)/p_{t+1} \tag{10.10}$$

Equation (10.10) states that the household's beginning period real wealth, $\theta_t(x_t)$, must be spent on money, taxes ($\tau_t$), and government claims (at current price $n(x_{t+1}, x_t)$ for contingency $x_{t+1}$); that consumption can only be carried out by money; and that next period's beginning wealth will be produced by this period's income (in the form of money $= p_t d_t s_t$) deflated by next period's prices, next period's value of the trees and government claims acquired this period, and the value of any money acquired by the household before the goods trading session but not used for consumption then. If we assume, as we will, that the nominal return on bonds is positive, then there will be no such surplus money balance, because money is only useful for buying consumption goods, and the cash-in-advance constraint is binding: $m_t^p = p_t c_t$. In this case we have the Quantity Theory:

$$M_{t+1} = p_t d_t \tag{10.11}$$

The consumer's Lagrangean is then:

$$L = E_{t=0} \sum_{t=0}^{\infty} \beta^t u(c_t) - \mu_t(c_t + \tau_t + r_t(x_t)s_t$$

$$+ 1/p_t \int l_{t+1}^p(x_{t+1}) \, n(x_{t+1}, x_t) \, dx_{t+1}$$

$$- (d_{t-1}p_{t-1}s_{t-1})/p_t - r(x_t)s_{t-1} - l_t^p(x_t)/p_t) \tag{10.12}$$

The first order conditions yield:

$$n(x_{t+1}, x_t)$$

$$= \frac{\beta u'(d_{t+1} - g_{t+1}) M_{t+1} d_{t+1}}{[u'(d_t - g_t)] [M_{t+2} d_t]} f(x_{t+1}, x_t) \tag{10.13}$$

$$r_t(x_t) = \int \{\beta u'(d_{t+1} - g_{t+1})/u'(d_t - g_t)\}.$$

$$\{r_{t+1}(x_{t+1}) + M_{t+1}d_{t+1}/M_{t+2}\} f(x_{t+1}, x_t) dx_{t+1} \qquad (10.14)$$

Equation (10.13) is the price of a nominal bond which pays out when $x_{t+1}$ occurs and it is set just as it was earlier, as the expected domestic marginal utility of consumption in that event relative to its current marginal utility; except that in this case it is the marginal utility of consumption of a nominal rather than a real unit that is assessed, so that it is deflated by the price level when $x_{t+1}$ occurs. (Of course $c_t = d_t - g_t$ by the market-clearing condition.)

Equation (10.14) is the price of a real asset (the tree). Again the pricing method is the same as before but now the asset's dividend is in monetary form $(p_t d_t)$ as it can only be exchanged for money. So apart from the expected future real price

$$\int r_{t+1}(x_{t+1}) f(x_{t+1}, x_t) dx_{t+1}$$

its value depends on the expected value of the dividend received this period but spent next,

$$\int d_t p_t/p_{t+1} f(x_{t+1}, x_t) dx_{t+1}.$$

What effects does government policy have on this economy?
The government's budget constraint is:

$$g_t = \tau_t + 1/p_t \int l_{t+1}(x_{t+1}) n(x_{t+1}, x_t) dx_{t+1}$$

$$- l_t(x_t)/p_t + (M_{t+1} - M_t)/p_t \qquad (10.15)$$

Government policy consists of choosing sequences for $g_t$, $\tau_t$ and $M_t$, conditional on $x_t$, and consistently with (10.15). Now because in this economy the output must be shared between government and private consumption, it is impossible for consumption to be affected by the pattern of taxation or money supply, given the government consumption sequence. However, the money supply sequence (and so also the taxation sequence if it is altered as a result) does affect the real value of real assets (trees). Hence there are real effects of monetary policy and taxation, because the returns from real assets can only be enjoyed by being exchanged for money and then spent. It follows that if there was investment in this economy, but the returns from investment could only be enjoyed by exchange for money, then private consumption would be affected by taxation and monetary policy: the mix between private investment and consumption would be changed. Only if there were an investment vehicle (such as an indexed bond) offering consumption possibilities quite independent of the price level would this cease to be the case. But such a vehicle may be ruled out in this cash-in-advance world (even on an indexed bond the indexed dividend has to be paid at a particular time to be exchanged later for goods in monetary exchange).

## Unpleasant Monetarist Arithmetic Revisited

Let us now return to the question addressed in chapter 6: whether tighter money today will reduce inflation permanently in the absence of changes in government spending and tax sequences. We can rewrite the government budget constraint:

$$K = \frac{M_1 - M_0}{p_0} + \sum_{j=1} \int q(x_{t+j}, x_t) \frac{(M_{t+j+1} - M_{t+j})}{p_{t+j}} \, dx_{t+j} \qquad (10.16)$$

where $K$ is the present value of the $(g_t - \tau_t)$ sequence and

$$q(x_{t+j}, x_t) = \frac{\beta^j u'(c_{t+j})}{u'(c_t)} f(x_{t+j}, x_t)$$

is the present ($t$-period) real discounted value of a unit of consumption if $x_{t+j}$ occurs (that is, it is a contingent real discount rate).

Using the quantity theory, we can rewrite this:

$$K = d_0 - M_0/p_0$$
$$+ \sum_{j=1} \int q(x_{t+j}, x_t)(d_{t+j} - p_{t+j-1} d_{t+j-1}/p_{t+j}) \, dx_{t+j} \qquad (10.17)$$

If $M_1$ is lowered, $p_0$ falls ($M_0$ is given), so $M_0/p_0$ rises and there is a lower current inflation tax which must be offset by a higher future inflation tax ($p_{t+j}/p_{t+j-1}$): but because $q(x_{t+j}, x_t)$ is of the order $\beta^j$ ($c_{t+j}$ being random and stationary), future inflation has to be higher by the order $\beta^{-j}$.

## Introducing Money into Bewley–Townsend and OLG Models

In chapter 9 we showed that both the Bewley–Townsend and OLG models gave government bonds a role in intermediating between groups which would not lend to each other. However, government bonds are a relatively sophisticated instrument, coming late in economic evolution. Money came first, as a government-backed medium of exchange and store of value. It is interesting to ask how these economies would behave if there were only money to perform this intermediary function.

If money is the only available store of value, then to achieve the optimal consumption-smoothing (i.e. intermediation) that bonds achieved (in chapter 9) we require prices to be falling at the rate of time preference.

Consider now the Bewley–Townsend model. Consumers with $T$-period lives maximize

$$J = \sum_{t=0}^{\infty} \beta^t u(c_t) - \mu_t^h (p_t c_t + m_t^h - p_t y_t - m_{t-1}^h) \qquad (10.18)$$

with $m_{-1}^A = 0, m_{-1}^B = m$ given; A agents receive $y^A = \varepsilon$ (odd periods), 0 (even); B agents receive $y^B = 0$ (odd), $\varepsilon$ (even). The first order conditions are:

$$0 = \delta J/\delta c_t = \beta^t u'(c_t) - \mu_t^h p_t$$

$$\delta J/\delta m_t^h = -\mu_t^h + \mu_{t+1}^h = 0 \text{ for } m_t^h > 0$$

$$\leqslant 0 \text{ for } m_t^h = 0$$

$$0 = \delta J/\delta m_T^h = -\mu_T^h = 0 \text{ for } m_T^h > 0$$

$$\leqslant 0 \text{ for } m_T^h = 0 \qquad (10.19)$$

The last, terminal, condition implies that for money to be held in $T$ (as it must be for market clearing, i.e. $N_A m_T^A + N_B m_T^B = M$), then $-\beta^T u'(c_T)/p_T = 0$. But with $\beta^T u'(c_T) > 0$ (since $c_T < \infty$, there can be no saturation of wants), $p_T$ must be infinite: money will all be spent in the last period until it is worthless. Working back to $T - 1$, since $\mu_T^h = 0$, so will $\mu_{T-1}^h = 0$, and money will become worthless throughout. So to have a monetary economy we have to let $T \to \infty$. Agents live forever (a parable for the household which treats the interests of its descendents as its own, subject to the constant rate of time preference, $\beta$).

In this case, the terminal condition becomes for $m_T^h > 0$ $\lim_{T \to \infty} -\mu_T^h = 0$.

If prices are falling at the rate $1 - \beta$, we know that all agents will smooth their consumption optimally (as in chapter 9): consumption will be constant. Whichever agents are holding money at time $t$ have

$$u'(c_t)/p_t = \beta u'(c_{t+1})/p_{t+1} \qquad (10.20)$$

But A and B agents hold money in alternate periods (as we saw with bonds in chapter 9). Hence (10.20) holds in alternate periods for A and B agents; so it always holds for *one* set of agents. Therefore since $c_t$ and $u'$ are constant, $p_{t+1}/p_t = \beta$. Unfortunately, this violates the terminal condition, since $\mu_t^h = \beta^t u'(c_t) / (p_0 \beta^t)$ and therefore $\lim_{T \to \infty} -\mu_T^h = -u'(c_t) / p_0 \neq 0$ (unless $p_0 = \infty$).

What this means is that as time goes on the present value of money holdings (discounted by the rate of time preference) does not diminish: so people find they have surplus money and spend it. This raises $p_T$ and the path before it, and $p$ does not fall by $(1 - \beta)$ each period. This solution is therefore not an equilibrium. It follows that the Pareto-optimal solution in this model is impossible if only money, not bonds, exists.

Only equilibria where prices fall more slowly than $(1 - \beta)$ are possible. One such equilibrium is a constant price one: this is obviously interesting as money evolved because of its great stability in purchasing power. Figure 10.1 illustrates how price stability (offering a zero rate of return) achieves less than perfect consumption smoothing.

Let $p$ be constant at $\bar{p} = 1$. Then A agents, for example, who get $\varepsilon$ in odd periods, will consume $c^{**}$ in odd periods, $c^*$ in even ($c^{**} < c^*$), so that

$$u'(c^{**})/u'(c^*) = 1/\beta \tag{10.21}$$

B agents consume $c^{**}$ in even periods, $c^*$ in odd (with (10.21) holding as for A agents). $c^{**} + c^* = y$ for both sets of agents, so that $c^* = y - c^{**}$. Since there are the same numbers ($N = N_A = N_B$) of each, this also satisfies market clearing.

B agents will hold enough money at the end of odd periods to buy $c^{**}$

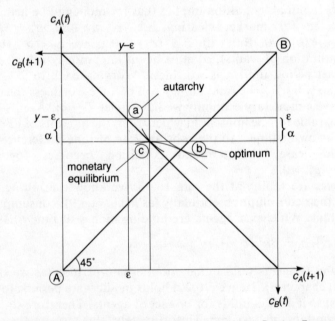

Figure 10.1 Monetary equilibrium with a static price level in the Bewley–Townsend model.

A agents move to an internal equilibrium at c, given zero interest rate: 'lend' $\alpha$ by acquiring money. B agents fail to reach an internal optimum.

in the even periods, but will run this money balance down totally in the even period. The reason is that in the even period $u'(c^{**}) > \beta u'(c^*)$, so that he would rather spend then than wait and will exhaust his money holdings in the attempt: in terms of the first order conditions, he is at a corner solution with $m_t^h = 0$ ($t$ even). A agents follow the same pattern in the alternate period. The result is that the money supply is passed from A to B each period.

It is possible to get to Pareto-optimal equilibrium if some way can be found to pay interest on money while still satisfying the terminal condition. For example, if prices fall at $1 - \beta$ per period and the money supply is reduced at this rate also by lump sum taxes, then this condition will be satisfied. But it is, of course, a highly artificial scenario.

## Money in the OLG Model

In the OLG example of chapter 9, we found that, if the government borrowed to finance a transfer to the initial old generation, and chose this transfer well, it could perfectly smooth each generation's consumption pattern across its youth and old age. By failing ever to pay off the loan it maintains this perfect smoothing for ever. The real interest rate is zero; because the economy is not growing, this is in this example the

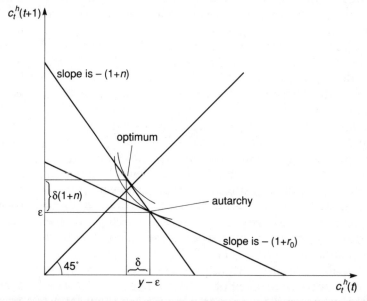

Figure 10.2   Feasible reallocation of consumption from zero saving (autarchy) to optimal intergenerational lending in government bonds – the overlapping generations model with growth, $n$.

Pareto-optimal outcome. In this model if the economy were growing at the rate $n$, the Pareto-optimum would be where $r = n$.

This is illustrated in figure 10.2, which shows the zero-saving equilibrium (consumption is $y - \varepsilon$ in youth and $\varepsilon$ in old age) with $r = r_0$ and the feasible reallocation along the line $- (1 + n)$, achieved when $r = n$. This reallocation is feasible because the next generation is $(1 + n)$ times the current; so if $\delta$ consumption is transferred by each of the young to the old each period, then each of the old, being less in number, will enjoy $\delta(1 + n)$. By giving up $\delta$ consumption to the old today then the young guarantee an old age in which they will enjoy $\delta(1 + n)$. (To achieve this equilibrium, the government must increase its debt and spending each period at the rate $1 + n$.)

In the example of chapter 9, where $n = 0$ and bonds paid zero interest, we could easily think of money performing exactly the same function as bonds. Let the government issue currency, $H(t)$, instead of bonds and let the price level be $p(t)$. Then we can treat $H(t)/p(t) = -L^g(t)$ as equivalent to the previous bonds, and the equilibrium would be the same. If currency issue were to be kept constant at $H_0, p(t)$ would then be constant at $p_0 : p(t + 1)/p(t) = 1$, implying a zero interest rate on money, the Pareto-optimal equilibrium as before.

So in this case, money could perform the same consumption-smoothing function as bonds, justifying its role in early societies with no growth and an unsophisticated financial market. It would also be possible for any government to swap bonds for money with no effect on anything (prices, consumption, interest rates) in the economy: since $H'(t)/p(t) + L^g{}'(t) = H(t)/p(t) + L^g(t)$ there is no need for the new mix of bonds and money $H'(t) + L^g{}'(t)$ to change $p(t)$ and, given that government liabilities are the same overall, nothing else changes either. This is the 'real bills' doctrine that open market operations altering the supply of money have no effect.

Matters become more complicated in growing economies, where the optimal $r = n > 0$. In an optimal monetary equilibrium prices would have to be falling (or money being printed and distributed) at the rate $n$. For this to occur the demand for real money balances (the net savings of the young) must be positive and the government's primary deficit must permit these balances to grow at exactly $n$; both conditions may fail to hold, and there may also be problems of stability. An enormous literature exists exploring the properties of these and other equilibria: for an introduction to it see Sargent (1987).

The main difficulty with using OLG models for the study of monetary economies is their emphasis on money as a store of value: this and the arbitrage between money and other financial assets produces somewhat strange results. For primitive economies without alternatives to money, however, OLG monetary models offer interesting insights.

## Conclusions

The models in this chapter do not attempt to explain why money exists, in preference to other financial instruments. But on the assumption that such other financial instruments have not been developed, the Bewley–Townsend model does explain how money permits two parallel communities, which are too remote from each other to lend directly to each other, to lend indirectly via money holding. The OLG model shows how money can be a store of value which permits one generation to lend to the next indirectly. The first model we looked at, the cash-in-advance, assumes, but does not explain, the use of money for transactions; given that, it models how an economy with its full panoply of other financial instruments would behave. Because returns on other assets have to be turned into money before they can be enjoyed, changes in monetary policy can alter the expected rate of return on these and so have real effects.

# 11

# Testing the Rational Expectations Hypothesis

A hypothesis is no better or worse than its empirical performance: as we indicated in chapter 1, the idea of rationality in the use of information is a noteworthy part of the methodology of economics which supposes Rational Economic Man (Brunner and Meckling, 1977; Cleaver, 1986), but it may well fail to perform empirically, like the rest of this methodology. In the remainder of this book, we consider the ways in which the RE hypothesis has been tested empirically. We begin in this chapter with the efficient market hypothesis, which is a joint hypothesis made up of rational expectations and a hypothesis about how expected returns are determined. In chapter 12, we discuss the evidence assembled by Robert Barro and others to test whether output is determined by the New Classical model or not. In chapter 13, we review direct tests of rational expectations using survey data on actual expectations. We then turn to the estimation of complete rational expectations models: some such models are 'deep structure' (where the parameters are those of tastes and technology, presumably invariant to changes in the processes driving the exogenous variables, including policy) but most are 'shallow structure', the parameters being those of aggregate supply and demand curves.

The purpose of this chapter is to consider the relationship between the concepts of financial market efficiency and rational expectations. A particular feature of financial markets is that trading can occur, in principle, almost continuously, and the market price is free to move to eradicate any imbalance between demand and supply. Furthermore, since the assets traded (stocks, bonds, commodities) can be resold or traded in future periods it follows that financial markets are, more obviously than others, speculative in the technical sense that expectations of future asset prices affect current asset prices.

We begin this chapter by defining the concept of an efficient capital market and contrast this with the concept of a perfect capital market. A brief review of the empirical evidence for efficiency in asset markets in general is then presented.

We then go on to consider two important applications of efficiency in macroeconomics and the evidence in these areas. First, we discuss a model of the open economy and the exchange rate based on that of

Dornbusch (1976), in which goods and labour markets are typified by sticky prices but financial markets, including the market for foreign exchange, are efficient. The model has the property that the exchange rate in response to permanent change in the money stock will, in the short run, 'overshoot' its long-run value. We extend the discussion to models in which the goods and labour markets are in continuous equilibrium; and we find that here too an efficient exchange market will exhibit overshooting.

Secondly, we consider the behaviour of long-run interest rates under market efficiency, and show that they will follow a random walk. We conclude with some general implications of efficiency for macroeconomic model building.

## Efficiency, Perfection and Asset Pricing in Capital Markets

A capital or asset market is defined to be efficient when prices (e.g. stock prices, bond prices or exchange rates) fully and instantaneously reflect all available relevant information. Fama (1970) has defined three types of market efficiency, according to the extent of the information reflected in the market:

1   *Weak-form efficient*   A market is weak-form efficient if it is not possible for a trader to make abnormal returns by developing a trading rule based on the past history of prices or returns.
2   *Semi-strong-form efficient*   A market where a trader cannot make abnormal returns using a trading rule based on publicly available information. Examples of publicly available information are past money supply data, company financial accounts, or reports in periodicals such as the *Investor's Chronicle*.
3   *Strong-form efficient*   Where a trader cannot make abnormal returns using a trading rule based on any information source, whether public or private.

These three forms of efficiency represent a crude partitioning of all possible information systems into three broad categories, the precise boundaries of which are not easily defined. However, they are useful, as we shall see, for classifying empirical research on market efficiency. As their names suggest, strong-form efficiency implies semi-strong efficiency which in turn implies weak-form efficiency, while of course the reverse implications do not hold.

It is useful to distinguish between the concept of an efficient capital market and that of a perfect capital market. A perfect capital market could be defined as one in which the following conditions hold (see Copeland and Weston, 1988):

1   Markets are informationally efficient; that is, information is costless and it is received simultaneously by individuals.
2   Markets are frictionless; that is, there are no transactions costs or taxes, assets are perfectly divisible and marketable and there are no constraining regulations.
3   There is perfect competition in product and securities markets, that is agents are price-takers.
4   All individuals are rational expected-utility maximizers.

If conditions 1 to 4 were met (and assuming no significant distortions elsewhere in the economy), the capital market would be allocationally efficient, in that prices would be set to equate the marginal rates of return for all producers and savers, and of course consequently savings are optimally allocated. The notion of capital market efficiency is therefore much less restrictive. An element of imperfect competition in product markets would imply capital market imperfection; nevertheless, the stock market could determine a security price which fully reflected the present value of the stream of expected future monopoly profits. Consequently the stock market could still be efficient in the presence of imperfection.

Asset prices, in order to give the correct signals to traders, must fully and instantaneously reflect all available information.[1] However, as pointed out by, for example, Grossman and Stiglitz (1976, 1980), it cannot be the case that market prices do fully and instantaneously reflect all available information. If this were so, agents would have no incentive for collecting and processing information, since it would already be reflected in the price, which each individual is assumed to be able to observe costlessly. It is the possibility of obtaining abnormal profits in the course of arbitraging which provides the incentive to collect and process new information. In the Grossman and Stiglitz model, individuals choose to become informed or remain uninformed, and in equilibrium each individual is indifferent between remaining uninformed on the one hand, and collecting information (or buying the expertise of brokers), so becoming informed, on the other. This is because after deducting information costs each action offers the same expected utility.

Nevertheless, a reasonable interpretation of empirical tests of the efficient market hypothesis is, given that the data are collected at discrete intervals, that the process of arbitrage has occurred *within* the period. Consequently the implications of different available information can then be analysed without modelling the process of arbitrage itself (Begg, 1982) and this is the usual assumption in empirical work.

Because all definitions of market efficiency invoke the concept of abnormal returns, we are also required, for empirical work, to have a theory of the equilibrium expected rate of return for assets. Tests of market efficiency are conducted after allowance for the equilibrium rate of return. If the riskiness of an asset does not change over time (or conversely if its risk changes randomly over time) then, for example, weak-form efficiency implies that there should not be an extrapolative pattern in the time series of returns. If there were a recurring pattern of any type, traders who recognized the pattern would use it to make abnormal profits. The very effort to use such patterns would, under the efficiency hypothesis, lead to their elimination.

The equilibrium expected return on assets is a central topic in modern portfolio theory and the interested reader is directed to, for example, Copeland and Weston (1988) for a full discussion (Allen (1985) provides a helpful introduction). The following brief account of one such and widely used theory, the capital asset pricing model (CAPM), must suffice here.

## The Capital Asset Pricing Model

Only if traders are risk neutral[2] will they be indifferent to the variability of the returns (i.e. the risk) on their portfolio. Risk averse individuals will be concerned about aggregate portfolio risk and will require a risk premium on each asset (or class of assets). By combining assets in the portfolio it is possible to diversify away some of the risk (the 'unsystematic' risk) associated with an asset. However, to the extent that the returns on an asset move with the market, there will be a component of risk (systematic risk) that cannot be diversified away. Assuming optimal portfolio diversification, the risk premium reflects the asset's systematic risk and hence its contribution to the overall variability of returns on the portfolio. This premium will be included in the equilibrium expected rate of return on this asset, in addition to the general rate of return on the portfolio.

The algebra of the CAPM theory is straightforward. All investors are assumed, as in standard portfolio analysis, to maximize their expected utility subject to their portfolio wealth constraint: this yields for each investor an optimally diversified holding of each asset in terms of the expected returns on all assets. It is convenient to aggregate this equation across investors and refer to the result as the asset demand of a 'typical' investor (but this does not imply that all investors are the same; it is merely an expression indicating averaging). The CAPM's contribution is then to note that at any time there will be a certain stock of each asset outstanding in the market which must be held in equilibrium. To be held, its expected return (and so its price) must satisfy the asset demand equation of the typical investor: in other words, this equation is turned round and solved for the necessary expected return in terms of the outstanding asset quantity. As the quantity of each asset rises, however risky it may be, it contributes only a little to the total risk on the whole market portfolio because it forms only a small part of this diversified whole; hence the rise in necessary expected return (fall in price) is negligible and we can talk of 'the' required expected return on an asset, independently of its quantity outstanding. Clearly this must not be pushed too far: some assets (e.g. dollar liabilities in currency portfolios) are outstanding in very large quantities and their own risk cannot be fully diversified away.

Assume three assets, one of which yields a safe return (ignore inflation risk, on the grounds that inflation can be easily predicted over short time horizons). The typical investor maximizes then:

$E_t \, U(W_{t+1})$ with respect to $w_1$ and $w_2$ subject to

$$W_{t+1} = w_1 \, R_{1t} + w_2 R_{2t} + (1 - w_1 - w_2) \, R_t \qquad (11.1)$$

where $w_i$ is the share in the investor's portfolio of asset $i$, $R_{it}$ is the actual return during the period, $W_{t+1}$ is his end-period wealth expressed as an index (beginning period wealth = 1), $U$ is his utility function $(U' > 0, U'' < 0)$, and $E_t$ is his expectation formed at the beginning of the period when he takes his investment decision.

Take a second order Taylor series expansion $U(W_{t+1})$ around $E_t (W_{t+1})$:

$$U(W_{t+1}) = U(E_t \, W_{t+1}) + U' \cdot (W_{t+1} - E_t \, W_{t+1})$$
$$+ \tfrac{1}{2} U'' \cdot (W_{t+1} - E_t \, W_{t+1})^2 + \dots \qquad (11.2)$$

Ignoring higher order terms, the expectation of this is:

$$E_t \, U(W_{t+1}) = U(E_t \, W_{t+1}) + U' \cdot (E_t \, W_{t+1} - E_t \, W_{t+1})$$
$$+ \tfrac{1}{2} U'' \cdot E_t \, (W_{t+1} - E_t \, W_{t+1})^2$$
$$= U(w_1 \, E_t \, R_{it} + w_2 \, E_t \, R_{2t} + \{1 - w_1 - w_2\} R_t)$$
$$+ \tfrac{1}{2} U'' \, (w_1^2 \, \sigma_1^2 + w_2^2 \sigma_2^2 + 2w_1 w_2 \sigma_{12}) \qquad (11.3)$$

where $\sigma_{ij} = E_t \, ([R_{it} - E_t \, R_{it}][R_{jt} - E_t \, R_{jt}])$, the covariance between the returns of assets $i$ and $j$, and $\sigma_i^2 =$ the variance of $i$'s return.

The first order conditions are:

$$\begin{bmatrix} E_t \, R_{1t} - R_t \\ E_t \, R_{2t} - R_t \end{bmatrix} = \frac{-U''}{U'} \begin{bmatrix} \sigma_1^2 & \sigma_{12} \\ \sigma_{12} & \sigma_2^2 \end{bmatrix} \begin{bmatrix} w_1 \\ w_2 \end{bmatrix} \qquad (11.4)$$

expressed in the CAPM manner with required expected asset returns as the dependent variable vector (the standard portfolio analysis has the asset shares as the dependent variables): $w_1$ and $w_2$ are given by the outstanding stocks of assets 1, 2 and the safe asset in the overall market. $\dfrac{-U''}{U'} = p$ measures risk aversion.

The expected return on asset 1, for example, is:

$$E_t\, R_{1t} = R_t + p(w_1\sigma_1^2 + w_2\sigma_{12})$$
$$= R_t + pw(x_1[\sigma_1^2 - \sigma_{12}] + \sigma_{12}) \tag{11.5}$$

where $x_1$ is the share of asset 1 in the risky part of the market portfolio and $w$ is the share of the risky part in the total market. Suppose we regard asset 1 as being a single asset and asset 2 as being an average of all the other assets in the risky market, that is essentially 'the' risky market portfolio. Then (11.5) reveals that the expected return on a single asset consists of the safe return plus a risk premium reflecting risk aversion ($p$), the overall share of risky assets in the whole market ($w$) and the covariance between asset 1 and the risky market ($\sigma_{12}$), 'systematic risk': there is also a small component in the risk premium for the extent to which risk on asset 1 exceeds this covariance – 'diversifiable risk' – but this has a negligible effect because it is multiplied by $x_1$, the small share of asset 1 in the risky market. So provided asset 1 is small in relation to the market, its risk can be virtually totally diversified away and barely affects the expected return.

We can make (11.5) observationally operational by now letting asset 1 embrace the whole risky market. Then $x_1 = 1$ and we have:

$$E_t\, R_{mt} = R_t + pw\sigma_m^2 \tag{11.6}$$

where $m$ is the whole risky portfolio. From this it follows that:

$$pw = (E_t\, R_{mt} - R_t)/\sigma_m^2 \tag{11.7}$$

This means we can rewrite our single asset's required return as

$$E_t\, R_{it} = R_t + \{x_i[\sigma_i^2 - \sigma_{im}] + \sigma_{im}\}(\sigma_m^2)^{-1}(E_t\, R_{mt} - R_t)$$
$$= R_t + \beta_i(E_t\, R_{mt} - R_t) \tag{11.8}$$

$(E_t\, R_{mt} - R_t)$ is the excess return required on a unit of the average portfolio: it is therefore 'the cost of average risk'. Individual assets command higher or lower excess returns according to their 'beta', $\beta_i$, which measures their systematic risk – as illustrated in figure 11.1.

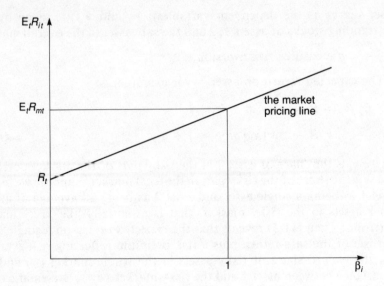

Figure 11.1   The pricing of a security.

## Other Models of Equilibrium Expected Returns

A related idea to the CAPM assumes that aggregate market risk is dominated by several sources of risk: principal component analysis can be used to separate these out. Thus there is not one but several market 'risks' or variables which are uncorrelated (for example, one variable might be a measure of the world business cycle, another might be the North–South terms of trade): the expected return associated with taking each risk is priced exactly as above – now think of 'asset 1' and 'asset 2' as being respectively 'exposure' to 'risk 1' and 'risk 2': that is, you buy £1 worth of assets combined in such a way that their return is correlated perfectly with variable 1, and similarly for variable 2. These fundamental risks being priced, each asset is then priced, by arbitrage, according to its amount of each risk. This is the arbitrage pricing theory (APT), due to Ross (1976).

In chapters 9 and 10 we dug deeper still, with Lucas's theory of asset pricing. In this, the expected gross return on any asset equals the expected ratio of the marginal utility of current consumption to that of the future consumption the asset will yield, discounted by time preference. Theoretically compelling as this is, it is not empirically operational until we have detailed the error structure of the model and the shape of the utility function. It is best thought of as a way of giving a theoretical basis for $U(W_{t+1})$ and so of $p$ in the above empirical CAPM and APT analyses.

## Rational Expectations and Market Efficiency

The semi-strong-form efficient markets model, i.e. that based on publicly available information, is an application of the concept of rational expectations, although this was not stressed in the early literature on efficiency, which goes back much further than the rational expectations literature. If expectations are non-rational, then publicly available information will not be reflected in asset prices and systematic abnormal profit opportunities will be available. This can be seen simply enough by noting that market agents have to know the model governing prices (or act as if they know it) in order to eliminate abnormal expected returns; if the model governing expected prices is different from that governing actual prices, there will be systematic abnormal returns available in the market.

Strong-form efficiency also implies that agents have rational expectations, since they must know how to use all sorts of private information as well as public; where strong-form efficiency differs from semi-strong is about the effects of private information on the market (fully discounted in strong-form, not at all in semi-strong), but this is a difference of assumptions about behaviour in response to expectations, not about expectations-formation itself.

Not quite the same is true of weak-form efficiency. In this case, since they make efficient use only of the past history of prices, they must know the time series model governing prices; strictly speaking this does not imply knowledge of the underlying structural model, since there will be generally insufficient identifying restrictions. Nevertheless, in practice, with limited samples and structural change, recovery of the time-series parameters by market agents from the data can effectively be ruled out. It is therefore natural, if not necessary, to assume in this case too that agents have rational expectations and so know the underlying model, from which they are then able to derive the time-series parameters.

While, therefore, market efficiency can be regarded as implying rational expectations, rational expectations does not imply market efficiency. Market efficiency is a joint hypothesis about expectations and market behaviour (specifically, the model of equilibrium expected returns). The main hypothesis about behaviour is the capital asset pricing model; and in empirical tests more detailed assumptions must also be made about how equilibrium returns will move. Further hypotheses concern the behaviour of the agents with access to different sets of 'available' information. Under weak-form efficiency, active market participants are assumed to make effective use only of the past history of prices in their market; one theoretical basis for this has been in the costs of obtaining and processing wider information (Feige and Pierce, 1976). Under semi-strong-form efficiency, the assumption made is the usual one in rational expectations macro models that active agents use all publicly available information, presumed to be useable at zero or low cost. Finally, in the strong-form case it is assumed that those agents with access to private information deploy or influence indirectly funds to eliminate expected returns from this source of information; there are, however, problems with this, since private information cannot be sold at a fair price (once divulged it is valueless, but before divulgence it is impossible for the buyer to assess) and those with access have, by definition, in general only limited funds.

While rational expectations macro models do not always assume market efficiency, it has become increasingly common for them to assume semi-strong efficiency in financial markets. The capital asset pricing model is widely accepted by macroeconomists, the assumption of costless public information is of course shared and the equilibrium expected rate of return is easily endogenized within the model. We will be examining examples of these macro models later in this chapter.

### Empirical Evidence on Market Efficiency

Our interest here is in the empirical evidence that testing for market efficiency yields on the rational expectations hypothesis. In these tests, either part of the joint hypothesis may fail: the model of equilibrium expected returns or the RE hypothesis. But this is unavoidable in testing a hypothesis about expectations which are not directly observable.

The basis of the tests is the property of rational expectations that any difference of outcome from the expected outcome is unforecastable from available information. Thus:

$$R_{it} = E_t R_{it} + v_{it} \tag{11.9}$$

So that $v_{it}$ is independent of $E_t R_{it}$, the rational expectation. Substituting the determinants of $E_t R_{it}$ from CAPM, for example, gives:

$$R_{it} = R_t + q_{it} + v_{it} \tag{11.10}$$

where $q_{it} = pw[x_1(\sigma_1^2 - \sigma_{12}) + \sigma_{12}]$ from (11.5) could be posited as a constant risk-premium, $q_i$. In that case (11.10) can be estimated by ordinary least squares (with the coefficient on $R_t$ constrained to unity), and the estimated error term, $\hat{v}_{it}$, should be independent of all information available at the beginning of period $t$: not merely past $\hat{v}_{it}$ (weak form), but also all relevant data (such as money supply, inflation and growth). It is also possible to estimate (11.10) freely, in which case the coefficient on $R_t$ should not be significantly different from unity, a further check on the joint hypothesis: the other tests apply as before.

A variant of this test exploits the identity:

$$R_{it} = \log p_{it+1} - \log p_{it} + d_{it} \tag{11.11}$$

where $p_{it+1} =$ price of asset $i$ at end of period $t$, and $d_{it} =$ any payment made during period $t$ (such as a dividend). Equation (11.10) can then be rewritten:

$$\log p_{it+1} - \log p_{it} = R_t - d_{it} + q_{it} + v_{it} \tag{11.12}$$

If $d_{it}$ is known at the start of $t$, as is often the case, then (11.12) can be estimated as (11.10) but treating $(R_t - d_{it})$ as a single variable. If $d_{it}$ is not known, then $(v_{it} - d_{it})$ is obtained as the estimated error. In either case the log of $p_{it}$ follows a random walk with drift, i.e. the percentage change in the asset price is independent of previous information. A further implication of (11.10) is that any trading rule, $TR$, which uses information at the start of $t$, including past $\hat{v}_{it}$, to buy and sell asset $i$, intending to make profits because

$$E[R_{it} - E_t \, R_{it}] \mid TR > 0 \tag{11.13}$$

must fail since, by (11.9),

$$E[R_{it} - E_t \, R_{it}] = 0 \tag{11.14}$$

whatever trading strategy is followed, including buy and hold (do nothing). When transactions costs of trading are added in, such trading rules will do worse, therefore, than buy and hold.

All the above tests have been applied across the whole spectrum of asset markets in a very large literature. Any market clearly can be treated, provided the asset return and the safe asset return can be suitably defined. This is not in general difficult for domestic markets, where the safe return is usually taken to be the rate of interest on short-term deposits: inflation risk is usually ignored on the grounds that inflation is forecast over short-term horizons (mostly of a quarter or a month in these studies). One such market of great importance for macroeconomics is long-term bonds: we discuss this and how it relates to the economy later in this chapter.

For international markets there is more of a problem. This can be overcome by arbitrarily deciding on a numeraire currency in which there is a safe return: other assets' returns are then defined in this currency and the risk premia derived using covariances in terms of this currency. This gives a straightforward required expected return for investors residing in this currency area. However, investors residing in currency areas other than that of the numeraire currency will obtain utility by converting returns into their own currencies for consumption in their area of residence: their exchange risks create an additional risk-premium for them. The equilibrium expected return on an international asset is a weighted average of the required expected returns across investors residing in all currency areas (Adler and Dumas, 1984).

The foreign exchange market in particular has been looked at particularly exhaustively in this way, and is clearly of crucial interest for macroeconomics. Later in this chapter we develop an example of a macroeconomic model of the generic type discussed in chapter 9 and discuss some macroeconomic implications of efficient markets. To test the efficiency of the foreign exchange market, it is usual to take the market in short-term deposits and treat

$$R_{it} = R_t + S_{t+1} - S_t \tag{11.15}$$

that is, the return on a country's deposits adjusted for exchange rate conversion into a numeraire currency, say the dollar: $S_t$ is the exchange rate (dollars per domestic currency) at the start of the period, $R_t$ is the domestic deposit interest rate. Then the equivalent of (11.10) will be

$$(R_t + S_{t+1} - S_t) = R_t^\$ + q_{it} + v_{it} \tag{11.16}$$

where $q_{it}$ is the international risk-premium on a domestic currency deposit. Clearly, treating this as constant is a far more heroic assumption than doing the equivalent for domestic assets. It is possible to concentrate the test of efficiency on the exchange market alone. Under normal assumptions of currency convertibility, arbitrage between the spot rate, $S_t$, forward rate, $F_t^{t+1}$ (at the beginning of $t$ for the beginning of $t + 1$) and the interest differential implies that the following covered arbitrage condition must hold:

$$R_t + F_t^{t+1} - S_t = R_t^\$ \tag{11.17}$$

Substituting this into (11.16) yields

$$S_{t+1} = F_t^{t+1} + q_{it} + v_{it} \tag{11.18}$$

which too can be tested in the same way as (11.10).

It is impossible to do justice to the empirical results from this vast literature, even in the areas of most interest to macroeconomics, i.e. foreign exchange and international bond markets. Large scale surveys available include Baillie and MacMahon (1989), Macdonald (1988), Levich (1985) and Adler and Dumas (1984).

In the early days of these tests, the general opinion of researchers emerged in favour of market efficiency. A typical view was expressed by Mussa (1979, p. 51): 'spot and forward exchange rates exhibit many of the behavioural characteristics . . . that are consistent with the efficient markets theory.'

More recently, doubts have grown as more and more tests have rejected the basic model in (11.10) with $q_{it}$ constant at $q_i$. Given the difficulty of sustaining this, debate has revolved around whether the model of equilibrium expected returns or the RE hypothesis is at fault. Yet another possibility – discussed in the appendix to this chapter – is that the available information set has not accurately allowed for only partial information: full knowledge of some data, including revisions, is often not available for a long time.

One major possible fault in the equilibrium model is that $q_{it}$ is variable; since it is of course necessarily correlated with currently available data, that would account for the non-independence of such data of $\hat{v}_{it}$. At this time, in spite of numerous suggested models for such variability, no conclusive way of discriminating between a variable risk premium and failure of the REH has been found.

We now turn from direct testing of market efficiency to some further implications in macroeconomic models, both for other tests of a less direct sort and for overall model properties.

## Aspects of Macroeconomic Behaviour under Market Efficiency

### Long-run Interest Rates under Market Efficiency

Government bonds can typically be regarded by investors as free of default risk. Bonds do have different coupon rates, but are essentially similar except that the various bonds differ in their term to full maturity. For an individual trader, long-run bonds are substitutable for short-run bonds, since it is possible for him to hold a series of short bonds rather than a long bond over the same holding period, or conversely to hold a long bond for a short period and then sell it rather than hold a short bond to maturity.

More formally, assume initially that traders are completely certain of the future and that we can ignore the complication which can occur due to periodic coupon payments; that is, we treat all bonds as pure discount bonds, so that the return is simply the discount from par at which the bond is sold at the beginning of the period relative to the redeemed par price at the end of the period. Then the following condition must hold:

$$(1 + R_t^k)^k = (1 + R_t)(1 + R_{t+1})(1 + R_{t+2}) \ldots (1 + R_{t+k-1})$$

$$(11.19)$$

The left hand side of (11.19) is simply the rate of return on holding a $k$-period bond until maturity. The right side of (11.19) is the rate of return implied by holding a one-period bond for one period, then reinvesting the proceeds (principal plus interest) in a one-period treasury bond for the next period and so on.

By taking logarithms and recalling that for small values of $Z$, log $(1 + Z)$ can be approximated by $Z$, we can rewrite (11.19) as:

$$R_t^k = 1/k(R_t + R_{t+1} + R_{t+2} + \ldots + R_{t+k-1}) \tag{11.20}$$

In other words (11.20) tells us that long-run interest rates are simply averages of future interest rates over the time period to maturity. It tells us, for instance, that if short-run interest rates remain constant for the indefinite future, then long rates will be equal to short rates. Conversely, if future short rates are expected to fall, the current long rate will be below the short rate. The relationship is known as the expectations theory of the term structure of interest rates.

When we relax the assumption of perfect knowledge of the future and recognize that traders can observe the current long rate $R_t^k$ and the current one-period short rate $R_t$, it follows if traders are risk neutral that:

$$R_t^k = 1/k[R_t + \mathsf{E}_t \, R_{t+1} + \mathsf{E}_t \, R_{t+2} + \ldots + \mathsf{E}_t \, R_{t+k-1}] \tag{11.21}$$

If traders are risk averse, then we must add a risk-premium $r$ to the right-hand side of (11.21), but this does not affect the argument, provided it is constant. Consequently:

$$R_{t-1}^k = 1/k[R_{t-1} + \mathsf{E}_{t-1} \, R_t + \mathsf{E}_{t-1} \, R_{t+1} + \ldots + \mathsf{E}_{t-1} \, R_{t+k-2}] \tag{11.22}$$

Subtracting (11.22) from (11.21) we obtain:

$$R_t^k - R_{t-1}^k = 1/k[\, (R_t - \mathsf{E}_{t-1} \, R_t) + (\mathsf{E}_t \, R_{t+1} - \mathsf{E}_{t-1} \, R_{t+1})$$

$$+ \ldots + (\mathsf{E}_t \, R_{t+k-2} - \mathsf{E}_{t-1} \, R_{t+k-2})] + 1/k(\mathsf{E}_{t-1} \, R_{t+k-1} - R_{t-1}) \tag{11.23}$$

It follows from the assumption of rational expectations that the revision terms in square brackets can occur only as a consequence of news. Thus (11.23) simplifies to:

$$R_t^k - R_{t-1}^k = \varepsilon_t + 1/k(\mathsf{E}_{t-1} \, R_{t+k-1} - R_{t-1}) \tag{11.24}$$

Clearly, if $k$ is sufficiently large, as it would be for, say, undated securities $(k \to \infty)$, then, since the difference between $\mathsf{E}_{t-1} \, R_{t+k-1}$ and $R_{t-1}$ cannot be infinite (owing to the usual terminal conditions), (11.24) simplifies to :

$$R_t^k - R_{t-1}^k = \varepsilon_t \tag{11.25}$$

This striking result tells us that for sufficiently long dated bonds, assuming that risk-premiums are relatively constant, the long-run interest rate should follow a random walk. Consequently, no information available at time $t - 1$ should allow us to predict systematic changes in the long-run interest rate.

We notice that market efficiency does not imply that changes in *short-run* nominal rates of interest need be random. Movements in short-run rates will be dependent on the precise model structure. The random walk property only applies to long-term interest rates under the precise assumptions outlined above.

### Open Economy Models with Efficient Financial Markets

In Chapter 8 we set out the general behaviour of macro models of the open economy with efficient markets and New Classical price behaviour, under fixed and floating exchange rates. Here we focus in more detail on the behaviour of nominal exchange rates under floating, under varying assumptions about price behaviour. This will illustrate the role of financial efficiency *per se* in open macro models.

Our first model is based on that outlined by Dornbusch (1976) in his seminal paper. For simplicity it is assumed that (11.16) holds exactly with risk-premium $q_{it} = 0$ (i.e. transactions costs are negligible and international assets are perfect substitutes). Consider an agent who is faced with the choice between holding a domestic or foreign bond for the duration of one period (say 90 days). The rates of interest in the foreign country and in the domestic country are given by $R_F$ and $R$ respectively. Since the bonds are perfect substitutes, asset market equilibrium requires that the expected rates of return on the two bonds be equal. This expected rate of return has two components. The first component is the interest rate on the bond, which we can assume to be known at $t$; the second component is the expected capital gain or loss from exchange rate changes during the 90-day period.

It follows that the condition for equilibrium is:

$$R_t = R_{Ft} - E_t S_{t+1} + S_t \tag{11.26}$$

where $S$ is the logarithm of the current exchange rate (foreign currency per domestic unit) and $E_t S_{t+1}$ is the expectation of the rate in period $t + 1$. A rise in $S$ in our notation represents an appreciation of the home currency. Equation (11.26) therefore states that the interest rate differential in favour of domestic bonds must be equal to the expected depreciation of the exchange rate.

For example, if the domestic currency pays 12 per cent interest and the foreign currency pays 4 per cent interest, a domestic investor buying foreign currency at the beginning of the period and converting back at the end of the period will, assuming the domestic currency depreciates by 8 per cent, expect to finish up with sufficient domestic currency to make him indifferent between holding domestic or foreign bonds.

We may note as above that there is a forward market for foreign exchange (i.e. traders can at time $t$ contract to trade foreign currency at time $t + 1$), and that the forward rate is the direct measure of the market's expectation of the future exchange rate (since, in the forward market, large transactors are required to put up only very small amounts of money as 'margin requirements', there is no need to discount). Under expectations, the forward rate should be an unbiased predictor of future spot rates, as in (11.18).

In the Dornbusch model it is assumed that prices in goods or labour markets are in the short term 'sticky' with respect to changes in market conditions. This could, for instance, be because of the existence of multi-period wage or price contracts, as in the New Keynesian model. It follows from this assumption that purchasing power parity does not hold in the short run. Purchasing power parity (PPP), or the 'law of one price', states that in the absence of transport costs and other transactions costs, international arbitrage in goods should eliminate differentials between the prices of goods in different countries. We discussed in chapter 8 on the open economy how this would not hold in the short run (as is confirmed by numerous tests, e.g. Krugman, 1978) but should hold in the long run, whether traded goods are homogeneous across countries or differentiated and imperfectly competitive.

Under PPP we would have:

$$- S_t = p_t - p_{Ft} \tag{11.27}$$

where $p, p_F$ are the logarithms of the domestic and foreign price level. It immediately follows, with efficient capital markets and PPP, that (11.26) and (11.27) imply the equalization of expected real rates of interest.

$$R_t - E_t\, p_{t+1} + p_t = R_{Ft} - E_t\, p_{Ft+1} + p_{Ft} \tag{11.28}$$

Absence of PPP in the short run means that we may examine the behaviour of the real exchange rate, $x$, defined as:

$$x_t = S_t + p_t - p_{Ft} \tag{11.29}$$

For simplicity we assumed that output (in logs), foreign interest rates, real and nominal, and the foreign price level (in logs) are fixed and set at zero; but this does not affect the features of the model on which we focus here. The model is given by

$$R_t = - E_t\, S_{t+1} + S_t \tag{11.30}$$

$$m_t + \bar{m} = p_t - \delta R_t \tag{11.31}$$

$$p_t - p_{t-1} = -k(S_{t-1} + p_{t-1}) + u_t \qquad (11.32)$$

where $m_t$ is a random monetary shock around $\bar{m}$, the constant average money supply, and $u_t$ is a supply shock; the exogenous foreign interest rate and price level, as well as domestic output, are normalized at zero for simplicity. Equation (11.31) is a conventional demand for money function equated to money supply. Equation (11.32) is a price adjustment mechanism, in which inflation depends upon aggregate demand, this in turn depending on the real exchange rate via its effects on the volume of net trade.

We solve this model under the assumption that agents have full current information. Following the procedure outlined in chapter 2, the solution for the exchange rate in the full-information case is given by

$$S_t = -(1 - z)\bar{m} + zS_{t-1} + a_0 m_t + a_1 m_{t-1} + a_2 u_t \qquad (11.33)$$

where $z$ is the stable root of the equation:

$$z^2 + (k - 2)z + 1 - \frac{k(1 + \delta)}{\delta} = 0 \qquad (11.34)$$

$$a_0 = \frac{-(1 - z)}{\delta(1 - z) + k} \qquad (11.35)$$

$$a_1 = \left(\frac{1 + \delta}{\delta}\right) a_0 \qquad (11.36)$$

$$a_2 = \frac{1}{\delta(1 - z)} \qquad (11.37)$$

We notice from (11.33) that, in the long run, the elasticity of the exchange rate with respect to an increase in the permanent level of money supply is unity. In other words, in the long run the exchange rate depreciates by the change in $\bar{m}$. Given that $\bar{m}$ is a constant (11.30) implies that $R$ is zero in the long run, and hence (11.31) that prices have the same response to $\bar{m}$ as the exchange rate. Equation (11.32) implies that in the long run PPP must hold. Leading (11.33) one period and taking expectations we obtain:

$$E_t S_{t+1} - S_t = (1 - z)(\bar{m} - S_t) + a_1 m_t \qquad (11.38)$$

Equation (11.38) defines an expectations mechanism known as regressive expectations. It tells us that when the equilibrium exchange rate is above the current exchange rate, then expectations are revised upwards and vice versa. The fact that regressive expectations can by choice of the regressive parameter $(1 - z)$ be rational is the implication of this Dornbusch model. However, we should note that this property can hold in rational expectations models only where there is one stable root; it does not hold generally.[3]

We can substitute (11.38) into (11.30) and (11.31) to obtain

$$S_t = -[\delta(1 - z)]^{-1}\{(1 + \delta(1 - z))\bar{m} + (1 - \delta a_1)m_t - p_t\}$$

$$(11.39)$$

Equation (11.39) illustrates another key insight of Dornbusch.

The impact of a change in the permanent level of money supply ($\bar{m}$) in the short run is greater than unity and consequently greater than the long-run impact. This phenomenon is known as 'overshooting'. The rationale for this effect is that because, in the short run, prices are at a point in time fixed (or sticky), the only way the money market can remain in equilibrium as the permanent level of the money supply is increased is for the interest rate to fall. However, a falling interest rate has to be associated with an expected appreciation of the currency. Consequently the current exchange rate has to depreciate further than its long-run value in order to give rise to anticipations of an appreciation as it moves to its ultimate long-run value.

This mechanism is illustrated diagrammatically in figure 11.2. Suppose that at time $t = 0$ the pound/dollar rate is $\$1 = \pounds1$. At time $t = N$ the authorities increase the level of the money supply by 100 per cent. In the long run this causes the pound to depreciate against the dollar to $\$1 = \pounds2$. However, in the short run the pound depreciates further, to say $\$1 = \pounds3.20$, and then follows the arrowed path back to long-run equilibrium. We notice that along the arrowed path the pound is appreciating, but has always depreciated relative to $t = 0$. The possibility that

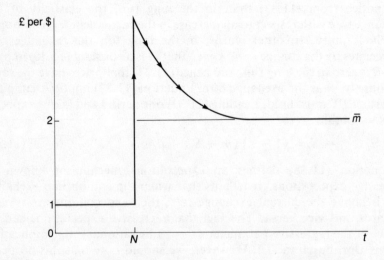

Figure 11.2   Exchange rate overshooting.

efficient assets markets, in conjunction with sticky wages or prices, could give rise to volatile behaviour of asset prices was a principal insight of Dornbusch and has been influential (see e.g. Buiter and Miller, 1981).

We should also note from the solution for the exchange rate that, while a positive monetary shock causes a depreciation of the currency, its impact can be greater or less than unity, but since $\bar{m}$ has not changed, there will always be an 'overshoot' of the long-run equilibrium. The Dornbusch result applies to permanent (unanticipated) changes in the money stock ($\bar{m}$).

A number of authors have attempted to test the Dornbusch model (see e.g. Driskill, 1981; Frankel, 1979; Haache and Townsend, 1981; Demery, 1984), by examining the properties of reduced form exchange rate equations derived from structural models of the Dornbusch type. The empirical results the authors report are unfavourable to the model. However, there are a number of problems with these tests, the main one being that they all assume the regressive form for expectations, which is in general incorrect (Minford and Peel, 1983). For example, Haache and Townsend (1981) and Frankel (1979, 1982) specify models in which lagged adjustment or wealth effects are introduced into the demand for money function or lagged adjustment is introduced into the interest arbitrage condition (11.30); in these models, expectations will not be regressive.

## Exchange Rate Overshooting in Equilibrium Models

We now turn to the issue of whether exchange rate overshooting, which occurs in the Dornbusch model as a result of disequilibrium in goods or labour markets, must always be regarded in a real economy as occurring as a consequence of such features. We will demonstrate that this is not the case. Overshooting can indeed, and generally will, occur in equilibrium open economy models. In order to explain this, we adopt the model of the previous section.

In keeping with the equilibrium framework, we assume that all agents form expectations on the basis of the same set of macro information. This we date at $t - 1$, and for simplicity ignore current global information (but this does not alter our point). Hence the exchange market equilibrium condition becomes:

$$-E_{t-1} S_{t+1} + S_t = R_t \tag{11.40}$$

and the real interest rate differential, $r$, is defined as:

$$r_t = R_t - E_{t-1} p_{t+1} + p_t \tag{11.41}$$

(We have for simplicity set the foreign real interest rate to zero.) Demand for money is:

$$m_t = p_t + \phi y_t - aR_t \tag{11.42}$$

Money supply is:

$$\Delta m_t = \varepsilon_t + \Delta \bar{m}_t + \Delta v_t \tag{11.43}$$

where

$$\Delta^2 \bar{m}_t = u_t$$

This money supply function now allows not only for (unanticipated) temporary changes in the level of money ($v$) and once-for-all changes in the level ($\varepsilon$) but also for once-for-all changes in the steady state rate of increase ($u$). It will thus permit us to examine the different reactions to these shocks.

From the definition of real interest rates and the real exchange rate, $x_t = S_t + p_t$, and from (11.40) we have:

$$(R_t - E_{t-1} p_{t+1} + p_t) = -E_{t-1} S_{t+1} - E_{t-1} p_{t+1} + (S_t + p_t)$$

$$= -E_{t-1} x_{t+1} + x_t \tag{11.44}$$

i.e. the real interest differential must equal the expected real depreciation.

Now complete the model with an *IS* and Phillips curve:

$$y_t = -\alpha r_t - \delta x_t \tag{11.45}$$

$$y_t = \beta r_t + b(p_t - E_{t-1} p_t) + \sigma y_{t-1} \tag{11.46}$$

Equation (11.46) has the full classical form discussed in chapter 4. Note that neither $\alpha$ nor $\beta$ is infinite, so that $r$ will vary.[4] The model has been set up so that $y = r = x = 0$ in equilibrium.

Define the superscript *ue* as 'unanticipated at $t - 1$'; hence, for example, $p_t^{ue} = p_t - E_{t-1} p_t$. Equations (11.44) to (11.46) can be solved as a recursive block in terms of $p_t^{ue}$ to give:

$$x_t = \mu x_{t-1} + \pi_0 p_t^{ue} + (\pi_1 - \mu \pi_0) p_{t-1}^{ue} \tag{11.47}$$

where

$$\pi_0 = -b/(\alpha + \beta + \delta), \quad \pi_1 = \sigma \pi_0 (\alpha + \delta)/[(\alpha + \beta)(1 - \mu) + \delta]$$

and $\mu$ is the (assumed unique) stable root of the characteristic equation

$$\mu^2 - 1 + \frac{\alpha \sigma + \delta}{\alpha + \beta} \mu + \frac{\sigma(\alpha + \delta)}{\alpha + \beta} = 0 \tag{11.48}$$

$r$ and $y$ have similar solutions: a first order moving average in $p^{ue}$ and first order autoregressive coefficient $\mu$. From (11.42) using these, we obtain:

$$p_t^{ue} = qm_t^{ue} \tag{11.49}$$

$$x_t^{ue} = \pi_0 qm_t^{ue} \tag{11.50}$$

where $q = [1 + a - a\pi_0 - \phi(\alpha + \delta)\pi_0]^{-1}$ is greater than 0 and less than 1. The nominal exchange rate depreciation is:

$$S_t^{ue} = x_t^{ue} - p_t^{ue} = -q(1 - \pi_0)m_t^{ue} \tag{11.51}$$

where

$$m_t^{ue} = e_t + u_t + v_t$$

We can usefully rewrite

$$q(1 - \pi_0) = [\alpha + \beta + \delta + b]/(\alpha + \beta + \delta)(1 + a)$$
$$+ b(a + \phi\alpha + \phi\delta)$$

which makes it clear that the value is positive and greater or less than unity depending on all the impact parameters. Notice that overshooting properties occur in the broad sense that both the nominal and the real exchange rate depreciate in a 'volatile' manner in response to positive money shocks.

For the case where the money supply is growing over time we define overshooting as a reaction of the nominal exchange rate by a greater proportion than the change in the (current) equilibrium nominal exchange rate, i.e. that which would prevail were the present money supply difference to be maintained in perpetuity, apart from elements expected to be reversed ($v_t$).

On this basis, we can determine from (11.51) that:

1   The exchange rate may respond more than proportionately to a *once-for-all* change in $m(\varepsilon)$, and so the equilibrium exchange rate. This is the overshooting considered by Dornbusch (1976), which deals with surprise shifts in the permanent level of $m$.

2   It also may respond more than proportionately to a rise in $m$ which is due to a permanent rise in its *growth rate* ($u$), However, since there is no way that speculators can distinguish between $\varepsilon$ and $u$ shocks *when they occur*, the reactions to both are the same.

3   It also responds to a temporary change in $m(v)$, which on our definition does *not* change the equilibrium exchange rate. This is also a form of overshooting, though not that dealt with by Dornbusch.

All these types of overshooting in response to monetary shocks are qualitatively the same as those in the 'sticky price' models of Dornbusch and Frankel, yet they emerge from an equilibrium model. By altering our assumptions about the availability of current global information, these results could be easily 'enriched' to give a variety of potential over-shooting responses; substantial overshooting is exhibited in empirical application by an equilibrium model of the UK economy (Minford, 1980; the Liverpool model). To sum up, volatility of the nominal exchange rate (overshooting), as well as of the real exchange rate and real interest differentials, is not prima facie evidence of 'price stickiness', 'disequilibrium' or 'inefficiency' in goods or labour markets.

### Distinguishing Equilibrium from Disequilibrium Models of the Exchange Rate?

It is of some interest now to ask whether on the basis of a reduced form exchange rate equation on its own it is possible to determine whether it comes from an equilibrium or disequilibrium model. For this purpose, we set up two models identical in all respects except in their 'supply' behaviour. The first model is the one just dealt with; it consists of the demand for money function (11.42), money supply function (11.43), efficient market condition (11.40) and *IS* curve (11.45), and its supply curve is an equilibrium one (11.46). The second model consists of the same equations apart from (11.46), where it has a sticky price Phillips curve like Frankel's, namely:

$$p_t - p_{t-1} = -bx_{t-1} + \Delta \bar{m}_t \tag{11.46$^s$}$$

(We also assume in the spirit of disequilibrium models that speculators have full current information, and condition the expectations operator throughout on the basis of current information.) It turns out that the solution for $x_t$ in this model is:

$$x_t = \mu_2 x_{t-1} - \frac{[\varepsilon_t + au_t + (1 - \mu_1^{-1})(v_t - v_{t-1})]}{(a + \phi\alpha)(1 - \mu_2) - (a + \phi\alpha)} \tag{11.52}$$

where $\mu_2$ is the stable, $\mu_1$ the unstable root of the characteristic equation:

$$\mu^2 - \left\{ 2 - \frac{(ba - \phi\delta)}{(a + \phi\alpha)} \right\} \mu + 1 - \left\{ \frac{b[1 + a] + \phi\delta}{a + \phi\alpha} \right\} = 0 \tag{11.53}$$

Compare this to the solution for the equilibrium model:

$$x_t = \mu x_{t-1} + \pi_0 q m_t^{ue} + q(\pi_1 - \mu\pi_0) m_{t-1}^{ue} \tag{11.54}$$

This shows that it is not possible to distinguish between the equilibrium and disequilibrium models on the basis of the reduced form (real) exchange rate equations alone. It follows that the models can only be distinguished, it at all, on the basis of full structural estimation. This is another example of 'observational equivalence' (see chapter 12).

This concludes our discussion of the behaviour of exchange rates in an economy in which the exchange market is efficient. We have shown that evidence of overshooting does not imply that the economy is typified by disequilibrium in goods or labour markets; equilibrium models will make similar predictions under a wide range of parameter values.

## Conclusions

In this chapter we have discussed some of the implications of the proposition that financial markets are efficient. As particular applications of the proposition we examined the behaviour of exchange rates and bond markets.

In general the empirical evidence does not fully support semi-strong efficiency in the capital market but does suggest at least a strong tendency towards it. Consequently, macroeconomic model builders cannot in our view legitimately continue to simulate or forecast the impact of changes in government policy within models that assume serious capital market inefficiency. Mishkin (1978a, b), for example, shows how the imposition of the assumption of market efficiency radically changes the simulation properties of models without it. The reason is clear. Take, for instance, an announced permanent increase in monetary growth which within conventional models would have its effects with long lags: with market efficiency this will cause an immediate jump in very long-run interest rates (to their equilibrium value) and also jumps in the exchange rate (and stock market prices). The transmission mechanism of monetary policy will be radically altered.

## Appendix

The purpose of this appendix is to show the manner in which the standard test of efficiency based on (11.9) of this chapter has to be modified if agents have an incomplete current information set. For analytical simplicity (though the argument is quite general), we write a series $y_t$ as the summation of two infinite moving average error processes in the two white noise errors, $\varepsilon_t$ and $z_t$. Consequently:

$$y_t = \bar{y} + \sum_{i=0}^{\infty} \pi_i \varepsilon_{t-i} + \sum_{i=0}^{\infty} \delta_i z_{t-i} \tag{11.A.1}$$

where $\bar{y}$ is the mean of the series, and the $\pi_i$ and $\delta_i$ are constant coefficients.

Consider the rational expectation of $y_{t+1}$ formed at time $t$. If there is full current information at time $t$ the expectation will be given by:

$$E_t \, y_{t+1} = \bar{y} + \sum_{i=1}^{\infty} \pi_i \, \varepsilon_{t-i+1} + \sum_{i=1}^{\infty} \delta_i z_{t-1+i} \qquad (11.\text{A}.2)$$

In this case, given the one-period forecast horizon, the *ex post* forecast error will be given by a white noise error:

$$y_{t+1} - E_t \, y_{t+1} = \pi_0 \, \varepsilon_{t+1} + \delta_0 \, z_{t+1} \qquad (11.\text{A}.3)$$

Consequently the standard tests based on (11.9) are correct in these circumstances.

Suppose next that agents have incomplete current information at time $t$, and instead observe some current global information (for instance via asset markets), but other global information with a one-period lag. In particular we will assume for simplicity (though the argument is easily generalized) that there is one global indicator (say the interest rate) which is given the representation:

$$R_t = \bar{r} + \sum_{i=0}^{\infty} d_i \, \varepsilon_{t-i} + \sum_{i=0}^{\infty} h_i \, z_{t-i} \qquad (11.\text{A}.4)$$

where $\bar{r}$ is the mean of the series and the $d_i$ and $h_i$ are constant coefficients.

In this incomplete current information case the one-period-ahead expectation of $y_t$ is given by:

$$E_t \, y_{t+1} = \bar{y} + \pi_1 \, E_t(\varepsilon_t) + \sum_{i=2}^{\infty} \pi_i \, \varepsilon_{t-i+1} + \delta_1 \, E_t(z_t) + \sum_{i=2}^{\infty} \delta_i z_{t-i+1}$$
$$(11.\text{A}.5)$$

Consequently the forecast error is given by:

$$y_{t+1} - E_t \, y_{t+1} = \pi_0 \varepsilon_{t+1} + \delta_0 z_{t+1} + \pi_1 [\varepsilon_t - E_t(\varepsilon_t)] + \delta_1 [z_t - E_t(z_t)]$$
$$(11.\text{A}.6)$$

Given current observation of the global indicator $R_t$, and using the usual signal extraction formulae (as discussed in chapter 3) we obtain:

$$E_t(\varepsilon_t) = 1/d_0 \, \phi_\varepsilon (d_0 \, \varepsilon_t + h_0 z_t) \qquad (11.\text{A}.7)$$

$$E_t(z_t) = 1/h_0 (1 - \phi_\varepsilon)(d_0 \, \varepsilon_t + h_0 z_t) \qquad (11.\text{A}.8)$$

where

$$\phi_\varepsilon = d_0^2 \, \sigma_\varepsilon^2 / (d_0^2 \sigma_\varepsilon^2 + h_0^2 \sigma_z^2)$$

where $\sigma_\varepsilon^2$ and $\sigma_z^2$ are the variances of the two errors, $\varepsilon$ and $z$ respectively. Consequently the forecast error ($K_{t+1}$) is given by:

$$K_{t+1} = \pi_0 \, \varepsilon_{t+1} + \delta_0 z_{t+1} + \pi_1 \left[ (1 - \phi_\varepsilon)\varepsilon_t - \frac{d_0}{h_0}\phi_\varepsilon z_t \right]$$

$$+ \delta_1 \left[ \phi_\varepsilon z_t - \frac{d_0}{h_0}(1 - \phi_\varepsilon)\varepsilon_t \right] \qquad (11.A.9)$$

### Serial Correlation of Forecast Errors

If we take expectations of two successive errors we find:

$$\mathsf{E}(K_{t+1}, K_t) = \{\sigma_z^2 \sigma_\varepsilon^2/(d_0^2\sigma_\varepsilon^2 + h_0^2\sigma_z^2)\}.[\pi_1 h_0 - d_1 d_0].[\pi_0 h_0 - \delta_0 d_0]$$
$$(11.A.10)$$

Consequently, in general, incomplete current information will give rise to a moving average error process. This will not be the case if, first, we have implicitly full current information (for example, if there are as many global indicators in the economy as random shocks; see Karni, 1980), or if, secondly, we observe the current value of the variable to be forecast (it being itself a global indicator). In this latter case $\pi_0 = d_0$, $\delta_0 = h_0$ (also $\pi_1 = d_1$, $\delta_1 = h_1$) and the expected correlation in (11.A.10) is equal to zero.

It would appear from this result that standard tests of efficiency based on (11.9) will have the usual properties for asset prices in particular (which it can be assumed are observed currently), even under incomplete current information. However, the general point remains that variables not currently observed (i.e. the majority) will under incomplete information be inappropriately tested for efficiency by these methods. Furthermore, one needs to scrutinize carefully the assumption that the asset prices in question are contemporaneously observed. In very high frequency data (e.g. hourly) this will obviously not be so except for a few continuously broadcast asset prices; it will also not be so in lower frequency data for averages of variables (e.g. the level of all short-term interest rates), which are often examined in these studies.

In general, in circumstances of incomplete current information the moving average error in equation (11.A.9) will be given by $s + j - 1$, where $s$ is the time horizon of the forecast and $j$ is the longest lag on global information relevant for forecasting $y_t$. Clearly there may be some *a priori* doubt as to the magnitude of $j$, which may cause some problems in interpretation of tests based on (11.9). As a consequence of the moving average error process, least squares estimates of (11.9) under incomplete current information will be inefficient but unbiased, since

$$\mathsf{E}(K_{t+1}, \mathsf{E}_t(y_{t+1})) = 0 \qquad (11.A.11)$$

and least squares estimates have the property of unbiasedness even in the presence of moving error processes. This situation is the same as that of overlapping information in the usually assumed case of full current information; overlapping information here occurs with $s > 1$, familiarly introducing a moving average process with the same effects.

These results have potential implications for a number of empirical studies (see e.g. Holden and Peel, 1977; Turnovsky, 1970) in which an implicit assumption of full current information has been made when studying directly observed consumer price expectations data which cannot readily be assumed to be part of the current information set. The point here is that price data are not currently observable on any reasonable assumptions. Consequently, the 'expectations errors' should be serially correlated, as indeed has often been found in these tests. It is possible that these survey data may well reveal rationality after all. For further implications of partial current information sets for the testing of efficiency, see Minford and Peel (1984).

## Notes

1 Hellwig (1982) challenges the Grossman and Stiglitz proposition that the informativeness of market prices in equilibrium is bounded away from full informational efficiency. Hellwig points out that this proposition rests on the assumption that agents learn from current prices at which transactions have actually been completed. This is a model in which investors learn from past equilibrium prices but not from the auctioneer's current price offer. Hellwig is able to show that if the time span between successive market transactions is short, the market can approximate full informational efficiency arbitrarily closely and yet the return to being informed remains bounded away from zero. This results from the fact that informed agents can utilize this information before uninformed agents have an opportunity to infer it from current market prices.

Hellwig also pursues the implications that arise if one relaxes the assumption that agents cannot assure themselves of being informed in a given period, but rather agents choose the frequency on average at which they obtain information. It appears that relaxing such assumptions leaves his main result above unimpaired – see also the survey by Jordan and Radner (1982).

2 Consider an individual faced with a possible gamble; he may choose either to receive £100 for sure, or to toss a coin and receive £50 if heads occur and £150 if tails occur. The expected outcome of this latter choice is £100 = 0.5(£50) + 0.5(£150). The question is will the individual prefer the actuarial value of the gamble (this is its expected outcome) with certainty or will he prefer the gamble itself? If he prefers the gamble he is a risk lover; if he is indifferent he is risk neutral; and if he prefers the sure outcome he is risk averse. It is also possible to compute the maximum amount of wealth an individual would be willing to give up in order to avoid the gamble. This is the notion of a risk

premium (see Pratt, 1964; Arrow, 1971; Markowitz, 1959).

3 This can be seen by solving any model in which two stable roots are required for a unique solution. The analogue of $E_t \, s_{t+1}$ would then depend not only on $s_t$ but also on $s_{t-1}$.

4 For the real interest rate differential to be constant, as investigated by Mishkin (1981), an infinitely large intertemporal substitution response is required for either $\alpha$ or $\beta$. The evidence does not support such responses; it is therefore not surprising that Mishkin concludes from his reduced form work that the differential varies over time. Similar arguments apply to variation of the real interest rate within a closed economy, as investigated by Fama (1975) for the USA; this evidence has now been found (by Nelson and Schwert, 1977) to support non-constancy, which again is not surprising. We may also note that the size of variation in both the differential and the closed (e.g. world) economy level of real interest rates cannot be suggested *a priori*; nor can the length of time to convergence (determined by $\mu$ in this model as influenced by all the parameters).

# 12

# Interpreting the Evidence: The Problem of Observational Equivalence

As was shown in chapter 3, it is a key implication of an economy embodying a Sargent–Wallace supply curve, rational expectations and identical information sets of public and private agents that, from a stabilization perspective, output (or the unemployment rate) will be invariant to anticipated rates of monetary change. Only unanticipated changes in the money stock will have any impact on output. Barro (1977) in a seminal paper attempted to determine empirically the relative impacts of unanticipated and actual rates of monetary change on the unemployment rate in the USA over the period 1946–73. Since his initial paper, he and others have carried out similar tests for a number of other countries, as well as repeating the US tests in different ways. Barro wished to test whether the economy was New Classical in the manner of Sargent and Wallace.

Barro's empirical procedure involved two stages. First, a policy reaction function was determined for the authorities. This involved explaining the actual rates of change of the money stock in terms of variables previously known to the authorities. The residuals, or unexplained part of monetary change, from this reaction function are interpreted as the unanticipated rate of monetary change.

Thus if the reaction function of the authorities is given by

$$m_t = \mu X_t + \varepsilon_t \tag{12.1}$$

where $m$ is the rate of monetary expansion, $X$ is a vector of variables, $\mu$ a vector of coefficients, $\varepsilon$ is a random residual, then

$$m_t - \mathrm{E}_{t-1}\, m_t = \mu(X_t - \mathrm{E}_{t-1}\, X_t) + \varepsilon_t \tag{12.2}$$

and assuming $X_t = \mathrm{E}_{t-1}\, X_t$:

$$m_t - \mathrm{E}_{t-1}\, m_t = \varepsilon_t \tag{12.3}$$

Having obtained estimates of the monetary innovations, Barro proceeds to use these innovations (current and lagged) to explain (along with other postulated determinants of the natural rate of unemployment, such as a minimum wage variable and a measure of military conscription) the rate of unemployment.

Barro's empirical results appear impressive. They suggest that the current and previous two years' monetary innovations are significant determinants of the rate of unemployment with the correct negative sign. Moreover, when Barro adds previous rates of change of the money supply to his unemployment equation, they are found not to be statistically significantly different from zero at normal levels of significance.

The basic type of analysis conducted by Barro has been replicated by a large number of different authors for a number of different countries (see e.g. Barro and Rush, 1980; Leiderman, 1980; Attfield et al., 1981a, b; Mishkin, 1982). The results reported by almost all these authors, but not Mishkin, seem to suggest that real variables, either unemployment or output, are responsive only to unanticipated rates of monetary change and not the actual rate. Consequently, it would appear from this empirical evidence that there is powerful support for the joint hypothesis of rational expectations and independence of unemployment or output from anticipated rates of monetary change.

Sargent (1976b), in an important paper, showed that this interpretation of the empirical evidence may be incorrect. Sargent demonstrated that the reduced form for output or unemployment in a Keynesian model, in which systematic monetary policy will influence the variance of output, may be statistically indistinguishable from that of a classical model in which only unanticipated movements in the money stock impact on output or unemployment. The Keynesian and classical models are said to be observationally equivalent in their reduced forms.

Sargent's main point can be made most simply by consideration of the following model. Suppose the 'true' reduced form equations for an economy are given by the equations:

$$y_t = a(m_t - E_{t-1}\, m_t) + \delta y_{t-1} + u_t \tag{12.4}$$

$$m_t = gm_{t-1} + \varepsilon_t \tag{12.5}$$

where $a$, $\delta$, $g$ are positive constants, $y$ is real output and $u$, $\varepsilon$ are random variables; all mean values of variables are put equal to zero for simplicity. Since

$$m_t - E_{t-1}\, m_t = \varepsilon_t = m_t - gm_{t-1} \tag{12.6}$$

Equation (12.1) can be rewritten as:

$$y_t = am_t - agm_{t-1} + \delta y_t + u_t \tag{12.7}$$

It would appear from equation (12.7) that the current and lagged values of the money stock have an impact on real output, when in fact we know from equation (12.4) that this is not the case, since only unanticipated changes in the money stock have an impact on output.

It is obvious from Sargent's analysis that 'unrestricted' single equation reduced forms for output have no information content, at least with respect to the manner in which changes in the money supply impact on an economy. A simple regression of output on current and past money supplies simply cannot inform us of the true nature of the impact of monetary change on these variables.

The point that Sargent is making is that two quite different types of model, Keynesian and classical, have indistinguishable reduced forms for output in terms of either actual or unanticipated money stock, current and lagged. This does not imply that the models *in toto* are not distinguishable; clearly they are, on the basis of a variety of tests on structural coefficients and also on reduced form equations for *more* variables than simply output. Therefore the point is a narrow but important one, related to this *particular* test carried out by economists (remember that there has been great interest in money-supply/output relationships ever since the debate over Friedman and Meiselman, 1963).[1]

In particular, it needs to be stressed, because there has been some confusion on the point, that Sargent's point is not about 'identification' as such. Both the Keynesian and classical models may be fully identified; that is, the parameters of each may be individually retrieved by estimation of the full model (i.e. subject to all its restrictions). However, there is a useful potential connection with the concept of identification. If two models can be 'nested' in a more general model (usually, a linear combination of the two), then, provided the coefficients of each model can be identified in this general model, it is possible to test for their significance and accordingly that of each model. In this situation, if (and only if) the coefficients cannot be identified, the models will be 'observationally equivalent'.

Sargent's point has provoked a lively literature attempting to establish conditions under which a limited number of reduced forms *can* distinguish between the two models. These attempts have centred on identification within such a general model, in this case one which nests two distinct reduced forms.

### Identification

In order to discuss this issue more fully it is necessary first to set out the basic issues which arise in indentification of an economic system. (For a comprehensive outline the reader should consult a standard econometric text such as Johnston (1984).)

Suppose that the demand and supply for a commodity is given by:

$$q_t = \alpha_{11}p_t + \alpha_{12}y_t \quad \text{(demand)} \tag{12.8}$$

$$q_t = \alpha_{12}p_t + \alpha_{22}z_t \quad \text{(supply)} \tag{12.9}$$

where the $\alpha$s are constants, $p$ is price, $q$ quantity, and $y$ and $z$ are exogenous variables which affect demand and supply respectively. Demand and supply are assumed to be equal. Random disturbances and constants are omitted for simplicity. Equations (12.8) and (12.9), which specify the behaviour of demand and supply respectively, are treated here as structural or behavioural equations and the $\alpha$s as structural coefficients.

From (12.8) and (12.9) we can solve for $p$ and $q$ to obtain

$$p_t = (\alpha_{22}z_t - \alpha_{12}y_t)/(\alpha_{11} - \alpha_{21}) \tag{12.10}$$

and

$$q_t = (\alpha_{11}\alpha_{22}z_t - \alpha_{21}\alpha_{12}y_t)/(\alpha_{11} - \alpha_{21}) \tag{12.11}$$

We can also write equations (12.10) and (12.11) in their 'reduced form' as:

$$p_t = \pi_{11}z_t + \pi_{12}y_t \tag{12.12}$$

$$q_t = \pi_{21}z_t + \pi_{22}y_t \tag{12.13}$$

where

$$\pi_{11} = \alpha_{22}/(\alpha_{11} - \alpha_{21}) \qquad \pi_{12} = -\alpha_{12}/(\alpha_{12} - \alpha_{21}) \qquad \text{etc.}$$

When reduced forms are estimated, it is of course the $\pi$ coefficients that are retrieved with the objective of deriving estimates of the structural coefficients. It is clear that from sample estimates of these reduced form coefficients all the structural parameters $\alpha$ can be uniquely retrieved (thus $\pi_{21}/\pi_{11} = \alpha_{11}$ etc.).

In these circumstances our structural equations (12.8) and (12.9) are said to be exactly identified.

Consider the next model

$$q_t = \alpha_{11}p_t + \alpha_{12}z_t \tag{12.14}$$

$$q_t = \alpha_{21}p_t + \alpha_{22}z_t \tag{12.15}$$

The reduced form of this model is:

$$p_t = \pi_{11}z_t \tag{12.16}$$

$$q_t = \pi_{21}z_t \tag{12.17}$$

where

$$\pi_{11} = (\alpha_{22} - \alpha_{12})/(\alpha_{11} - \alpha_{21})$$

$$\pi_{21} = (\alpha_{11}\alpha_{22} - \alpha_{21}\alpha_{12})/(\alpha_{11} - \alpha_{21})$$

It is clear that, in this case, it is never possible to obtain estimates of the structural coefficients. The economic system (12.14) and (12.15) is said to be not identified and consequently there are an infinite number of parameter values in equations (12.14) and (12.15) that are consistent with the reduced form (12.16) and (12.17).

Finally, consider the system given by:

$$q_t = \alpha_{11}p_t + \alpha_{12}y_t + \alpha_{13}x_t \qquad (12.18)$$

$$q_t = \alpha_{21}p_t + \alpha_{22}z_t \qquad (12.19)$$

where $x$ is another exogenous variable. The reduced form of (12.18) and (12.19) is given by:

$$p_t = \pi_{11}z_t + \pi_{12}y_t + \pi_{13}x_t \qquad (12.20)$$

$$q_t = \pi_{21}z_t + \pi_{22}y_t + \pi_{23}x_t \qquad (12.21)$$

where

$$\pi_{11} = (\alpha_{22})/(\alpha_{11} - \alpha_{21}) \qquad \pi_{12} = (-\alpha_{12})/(\alpha_{11} - \alpha_{21})$$

$$\pi_{13} = (-\alpha_{13})/(\alpha_{11} - \alpha_{21})$$

In this case the system is identified but the parameters can be retrieved independently from alternative values of the reduced form coefficients; thus, two separate estimates of $\alpha_{21}$ are given by $\pi_{23}/\pi_{13}$ and $\pi_{22}/\pi_{12}$, while $\alpha_{22} = \pi_{11}(\alpha_{11} - \alpha_{21}) = \pi_{11}/[\pi_{21}/(\pi_{11} - \alpha_{21})] = \pi_{21} - \alpha_{21}\pi_{11}$, which gives two corresponding estimates of $\alpha_{21}$. Here the system is said to be over-identified. If a system is identified or over-identified, then a researcher can, in principle, estimate its structural coefficients (methods of estimation do not concern us here).

## Identification of Keynesian and Classical Reduced Form Coefficients

We now return to the problem raised by Sargent. Let us initially suppose that there are no lagged effects; the salient points can be made for this case. We know that a classical model with a Sargent–Wallace supply curve can be written in the 'semi-reduced' form (semi because expectations have not been eliminated):

$$y_t = a_{c1}X_t + b_{c1}(m_t - E_{t-1}\,m_t) + u_{c1t} \qquad (12.22)$$

and that a Keynesian model will have a reduced form:

$$y_t = a_{k1} X_t + c_{k1} m_t + u_{k1t} \tag{12.23}$$

where $u_{c1}$, $u_{k1}$ are error terms.

We now combine these two equations into a linear combination ($\mu = 0$ or 1)

$$y_t = [\mu a_{c1} + (1 - \mu) a_{k1}] X_t + (\mu b_{c1})(m_t - E_{t-1} m_t)$$
$$+ (1 - \mu) c_{k1} m_t + (\mu u_{c1t} + (1 - \mu) u_{k1t})$$

or

$$y_t = a_1 X_t + b_1 (m_t - E_{t-1} m_t) + c_1 m_t + u_{1t} \tag{12.24}$$

where $a_1 = \mu a_{c1} + (1 - \mu) a_{k1}$, etc. We would like to test whether $b_1$ or $c_1$ is significantly different from zero; if $b_1 > 0$, then $\mu = 1$ and the classical model prevails. If $c_1 > 0$, then $\mu = 0$ and the Keynesian model prevails (the other possibilities are disregarded here, although clearly if $b_1 = c_1 = 0$ or if $b_1 > 0 < c_1$, the problem must be reformulated if the test results are taken seriously).

Now suppose that the rest of the model is a policy reaction function for the money supply:

$$m_t = a_2 X_t + u_{2t} \tag{12.25}$$

where $u_2$ is a random error independent of $u_1$. (Much of the discussion which follows is based on Buiter (1983), to which the reader is referred for further analysis.)

Sargent's point can now be expressed as the impossibility of identifying $c_1$ and $b_1$ in this model. Assuming rational expectations, the reduced form of the model (12.24) and (12.25) is given by:

$$y_t = \beta_1 X_t + v_{1t} \tag{12.26}$$

$$m_t = \beta_2 X_t + v_{2t} \tag{12.27}$$

where

$$\beta_1 = a_1 + c_1 a_2$$

$$\beta_2 = a_2$$

$$v_{1t} = (b_1 + c_1) u_{2t} + u_{1t}$$

$$v_{2t} = u_{2t}$$

The effect of anticipated money on output is given by $c_1$, the effect of unanticipated money on output by $b_1 + c_1$.

We notice that the covariance between the error terms in the reduced form is given by:

$$\text{cov}(v_{1t}, v_{2t}) = (b_1 + c_1)\sigma^2 \qquad (12.28)$$

where $\sigma^2$ is the variance of the money supply error, $u_2$. Consequently an estimate of $b_1 + c_1$ is obtained as:

$$(\widehat{b_1 + c_1}) = [\text{cov}(v_1, v_2)]/\sigma^2 \qquad (12.29)$$

Even this requires independence of structural disturbances $u_1$ and $u_2^2$.

To identify the crucial parameter, $c_1$, we must set one of the elements in $a_1$ to zero (if $X$ is a single variable, $a_1 = 0$ is necessary); that is, at least one variable appearing in the monetary policy reaction function must *not* appear in the output equation. Suppose, for instance, that our model is given by:

$$y_t = a_1 X_{1t} + b_1 (m_t - E_{t-1} m_t) + c_1 m_t + u_{1t} \qquad (12.30)$$

$$m_t = a_2 X_{1t} + a_3 X_{2t} + u_{2t} \qquad (12.31)$$

where $X_1$, $X_2$ are subsets of $X$, the exogenous variable set. The reduced form is given by:

$$y_t = (a_1 + c_1 a_2)X_{1t} + c_1 a_3 X_{2t} + (b_1 + c_1)u_{2t} + u_{1t} \qquad (12.32)$$

$$m_t = a_2 X_{1t} + a_3 X_{2t} + u_{2t} \qquad (12.33)$$

Equation (12.30) is now identified.

This, however, is hard to visualize in any model, because the reduced form of output will generally contain all the exogenous variables of the model which are candidates for the money supply reaction function. Barro, in his work on the USA, assumes, with this in mind, that government expenditure enters the money supply function but not the output function. This is implausible, given that government expenditure appears in the GDP identity. It may be possible to develop the New Classical model to exclude exogenous variables, on the grounds that output depends only on supply shocks, $u_{c1t}$, and money shocks:

$$y_t = b_{c1} (m_t - E_{t-1} m_t) + u_{c1t}$$

Combining this with the Keynesian model (12.23) and the money supply model (12.25) gives a combined reduced form (12.24) in which $a_1 = (1 - \mu)a_{k1}$. Hence in (12.26) $\beta_1 = 0$ if and only if the model is New Classical. The exclusion restriction in the New Classical model is sufficient to identify $b_1$ and $c_1$: If $\beta_1 = 0$, then $c_1 = 0$ and (12.29) allows an estimate of $b_1$, while if $\beta_1 \neq 0$, then $b_1 = 0$ and (12.29) allows an estimate of $c_1$.

The difficulty with this is that the New Classical model supply curve also has the intertemporal substitution effect from real interest rates (and in open economy models the analogous effect from the real exchange rate); the real interest rate (or the real exchange rate) is impacted by all the exogenous variables in the model. Those using this test must (and in practice do) assume that these effects are negligible. But by so doing they restrict 'New Classical' to a limited class of model within the broader New Classical type; furthermore, some (intertemporal or other) substitution is a necessary component of the New Classical supply curve, otherwise no Phillips curve is possible. We also saw that there is scope for fiscal stabilization through government spending and (when there are wealth effects of government bonds) also for monetary stabilization in models with these effects. If Barro and his disciples were to demonstrate that the *limited* New Classical model held, they would be undermining the foundations of the New Classical model.

There remains the issue of partial macro information and signal extraction. This issue is assumed away in Barro's testing framework: none of the current money supply shock is assumed to be inferred from current information such as local prices, interest rates and exchange rates.

Yet again such signal extraction is at the core of the New Classical supply curve, as set out for example in Lucas's 'islands' model (Lucas, 1972b, 1973). If included, signal extraction implies that

$$E_t \, m_t = E_{t-1} \, m_t + (\phi_0 u_{2t} + \phi_1 u_{1t}) \tag{12.34}$$

where $\phi_0$ and $\phi_1$ are linear combinations of structural parameters and error variances. In the New Classical model, the output function becomes:

$$y_t = a_1 X_t + b_{c1} (m_t - E_t \, m_t) + u_{c1t} \tag{12.35}$$

so that the combined model is:

$$y_t = a_1 X_t + b_1 (m_t - E_t \, m_t) + c_1 m_t + u_{1t} \tag{12.36}$$

$\beta_1$, $\beta_2$ and $v_{2t}$ are as before, but

$$v_{1t} = [b_1 (1 + \phi_0) + c_1] u_{2t} + (1 + b_1 \phi_1) u_{1t} \tag{12.37}$$

Now:

$$\text{cov}(v_{1t}, v_{2t}) = [b_1 (1 + \phi_0) + c_1] / \sigma^2 \tag{12.38}$$

It can be seen that if the New Classical model has the exclusion restriction in it (on real interest rates and real exchange rate effects), then it is still possible from the $a_1$ parameter to tell whether the model is New Classical or not (although it is not possible to identify $b_1$ or $c_1$, without prior knowledge from the model structure of $\phi_0$, this is a secondary matter).

Nevertheless, the policy implications are different if there is signal extraction: stabilization policy may become effective, as discussed in chapter 4. The policy aspects of the Barro tests must therefore be approached with caution (this has also been stressed by Buiter, 1983).

The effectiveness of the test proposed by Barro really boils down, therefore, to the acceptability of the exclusion restriction he must make to allow the test to discriminate. With the exclusion restriction, the 'New Classical' model appears to be vitally impoverished: but without it the test is no use.

Sargent has suggested that a model such as (12.24) and (12.25) may be identified if a structural break is known to have occurred in the policy regime during the sample period. If the world is classical (i.e. $c_1 = 0$), then the reduced form output will be invariant to a change in the policy regime (when $a_2$ changes). Hence the coefficient $\beta_1$ will not change. Consequently, tests for stability of $\beta_1$ across the samples before and after the break will discriminate between Keynesian and classical models. Nevertheless, this is not helpful in general (when breaks in regime either do not occur or cannot be known to have occurred), and it has rarely been used.

This discussion can be extended to include lags. Write (12.24) and (12.25) generally as:

$$[1 - \delta_1^1(L)]y_t = a_1(L)X_t + b_1(L)(m_t - \mathsf{E}_{t-1}\, m_t) + c_1(L)m_t + u_{1t}$$
$$(12.39)$$

$$[1 - \delta_2^1(L)]m_t = a_2(L)X_t + u_{2t} \tag{12.40}$$

where $L$ is the lag operator and $a_1(L)$, for example, is a polynomial in $L$. The reduced form for $y_t$ (obtained by substituting from (12.40); i.e. for $m_t - \mathsf{E}_{t-1}\, m_t = u_{2t}$ and for $m_t = \delta_2^1(L)m_t + a_2(L)X_t + u_{2t}$) now becomes:

$$[1 - \delta_1^1(L)]y_t = [a_1(L) + c_1(L)a_2(L)]X_t + [b_1^1(L)$$
$$+ c_1^1(L)]u_{2t} + c_1(L)\delta_2^1(L)m_t + v_{1t} \tag{12.41}$$

where $v_{1t} = (b_1^0 + c_1^0)u_{2t} + u_{1t}$; $b_1^0$, $c_1^0$ are the leading terms, and $b_1^1(L)$, $c_1^1(L)$ are the terms of $L^i\,(i \geqslant 1)$ in $b_1(L)$, $c_1(L)$ respectively.

After substituting for lagged $u_{2t}$ in terms of observables (i.e. $u_{2t} = [1 - \delta_2^1(L)]m_t - a_2(L)X_t$ from (12.40)), (12.41) becomes:

$$[1 - \delta_1^1(L)]y_t = \{[a_1(L) + c_1^0\hat{a}_2(L) - b_1^1(L)\hat{a}_2(L)\}X_t$$
$$+ \{b_1^1(L)[1 - \hat{\delta}_2^1(L)] + c_1^1(L) + c_1^0\hat{\delta}_2^1(L)\}m_t + v_{1t} \tag{12.42}$$

The variance–covariance matrix will, as before, give an estimate of $(b_1^0 + c_1^0)$. The $\delta_2^1(L)$, $a_2(L)$ can be estimated from (12.40) and are hatted to show this. Even so, the $c_1(L)$ are not retrievable; they will only be retrievable if at least one of the $X_t$ variables is excluded from (12.39), as before in the no-lag case (for example, if $X_t$ is a single variable, then $a_1(L) = 0$ will suffice).

Another possibility for discrimination when there are lags has been pointed out by McCallum (1979). This is the special case, where the classical model contains only the current monetary innovation as a determinant of output. This case corresponds to having $b_1^1(L) = 0$ in (12.39). In this case we retrieve $c_1(L)$ from the coefficients on lagged money supply; for the model to be classical, lagged money supply should not enter the output reduced form.

The exclusion of past monetary innovations from the output equations may well not be valid; it places absolute reliance on the absence of a moving average process on the term $p_t - E_{t-1}\, p_t$ entering the Sargent–Wallace supply curve. Yet it only requires a one-period delay in one sector's observed response to such shocks to yield such a process; this surely cannot be ruled out, in view of decision and delivery lags.

This suggests a final problem: the difficulty of discriminating between a New Classical and a New Keynesian model with the Barro test, supposing that the Keynesian model can be rejected by it in some way. Barro's original test in fact included the current and lagged money innovation in the output equation, using normal data. Yet this is consistent with a simple overlapping contract model of the sort illustrated in chapter 2, where both the current and lagged money shock affected output. More complex models, such as Taylor (1979), add serial correlation to such moving averages of shocks, so that these shocks became an ARMA process. This is not obviously distinguishable from the processes Barro assumes. Only if an assumption is made, as in McCallum, about the New Classical error process, can the two be distinguished. Yet as we have seen, the basis for such an assumption is questionable, even without confronting the well-known empirical difficulties of testing between different error processes.


## Conclusions

The empirical evidence presented by Barro and others on the impact of unanticipated or actual money on real variables appears to give impressive support to the New Classical model, as set out in the Sargent–Wallace model of chapter 2.

Unfortunately, ingenious as Barro's original idea was and little as one would wish to ignore any empirical evidence, there are difficulties in the interpretation of these tests: it is impossible to distinguish a New Classical from a Keynesian reduced form equation for output unless it is assumed that at least in the New Classical model output is unaffected by exogenous variables which affect the money supply. This is a difficult assumption for a New Classical economist to make in view of the importance he or she attaches to intertemporal substitution and/or other mechanisms which induce relative price effects in the output supply curve. Various suggestions have been made to modify these tests but ultimately none has been successful in restoring credibility to this mass of empirical work. It should also be noted that even if the tests show a 'New Classical' model, that does not imply policy ineffectiveness because: (a) New Classical models with signal extraction in general create policy effectiveness and cannot be distinguished from New Classical models without signal extraction; (b) a New Keynesian model with overlapping contracts cannot be distinguished by these tests from a 'New Classical' model. To test for the restrictions which together give the full New Classical properties, the reduced form test of Barro is therefore inadequate. We turn next to estimation of structural models and how they may provide tests of these restrictions.

## Note

1  The analogous point also turns out to be applicable to reduced forms for the exchange rate (see chapter 11) as a means of distinguishing 'equilibrium' from 'disequilibrium' open economy models. It will also often be applicable when a reduced form on any single variable is appealed to as a means of distinguishing equilibrium from disequilibrium models; appeals to the 'stylized facts' about any single variable have accordingly to be treated with the greatest caution.

## 13

# Direct Tests of Rational Expectations

---

So far we have looked at two indirect ways of testing the rational expectations hypothesis: the test for market efficiency (a joint hypothesis of equilibrium expected returns and rational expectations) and the Barro reduced form test for whether only money surprises affect output (a joint hypothesis that the model has a 'Sargent–Wallace supply curve' and rational expectations). We now consider the two direct tests of the RE hypothesis: direct testing on whether surveys of expectations display the properties of rationality, and estimation of structural models with a test for the REH restriction.

### Survey Data

A number of surveys of industrialists and private consumers have been carried out over the years for inflation and for output. The best known are the Livingston series in the USA and Carlson and Parkin's (1975) interpretation of the Confederation of British Industry survey in the UK: another series which has been examined (Visco, 1984) is for Italy, the *Mondo Economico* magazine (with Confindustria) surveys of wholesale and retail prices.

These surveys have generally satisfied the unbiasedness property (a weak test of rationality since it is shared with most other expectations hypotheses, notably adaptive expectations) but not the efficiency property: that is, information available to the survey participants was not independent of the expectations errors. Some of them get close to efficiency. (Holden et al. (1985, chapter 3) review a number of these survey studies.) For example, Visco finds that, up to the 1973 oil crisis, the Italian survey inflation expectations were unbiased, serially uncorrelated and efficiently incorporated all available information; bias and inefficiency occur in the few sample years after the oil crisis but Visco argues that this reflected turbulence and learning.

There are two problems with tests based on surveys. First, are those surveyed the key participants in the markets? The RE hypothesis asserts that the 'average' participant has rational expectations: this is an 'as if' proposition which implies that the price should behave as if those active in the market have rational expectations. 'Those active in the market' means agents 'on the margin', to whom a decision whether to buy or sell matters at the time. We are all on many occasions not really interested in a particular market: for example, we are not most of the time buying a house, but when we are we become interested in being well-informed. It is clearly impossible for a survey to select those market participants who are at each time active in the market. To the extent that the survey does not, however, some of those who answer will not be well-informed and should not have rational expectations.

The second problem may be no less important: the veracity of participants' answers. The theory of revealed preference indicates that we should look at people's actions, not their words, to reveal their tastes or views. In answer to questions, either they may not wish to reveal their true tastes or views or they may not truly know them – not perhaps yet having gone through the decision process that would reveal it to themselves, or perhaps not even understanding their implicit views having done so (rather like a bicyclist who cannot explain how he has stayed upright).

For similar reasons, economists have paid little attention to surveys of whether firms maximize profits or consumers maximize utility. For example, Hall and Hitch (1939) and Wilson and Andrews (1951) found from questioning firms that they did not consider themselves to be setting prices in a manner consistent with profit maximization. Similarly, psychologists have found that some consumers are irrational (Akerlof and Yellen, 1987). Economists have preferred to use these maximizing models in spite of this evidence because the models have performed well empirically.

This reveals that it is the empirical performance of a hypothesis – the capacity to predict (past or future) conditionally on exogenous inputs – that matters to economists, if it is also attractive theoretically (that is, it is logical, tractable and based on non-absurd assumptions about behaviour). The RE hypothesis has obviously exercised considerable theoretical appeal, as argued earlier, indeed throughout this book implicitly in one way or another. It remains then to consider the last main predictive test: structural estimation subject to the REH.

## Structural Models with Rational Expectations

The natural way to test the RE hypothesis is in the context of a macro model. One may estimate the structural coefficients of the model subject to the RE hypothesis, and then test the restriction of the RE hypothesis against less restrictive alternatives, such as adaptive expectations or ARMA time series: this can be done by a likelihood ratio test if FIML is used or by an *F*-test within single equations estimation.

This is not the place to describe the technical econometrics for estimating an RE model: this has already been done by others (e.g. Wallis, 1980; Wickens, 1982; McCallum, 1976) and the techniques are available in software packages. There are two methods: limited and full information. In limited information (LI), the expectations variables are replaced by proxies generated from a first stage regression on the full set or a subset of the model's predetermined variables. In full information (FI), the expectations variables are the estimated model's own predictions: a package to do this written by Fair and Parke (1989) is available, implementing Fair and Taylor's (1983) procedure.

To carry out FIML estimation it is necessary to locate the set of parameters that generate maximum likelihood, taking account of the expectations they generate as well as their fit given any set of expectations. To find the expectations requires model solution (convergence) in every period of the sample: this is a very stringent requirement and Liverpool experience shows that it is frequently not met for a macroeconomic model, even of limited size (as with the Liverpool one), with arbitrarily chosen parameters. Hence the one available programme for estimating such models by FIML, that of Fair and Parke (1989), can easily break down if the initiating parameters do not permit convergence; the algorithm, finding non-convergence, may be unable to locate a parameter set which does converge and the estimation does not get off the ground.

For this reason, it appears necessary to begin with LI estimation and model simulation to locate a promising initial set of parameters. Movement towards maximum likelihood can then be achieved by iteration, as follows: (1) generate expectations (and equilibrium values) from the initial set of coefficients and compute their likelihood; (2) holding expectations and equilibrium values constant, run a standard FIML programme to convergence to obtain a new set of coefficients; (3) repeat steps (1) and (2) until the likelihood in step (1) is maximized (for more detail see Minford et al., 1990). At this point it should be possible to use the Fair and Parke (1989) program to fine-tune the results and compute appropriate standard errors which require the full search procedures of their program.

We do not yet know how much difference it makes, especially in small samples, to use FI rather than LI estimation. Asymptotically (i.e. in large samples), standard errors should fall in moving from single equation to FIML estimation (West (1986), for example, computes the asymptotic reduction in standard error for a small model as typically a rather small 20 per cent). However, although work on the Liverpool model is not yet complete, it seems likely that it will show a much bigger reduction, since outside a very narrow area around the estimated parameters the expectations series generated by model solution become highly erratic and the likelihood drops sharply, suggesting extremely small standard errors.

If this is so, then hypothesis testing will have much greater power with FI estimates. Minford et al. (1990) found, for example, that less restricted dynamics, which are accepted in LI estimation, are rejected in their provisional FI estimates (essentially because they give strange model solutions and so expectations). They also found that their very first stage estimates, based on instrumental variables, with varying sets of instruments being selected for each equation on statistical grounds, produced a low likelihood, so that the provisional FI estimates were generally distant from them. Thus LI estimation appears to have poor discrimination.

When structural coefficient estimates have been obtained the RE hypothesis restriction can then be tested. However, this has not been done at all widely. The reason is that for LI estimates the test has hardly any power: the less restricted expectations merely imply a different group of first step regressors and the test involved is the weak one of chi-squared on choice of instruments. Most RE models have been estimated by LI.

FI estimates can test the restriction with considerable power. But so far no large macro models have been estimated by FI. The closest to such estimates yet achieved are those discussed above for the Liverpool model from Minford et al. (1990), who report provisional results.

RE forces expectations to be generated by the model, whereas a generalized ARMA scheme, for example, relaxes this restriction, allowing several free lag coefficients to be estimated together with some arbitrarily normalized leading coefficient. Minford et al. tried two sorts of ARMA alternative to RE: one which was totally unrestricted and one ('restricted') where they forced the sum of the lagged inflation values generating expected inflation to equal unity (ensuring homogeneity).

They found that within the sample the ARMA expectations schemes, whether restricted or not, easily out-performed rational expectations. This is what they expected. So stringent is the RE assumption that, given likely model misspecification, it is unlikely to fit the data as well as the lags of the generalized ARMA, which can flexibly adjust for poorly fitting basic theory, even when restricted.

Out of sample, however, they found that the ARMA models massively reject stability for the expectations scheme parameters (they had insufficient degrees of freedom to test the stability of all the parameters). The fact that these parameters shift so much implies that no use can be made of the ARMA models for policy optimization or other analysis. At best they could be used for forecasting: the unrestricted ARMA turns out still to have a better fit out of sample than the RE model, even using the within-sample parameters. Nevertheless, given the parameter instability, there can be no confidence that this would generally be so: the estimated standard error of the parameters around the original means is underestimated by an unknown amount if the means shift unpredictably. As for the restricted ARMA, its within-sample parameters fitted worse outside sample than the RE ones, showing that this more relevant ARMA scheme performs significantly worse outside sample than RE. These results are consistent with rational expectations (together with a degree of model misspecification, which could well account for the superior within-sample performance of lags), and inconsistent with backward-looking expectations schemes, supposedly invariant to regime change.

## Conclusions

The rational expectations hypothesis is a modelling assumption. It does not assert that everyone everywhere and always has rational expectations any more than the marginal utility hypothesis asserts that all consumers everywhere maximize utility at all times. Therefore tests of the hypothesis through surveys are, though interesting, not persuasive, since they check what certain groups (say they) think rather than what their and others' behaviour is in the market. A modelling assumption can only ultimately be tested, as Friedman (1953) has stressed, by testing the goodness of fit of the model, with and without it. Such a test is still not widely practised; but some preliminary work reported here suggests that the RE hypothesis may not generate best fits to past data (and is rejected on these grounds within sample) but that it shows greater stability and better fit than less restricted alternatives outside sample. Since it is always with the intention of using their models outside sample that economists build them, this tentative conclusion, if borne out by future research, is favourable to the RE hypothesis. Certainly, most applied economists today seem to regard it as the best available assumption for carrying out policy analysis and in forecasting too it has gained considerable ground, especially in the UK.

# References

Adler, M. and Dumas, B. (1984) 'International portfolio choice and corporation finance', *Journal of Finance*, 39, 935–84.

Akerlof, G.A. and Yellen, J.L. (1987) 'Rational models of irrational behaviour', *American Economic Review*, 77, 137–42.

Alesina, A. (1987) 'Macroeconomic policy in a two-party system as a repeated game', *Quarterly Journal of Economics*, 102, 651–78.

Alesina, A. (1989) 'Macroeconomics and politics', in S. Fischer (ed.) *NBER Macroeconomics Annual 1988*. Cambridge, MA: MIT Press, 13–52.

Alesina, A. and Sachs, J. (1988) 'Political parties and the business cycle in the United States, 1948–1984', *Journal of Money, Credit and Banking*, 20, 62–82.

Alesina, A. and Tabellini, G. (1989) 'External debt, capital flight and political risk', *Journal of International Economics*, 27, 199–220.

Alesina, A. and Tabellini, G. (1990) 'A positive theory of fiscal deficits and government debt in a democracy', *Review of Economic Studies*, 57, 403–14.

Allen, D.E. (1985) *Introduction to the Theory of Finance*. Oxford: Basil Blackwell.

Aoki, M. and Canzoneri, M. (1979) 'Reduced forms of rational expectations models', *Quarterly Journal of Economics*, 93, 59–71.

Arrow, K.J. (1971) *Essays on the Theory of Risk Bearing*. Amsterdam: North Holland.

Arrow, K.J. and Hahn, F.H. (1971) *General Competitive Analysis*. San Francisco: Holden Day. (Reprinted, Amsterdam: North Holland.)

Attfield, C.L.F., Demery, D. and Duck, N.W. (1981a) 'A quarterly model of unanticipated monetary growth, output and the price level in the UK 1963–78', *Journal of Monetary Economics*, 8, 331–50.

Attfield, C.L.F., Demery, D. and Duck, N.W. (1981b) 'Unanticipated monetary growth, output and the price level', *European Economic Review*, 16, 367–85.

Backus, D. and Driffill, J. (1985) 'Inflation and reputation', *American Economic Review*, 75, 530–8.

Baillie, R.J. and McMahon, P.C. (1989) *The Foreign Exchange Market – Theory and Econometric Evidence*. Cambridge: Cambridge University Press.

Barro, R.J. (1972) 'A theory of monopolistic price adjustment', *Review of Economic Studies*, 39, 17–26.

Barro, R.J. (1974) 'Are government bonds net wealth?', *Journal of Political Economy*, 82, 1095–117.

Barro, R.J. (1976) 'Rational expectations and the role of monetary policy', *Journal of Monetary Economics*, 2, 1–33.

Barro, R.J. (1977) 'Unanticipated monetary growth and unemployment in the United States', *American Economic Review*, 67, 101–15.

Barro, R.J. (1980) 'A capital market in an equilibrium business cycle model', *Econometrica*, 48, 1393–417.

Barro, R.J. and Gordon, D. (1983) 'Rules, discretion and reputation in a model of monetary policy', *Journal of Monetary Economics*, 12, 101–22.

Barro, R.J. and Rush, M. (1980) 'Unanticipated money and economic activity', in S. Fischer (ed.) *Rational Expectations and Economic Policy*. Chicago: University of Chicago Press.

Bean, C., Layard, R. and Nickell, S. (1986) 'The rise in unemployment: a multi-country study', in *The Rise in Unemployment*, edited by the same authors. Oxford: Basil Blackwell, chapter 1.

Beenstock, M. (1980) *A Neoclassical Analysis of Macroeconomic Policy*. Cambridge: Cambridge University Press.

Begg, D.K.H. (1982) *The Rational Expectations Revolution in Macroeconomics – Theories and Evidence*. Oxford: Philip Allan.

Bell, S. and Beenstock, M. (1980) 'An application of rational expectations in the UK foreign exchange market', in D. Currie and W. Peters (eds) *Studies in Contemporary Economic Analysis, Volume 2*. London: Croom Helm.

Bewley, T. (1980) 'The optimum quantity of money', in J.H. Kareken and N. Wallace (eds) *Models of Monetary Economies*. Minneapolis: Federal Reserve Bank of Minneapolis, 169–210.

Bilson, J.F.O. (1980) 'The rational expectations approach to the consumption function', *European Economic Review*, 13, 273–99.

Black, S.A. (1973) *International Money Markets and Flexible Exchange Rates*. Studies in International Finance No. 32. Princeton, NJ: International Finance Section, Princeton University.

Blanchard, O.J. (1981) 'Output, the stock market and interest rates', *American Economic Review*, 71, 132–43.

Blanchard, O.J. and Wyplosz, C. (1981) 'An empirical structural model of aggregate demand', *Journal of Monetary Economics*, 7, 1–28.

Blinder, A.S. and Solow, R.M. (1973) 'Does fiscal policy matter?' *Journal of Public Economics*, 2, 319–37.

Borooah, V. and Van der Ploeg, R. (1982) 'British government popularity and economic performance. A comment', *Economic Journal*, 92, 405–10.

Brunner, K., Cukierman, A. and Meltzer, A.H. (1980) 'Stagflation, persistent unemployment and the permanence of economic shocks', *Journal of Monetary Economics*, 6, 467–92.

Brunner, K. and Meckling, W.H. (1977) 'The perception of man and the conception of government', *Journal of Money, Credit and Banking*, 9, 70–85.

Buiter, W.H. (1983) 'Real effects of anticipated and unanticipated money: some problems of estimation and hypothesis testing', *Journal of Monetary Economics*, 11, 207–24.

Buiter, W.H. and Miller, M. (1981) 'Monetary policy and international competitiveness: the problems of adjustment', *Oxford Economic Papers*, 33, 143–75.

Cagan, P. (1956) 'The Monetary dynamics of hyperinflation', in M. Friedman (ed.) *Studies in the Quantity Theory of Money*. Chicago: University of Chicago Press.

Canzoneri, M.B. (1980) 'Labour contracts and monetary policy', *Journal of Monetary Economics*, 6, 241–55.

Canzoneri, M.B. (1983) 'Rational destabilizing speculation and exchange intervention policy', *Journal of Macroeconomics*, 5, 75–90.

Carlson, J.A. and Parkin, M. (1975) 'Inflation expectations', *Economica*, 42, 123–38.

Cass, D. and Shell, K. (eds) (1976) *The Hamiltonian Approach to Dynamic Economics*. Philadelphia: University of Pennsylvania Press.

Chappell, D. and Peel, D.A. (1979) 'On the political theory of the business cycle', *Economics Letters*, 2, 327–32.

Chrystal, K.A. and Alt, J.E. (1981) 'Some problems in formulating and testing a politico-economic model of the United Kingdom', *Economic Journal*, 91, 730–6.

Cleaver, K. (1986) *The Crisis in Economics*. Unpublished PhD thesis, University of Liverpool, chapter 7.

Clower, R. (1965) 'The Keynesian counter-revolution: a theoretical appraisal', in F.H. Hahn and F.P.R. Brechling (eds) *Theory of Interest Rates*. London: Macmillan.

Copeland, T.E. and Weston, J.F. (1988) *Financial Theory and Corporate Policy*, 3rd edn. Reading, MA: Addison Wesley.

Crewe, I. (1988) 'Has the electorate become Thatcherite?' in R. Skidelsky (ed.) *Thatcherism*. Oxford: Basil Blackwell, 25–49.

Cukierman, A. and Meltzer, A. (1986) 'A positive theory of discretionary policy, the cost of a democratic government, and the benefits of a constitution', *Economic Inquiry*, 24, 367–88.

Davidson, J.E.H. and Hendry, D.F. (1981) 'Interpreting econometric evidence: the behaviour of consumers' expenditure in the UK', *European Economic Review*, 16, 177–92.

Davis, J. and Minford, P. (1986) 'Germany and the European disease' (Symposium on unemployment in Europe, eds J. Muysken and C. de Neubourg), *Recherches Economiques de Louvain*, 52, 373–98.

Demery, D. (1984) 'Exchange rate dynamics – the Swiss/US case', *European Economic Review*, 24, 151–9.

Dickinson, D.G., Driscoll, M.J. and Ford, J.L. (1982) 'Rational expectations, random parameters and the non-neutrality of money', *Economica*, 49, 241–8.

Dornbusch, R. (1976) 'Expectations and exchange rate dynamics', *Journal of Political Economy*, 84, 1161–76.

Downs, A. (1957) *An Economic Theory of Democracy*. New York: Harper and Row.

Driskill, R.A. (1981) 'Exchange rate dynamics: an empirical investigation', *Journal of Political Economy*, 2, 357–71.

Fair, R.C. and Parke, W.R. (1989) *The Fair-Parke Program for the Estimation and Analysis of Nonlinear Econometric Models*. Southborough, MA: Macro Inc.

Fair, R.C. and Taylor, J.B. (1983) 'Solution and maximum likelihood estimation of dynamic nonlinear rational expectations models', *Econometrica*, 51, 1169–86.

Fama, E.F. (1970) 'Efficient capital markets: a review of theory and empirical work', *Journal of Finance*, 25, 383–417.

Fama, E.F. (1975) 'Short term interest rates as predictors of inflation', *American Economic Review*, 65, 269–82.

Fama, E.F. (1976) *Foundations of Finance*, Oxford: Basil Blackwell.

Feige, E.L. and Pierce, D.K. (1976) 'Economically rational expectations: are innovations in the rate of inflation independent of innovations in measures of monetary and fiscal policy', *Journal of Political Economy*, 84, 499–52.

Fischer, S. (1977a) 'Long term contracts, rational expectations and the optimum money supply rule', *Journal of Political Economy*, 85, 191–205.

Fischer, S. (1977b) 'Long-term contracting, sticky prices, and monetary policy - a comment', *Journal of Monetary Economics*, 3, 317–23.

Fischer, S. (1980) 'Dynamic inconsistency, cooperation and the benevolent dissembling government', *Journal of Economic Dynamics and Control*, 2, 93–107.

Frankel, J.A. (1979) 'On the Mark: a theory of floating exchange rates based on real interest differentials', *American Economic Review*, 69, 610–22.

Frankel, J.A. (1982) 'The mystery of the multiplying marks: a modification of the monetary model', *Review of Economics and Statistics*, 64, 515–19.

Frey, B.S. and Schneider, F. (1978a) 'A politico-economic model of the United Kingdom', *Economic Journal*, 88, 243–53.

Frey, B.S. and Schneider, F. (1978b) 'An empirical study of politico-economic interaction in the United States', *Review of Economics and Statistics*, 60, 174–183.

Friedman, B.M. (1979) 'Optimal expectations and the extreme information assumptions of rational expectations macromodels', *Journal of Monetary Economics*, 5, 23–41.

Friedman, M. (1953) 'The methodology of positive economics' in *Essays in Positive Economics*. Chicago: University of Chicago Press.

Friedman, M. (1957) *A Theory of the Consumption Function*. Princeton, NJ: Princeton University Press.

Friedman, M. (1968) 'The role of monetary policy', *American Economic Review*, 58, 1–17.

Friedman, M. and Meiselman, D. (1963) 'The relative stability of monetary velocity and the investment multiplier in the US 1898–1958', in Commission on Money and Credit, *Stabilization Policies*. Englewood Cliffs, NJ: Prentice-Hall.

Frydman, R. and Phelps, E.S. (1983) *Individual Forecasting and Aggregate Outcomes - 'Rational Expectations' Examined*. Cambridge: Cambridge University Press.

Gourieroux, C., Laffont, J.J. and Montfort, A. (1982) 'Rational expectations in dynamic linear models - analysis of the solutions', *Econometrica*, 50, 409–25.

Graybill, F.A. (1961) *An Introduction to Linear Stochastic Models, Volume 1*. New York: McGraw-Hill.

Grossman, S.J. and Stiglitz, J.E. (1976) 'Information and competitive price systems', *American Economic Review*, 66, 246–53.

Grossman, S.J. and Stiglitz, J.E. (1980) 'On the impossibility of informationally efficient markets', *American Economic Review*, 70, 393–407.

Gurley, J. and Shaw, E.S. (1960) *Money in a Theory of Finance*. Washington, DC: Brookings Institution.

Hacche, G. and Townend, J. (1981) 'Exchange rates and monetary policy: modelling sterling's effective exchange rate', *Oxford Economic Papers*, 33, 201–47.

Hall, R.E. (1978) 'Stochastic implications of the life cycle–permanent income hypothesis: theory and evidence', *Journal of Political Economy*, 86, 971–88.

Hall, R.L. and Hitch, C.J. (1939) 'Price theory and business behaviour', *Oxford Economic Papers*, no. 2, May, 12–45. (Reprinted in Wilson and Andrews, 1951.)

Hansen, L.P. and Sargent, T.J. (1980) 'Formulating and estimating dynamic linear rational expectations models', *Journal of Economic Dynamics and Control*, 2, 7–46.

Hart, O.D. (1983) 'Optimal labour contracts under asymmetric information: an introduction', *Review of Economic Studies*, 50, 3–36.

Harte, C.P. (1986) *Political Economy and the New Macroeconomics*. Unpublished MPhil thesis, University of Liverpool, chapters 2 and 3.

Harte, C.P., Minford, A.P.L. and Peel, D.A. (1983) 'The political economy of government macroeconomic stabilisation policy', mimeo, University of Liverpool; also available as chapter 3 of Harte (1986).

Hayek, F.A. (1988) *The Fatal Conceit – the Errors of Socialism*. London: Routledge.

Hellwig, M.F. (1982) 'Rational expectations equilibrium with conditioning on past prices. A mean variance example', *Journal of Economic Theory*, 26, 279–312.

Hibbs, D.A. Jr (1978) 'Political parties and macroeconomic policy', *American Political Science Review*, 72, 981–1007.

Hillier, B. and Malcomson, J. (1984) 'Dynamic inconsistency, rational expectations and optimal government policy', *Econometrica*, 52, 1437–51.

Hoel, P.G. (1962) *Introduction To Mathematical Statistics*, 3rd edn. New York: John Wiley.

Holden, K. and Peel, D.A. (1977) 'An empirical investigation of inflationary expectations', *Oxford Bulletin of Economics and Statistics*, 39, 291–9.

Holden, K., Peel, D.A., and Thompson, J.L. (1985) Expectations – Theory and Evidence, Macmillan.

Holden, K. and Broomhead, A. (1990) 'An examination of vector autoregressive forecasts for the UK economy', *International Journal of Forecasting*, 6, 11–23.

Holly, S. and Zarrop, M.B. (1983) 'On optimality and time consistency when expectations are rational', *European Economic Review*, 20, 23–40.

Holt, C.C., Modigliani, F., Muth, J.F. and Simon, H.A. (1960) *Planning Production, Inventories and Work Force*. Englewood Cliffs, NJ: Prentice-Hall.

Johnson, H.G. (1968) 'Problems of efficiency in monetary management', *Journal of Political Economy*, 76, 971–90.

Johnston, J. (1972) *Econometric Methods*, 2nd edn. New York: McGraw-Hill.

Johnston, J. (1984) *Econometric Methods*, 3rd edn. New York: McGraw-Hill.

Jordan J.S. and Radner, R. (1982) 'Rational expectations in microeconomic models, an overview', *Journal of Economic Theory*, 26, 201-23.

Kalman, R.E. (1960) 'A new approach to linear filtering and prediction problems', Trans. ASME, *Journal of Basic Engineering*, Series D, 82, 35-45.

Karni, E. (1980) 'A note on Lucas's equilibrium model of the business cycle', *Journal of Political Economy*, 88, 1231-8.

Keynes, J.M. (1936) *The General Theory of Employment, Interest and Money*. London: Macmillan.

Keynes, J.M. (1939) 'Professor Tinbergen's method', *Economic Journal*, 49, 558-68.

King, R.G. (1982) 'Monetary policy and the information content of prices', *Journal of Political Economy*, 90, 247-79.

Koyck, L.M. (1954) *Distributed Lags and Investment Analysis*, Contributions to Economic Analysis no. 4. Amsterdam: North Holland.

Krugman, P.R. (1978) 'Purchasing power parity and exchange rates: another look at the evidence', *Journal of International Economics*, 8, 397-407.

Kydland, F.E. and Prescott, E.C. (1977) 'Rules rather than discretion: the inconsistency of optimal plans', *Journal of Political Economy*, 85, 473-91.

Kydland, F. and Prescott, E.C. (1982) 'Time to build and aggregate fluctuations', *Econometrica*, 50, 1345-70.

Layard, R. and Nickell, S. (1985) 'The causes of British unemployment' *National Institute Economic Review*, 111, Feb., 62-85.

Leiderman, L. (1980) 'Macroeconomic testing of the rational expectations and structural neutrality hypothesis for the United States', *Journal of Monetary Economics*, 6, 69-82.

Levich, R.M. (1985) 'Empirical studies of exchange rates: price behaviour, rate determination and market efficiency', in R.W. Jones and P.B. Kenen (eds) *Handbook of International Economics, Volume 2*, Amsterdam: North-Holland, 979-1040.

Lipsey, R.G. (1960) 'The relation between unemployment and the rate of change of money wage rates in the United Kingdom 1862-1957: A further analysis', *Economica*, NS, 27, 1-31.

Litterman, R.B. (1986) 'Forecasting with Bayesian vector autoregressions - five years' experience', *Journal of Business and Economic Statistics*, 4, 25-38.

Long, J.B. and Plosser, C.I. (1983) 'Real business cycles', *Journal of Political Economy*, 91, 39-69.

Lucas, R.E. Jr (1972a) 'Econometric testing of the natural rate hypothesis', in O. Eckstein (ed.) *Econometrics of Price Determination Conference*. Washington, DC: Board of Governors, Federal Reserve System.

Lucas, R.E. Jr (1972b) 'Expectations and the neutrality of money', *Journal of Economic Theory*, 4, 103-24.

Lucas, R.E. Jr (1973) 'Some international evidence on output-inflation trade-offs', *American Economic Review*, 68, 326-34.

Lucas, R.E. Jr (1975) 'An equilibrium model of the business cycle', *Journal of Political Economy*, 83, 1113-44.

Lucas, R.E. Jr (1976) 'Econometric policy evaluation: a critique', in K. Brunner and A.H. Meltzer (eds) *The Phillips Curve and Labour Markets, Carnegie Rochester Conference Series on Public Policy*, 1, 19-46, Supplement to the *Journal of Monetary Economics*.

Lucas, R.E. Jr (1978) 'Asset prices in an exchange economy', *Econometrica*, 46, 1426–45.

Lucas, R.E. Jr (1980) 'Equilibrium in a pure currency economy', *Economic Inquiry*, 18, 203–20.

Lucas, R.E. Jr and Rapping, L.A. (1969) 'Real wages, employment and inflation', *Journal of Political Economy*, 77, 721–54.

Lucas, R.E. Jr and Sargent, T.J. (1978) 'After Keynesian macroeconomics', in *After the Phillips Curve: Persistence of High Inflation and High Unemployment*, Minneapolis: Federal Reserve Bank of Minneapolis Quarterly Review, 3, no. 1. Reprinted in Lucas and Sargent (1981).

Lucas, R.E. Jr. and Sargent, T.J. (1981) *Rational Expectations and Econometric Practice*. London: George Allen and Unwin.

Lucas, R.E. Jr. and Stokey, N.L. (1983) 'Optimal fiscal and monetary policy in an economy without capital,' *Journal of Monetary Economics*, 12, 55–93.

McCallum, B.T. (1976) 'Rational expectations and the natural rate hypothesis: some consistent estimates,' *Econometrica*, 44, 43–52.

McCallum, B.T. (1979) 'On the observational inequivalence of classical and Keynesian models', *Journal of Political Economy*, 87, 395–402.

McCallum, B.T. (1983) 'On non-uniqueness in rational expectations models: an attempt at perspective', *Journal of Monetary Economics*, 11, 139–68.

McCallum, B.T. and Whittaker, J.K. (1979) 'The effectiveness of fiscal feedback rules and automatic stabilisers under rational expectations', *Journal of Monetary Economics*, 5, 171–86.

Macdonald, R. (1988) *Floating Exchange Rates – Theories and Evidence*. London: Unwin Hyman.

McNees, S.K. (1986) 'Forecasting accuracy of alternative techniques: a comparison of US macroeconomic forecasts', *Journal of Business and Economic Statistics*, 1, 3–24.

MacRae, D.C. (1977) 'A political model of the business cycle', *Journal of Political Economy*, 85, 239–63.

Markowitz, H. (1959) *Portfolio Selection: Efficient Diversification of Investment*. New York: John Wiley.

Marini, G. (1985) 'Intertemporal substitution and the role of monetary policy', *Economic Journal*, 95, 87–100.

Marini, G. (1986) 'Employment fluctuations and demand management', *Economica*, 53, 209–18.

Marshall, A. (1887) 'Minutes of evidence taken before the Royal Commission on Gold and Silver, Forty Third Day (19th Dec. 1887)', in *Final Report of the Royal Commission on Gold and Silver*. London: HMSO, 1–53.

Meltzer, A.H. and Richard, S.F. (1981) 'A rational theory of the size of government', *Journal of Political Economy*, 89, 914–27.

Meltzer, A.H. and Richard, S.F. (1983) 'Tests of a rational theory of the size of government', *Public Choice*, 41, 403–18.

Metzler, L.A. (1951) 'Wealth, saving and the rate of interest', *Journal of Political Economy*, 59, 93–116.

Minford, A.P.L. (1978) *Substitution Effects, Speculation and Exchange Rate Stability*, Studies in International Economics no. 3. Amsterdam: North Holland.

Minford, A.P.L. (1980) 'A rational expectations model of the United Kingdom under fixed and floating exchange rates', in K. Brunner and A.H. Meltzer (eds) *On the State of Macroeconomics, Carnegie Rochester Conference Series on Public Policy*, 12, 293–355, Supplement to the *Journal of Monetary Economics*.

Minford, A.P.L. (1983) 'Labour market equilibrium in an open economy', *Oxford Economic Papers*, 35, (supplement), 207–44.

Minford, A.P.L. (1986) 'Rational expectations and monetary policy', *Scottish Journal of Political Economy*, 33, 317–33.

Minford, A.P.L. (1988) 'Interest rates and bond financed deficits in a Ricardian two-party democracy', *Weltwirtschaftliches Archiv*, 124, 387–402.

Minford, A.P.L. Ashton, P.A., Davies, D.H., Peel, M.J. and Sprague, A. (1985) *Unemployment: Cause and Cure*, 2nd edn (1st edn, 1983, with Davies, Peel and Sprague. Oxford: Martin Robertson). Oxford: Basil Blackwell.

Minford, A.P.L., Brech, M. and Matthews, K.G.P. (1980) 'A rational expectations model of the UK under floating exchange rates', *European Economic Review*, 14, 189–219.

Minford, A.P.L., Ioannidis, C.E. and Marwaha, S. (1983a) 'Rational expectations in a multilateral macro model', in P. de Grauwe and T. Peeters (eds) *Exchange Rates in Multi-Country Econometric Models*. London: Macmillan, 239–66.

Minford, A.P.L., Ioannidis, C.E. and Marwaha, S. (1983b) 'Dynamic predictive tests of a model under adaptive and rational expectations', *Economics Letters*, 11, 115–21.

Minford, A.P.L., Matthews, K.G.P. and Marwaha, S. (1979) 'Terminal conditions as a means of ensuring unique solutions for rational expectations models with forward expectations', *Economics Letters*, 4, 117–20.

Minford, A.P.L., Matthews, K.G.P. and Rastogi, A. (1990) 'A quarterly version of the Liverpool model of the UK', working paper no. 90/06, Liverpool Research Group in Macroeconomics, University of Liverpool.

Minford, A.P.L. and Peel, D.A. (1982) 'The political theory of the business cycle', *European Economic Review*, 17, 253–70.

Minford, A.P.L. and Peel, D.A. (1983) 'Some implications of partial current information sets in macroeconomic models embodying rational expectations', *Manchester School*, 51, 235–49.

Minford, A.P.L. and Peel, D.A. (1984) 'Testing for unbiasedness and efficiency under incomplete current information', *Bulletin of Economic Research*, 36, 1–7.

Mishkin, F.S. (1978a) 'Efficient markets theory: implications for monetary policy', *Brookings Papers on Economic Activity*, 3, 707–52.

Mishkin, F.S. (1978b) 'Simulation methodology in macroeconomics: an innovation technique', *Journal of Political Economy*, 87, 816–36.

Mishkin, F.S. (1981) 'The real interest rate: an empirical investigation', in K. Brunner and A.H. Meltzer (eds) *The Costs and Consequences of Inflation, Carnegie Rochester Conference Series on Public Policy*, 15, 151–200, Supplement to the *Journal of Monetary Economics*.

Mishkin, F.S. (1982) 'Does anticipated monetary policy matter: an empirical investigation', *Journal of Political Economy*, 99, 22–51.

Modigliani, F. and Grunberg, E. (1954) 'The predictability of social events', *Journal of Political Economy*, 62, 465–78.

Mueller, D.C. (1979) *Public Choice*. New York: Cambridge University Press.

Mussa, M.H. (1979) 'Empirical regularities in the behaviour of exchange rates and theories of the foreign exchange market', *Carnegie Rochester Conference Series on Public Policy*, 11, 9–57.

Mussa, M. (1981) 'Sticky individual prices and the dynamics of the general price level', *Carnegie Rochester Conference Series on Public Policy*, 15, 261–96.

Muth, J.F. (1960) 'Optimal properties of exponentially weighted forecasts', *Journal of the American Statistical Association*, 55, 299–306.

Muth, J.F. (1961) 'Rational expectations and the theory of price movements', *Econometrica*, 29, 315–35.

Nelson, C.R. and Schwert, G.W. (1977) 'Short-term interest rates as predictors of inflation: on testing the hypothesis that the real interest rate is constant', *American Economic Review*, 67, 478–86.

Nerlove, M. (1958) 'Adaptive expectations and cobweb phenomena', *Quarterly Journal of Economics*, 72, 227–40.

Nordhaus, W.D. (1975) 'The political business cycle', *Review of Economic Studies*, 42, 169–90.

Olson, M. (1965) *The Logic of Collective Action*. Cambridge, MA: Harvard University Press.

Olson, M. (1982) *The Rise and Decline of Nations: Economic Growth, Stagflation, and Social Rigidities*. NewHaven, CT: Yale University Press.

Parkin, J.M. (1978) 'A comparison of alternative techniques of monetary control under rational expectations', *Manchester School*, 46, 252–87.

Parkin, M. (1986) 'The output inflation trade-off when prices are costly to change', *Journal of Political Economy*, 94, 200–24.

Parkin, M. and Bade, R. (1988) *Modern Macroeconomics*, 2nd edn (1st edn 1982). Oxford: Philip Allan.

Patinkin, D. (1965) *Money, Interest and Prices*, 2nd edn. New York: Harper and Row.

Peel, D.A. (1981) 'Non-uniqueness and the role of the monetary authorities', *Economics Letters*, 4, 117–20.

Phelps, E.S. (1970) 'The new microeconomics in employment and inflation theory', in E.S. Phelps et al. (eds) *Microeconomic Foundations of Employment and Inflation Theory*. New York: Norton, 1–27.

Phelps, E.S. and Taylor, J.B. (1977) 'The stabilizing powers of monetary policy under rational expectations', *Journal of Political Economy*, 85, 163–90.

Phillips, A.W. (1958) 'The relation between unemployment and the rate of change in money wage rates in the UK, 1861–1957', *Economica*, 25, 283–99.

Poole, W. (1970) 'The optimal choice of monetary instrument in a simple stochastic macro model', *Quarterly Journal of Economics*, 84, 197–221.

Popper, K.R. (1945/1966) *The Open Society and Its Enemies*, Routledge and Kegan Paul, 5th edition, 1966; 1st edition 1945.

Popper, K.R. (1988) 'The Open Society and Its Enemies revisited', *The Economist*, 23 April, 25–8.

Pratt, J.W. (1964) 'Risk aversion in the small and in the large', *Econometrica*, 32, 122–36.

Ramsey, F.P. (1927) 'A contribution to the theory of taxation,' *Economic Journal*, 37, 47–61.

Robinson, J.V. (1937) *Essays on the Theory of Employment*. London: Macmillan.

Rogoff, K. and Sibert, A. (1988) 'Equilibrium political business cycles', *Review of Economic Studies*, 55, 1–16.

Ross, S.A. (1976) 'The arbitrage theory of capital asset pricing', *Journal of Economic Theory*, 8, 343–62.

Rotemberg, J. (1983) 'Aggregate consequences of fixed costs of changing prices', *American Economic Review*, 73, 433–6.

Samuelson, P.A. (1958) 'An exact consumption-loan model of interest with or without the social contrivance of money', *Journal of Political Economy*, 66, 467–82.

Sargent, T.J. (1976a) 'A classical macroeconomic model of the United States', *Journal of Political Economy*, 84, 207–38.

Sargent, T.J. (1976b) 'The observational equivalence of natural and unnatural rate theories of macroeconomics', *Journal of Political Economy*, 84, 631–40.

Sargent, T.J. (1978) 'Estimation of dynamic labour demand schedules under rational expectations', *Journal of Political Economy*, 86, 1009–44.

Sargent, T.J. (1979) *Macroeconomic Theory*. New York: Academic Press.

Sargent, T.J. (1981) 'Interpreting economic time series', *Journal of Political Economy*, 89, 213–48.

Sargent, T.J. (1987) *Dynamic Macroeconomic Theory*. New York: Academic Press.

Sargent, T.J. and Wallace, N. (1975) 'Rational expectations, the optimal monetary instrument and the optimal money supply rule', *Journal of Political Economy*, 83, 241–54.

Sargent, T.J. and Wallace, N. (1981) 'Some unpleasant monetary arithmetic', *Quarterly Review, Federal Reserve Bank of Minneapolis*, Fall, 1–17.

Seater, J.J. (1982) 'Are future taxes discounted?', *Journal of Money, Credit and Banking*, 14, 376–89.

Shackle, G.L.S. (1958) *Time in Economics*. Amsterdam: North Holland.

Shiller, R.J. (1978) 'Rational expectations and the dynamic structure of macroeconomic models – a critical review', *Journal of Monetary Economics*, 4, 1–44.

Sims, C.A. (1979) 'Macroeconomics and reality', *Econometrica*, 48, 1–48.

Stern, R.M., Francis, J. and Schumacher, B. (1976) *Price Elasticities in International Trade – an Annotated Bibliography*. London: Macmillan.

Sugden, R. (1986) *The Economics of Rights, Co-operation and Welfare*. Oxford: Basil Blackwell.

Tabellini, G. (1987) 'Reputational constraints on monetary policy: a comment', *Carnegie Rochester Conference series on Public Policy*, 26, 183–90.

Taylor, J.B. (1977) 'Conditions for unique solutions to macroeconomic models with rational expectations', *Econometrica*, 45, 1377–85.

Taylor, J.B. (1979a) 'Estimation and control of a macroeconomic model with rational expectations', *Econometrica*, 47, 1267–86.

Taylor, J.B. (1979b) 'Staggered wage setting in a macroeconomic model', *American Economic Review, Papers and Proceedings*, 69, 108–13.

Taylor, J.B. (1980) 'Aggregate dynamics and staggered contracts', *Journal of Political Economy*, 88, 1–23.

Townsend, R. (1980) 'Models of money with spatially separated agents' in J.H. Kareken and N. Wallace (eds) *Models of Monetary Economies*. Minneapolis: Federal Reserve Bank of Minneapolis, 265–304.

Tullock, G. (1976) *The Vote Motive*, Hobart Paper no. 9. London: Institute of Economic Affairs.

Turnovsky, S.J. (1970) 'Empirical evidence on the formation of price expectations', *Journal of the American Statistical Association*, 65, 1441–54.

Turnovsky, S.J. (1980) 'The choice of monetary instrument under alternative forms of price expectations', *Manchester School*, 48, 39–63.

Visco, I. (1984) *Price Expectations in Rising Inflation*, Contributions to Economic Analysis, 152. Amsterdam: North-Holland.

Wallace, N. (1980) 'The overlapping-generations model of fiat money', in J.H. Kareken and N. Wallace (eds) *Models of Monetary Economies*. Minneapolis: Federal Reserve Bank of Minneapolis, 49–62.

Wallis, K.F. (1980) 'Econometric implications of the rational expectations hypothesis', *Econometrica*, 48, 49–72.

Wallis, K.F., Andrews, M.J., Bell, D.N.F., Fisher, P.G. and Whitley, J.D. (1985) 'Comparative model properties – section 2.4: terminal conditions in rational expectations models', in K.F. Wallis (ed.) *Models of the UK Economy*. Oxford: Oxford University Press, 57–66.

Walters, A.A. (1971) 'Consistent expectations, distributed lags and the quantity theory', *Economic Journal*, 81, 273–81.

Weiss, L. (1980) 'The role for active monetary policy in a rational expectations model', *Journal of Political Economy*, 88, 221–33.

West, K.D. (1986) 'Full versus limited information estimation of a rational expectations model,' *Journal of Econometrics*, 33, 367–85.

Wickens, M.R. (1982) 'The efficient estimation of econometric models with rational expectations', *Review of Economic Studies*, 49, 55–67.

Wilson, T. and Andrews, P.W.S. (eds) (1951) *Oxford Studies in the Price Mechanism*. Oxford: Clarendon Press.

# Index